Holt School Mathematics

HOLT, RINEHART AND WINSTON, PUBLISHERS
NEW YORK • TORONTO • LONDON • SYDNEY

W0011002

ABOUT THE AUTHORS

EUGENE D. NICHOLS is Professor of Mathematics Education and Lecturer in the Mathematics Department at Florida State University, Tallahassee, Florida.

PAUL A. ANDERSON is an elementary school teacher in the Clark County School District, Las Vegas, Nevada.

LESLIE A. DWIGHT is the former Head of the Department of Mathematics and Professor of Mathematics at Southeastern Oklahoma State University, Durant, Oklahoma.

FRANCES FLOURNOY is Professor of Elementary Education at the University of Texas, Austin, Texas.

ROBERT KALIN is Professor, Mathematics Education Program, at Florida State University, Tallahassee, Florida.

JOHN SCHLUEP is Associate Professor of Mathematics at State University College, Oswego, New York.

LEONARD SIMON is Assistant Director, Planning and Curriculum, for the New York City Board of Education.

Photo Credits
Pages 5, 35, 67, 87, 131, 207, 235, 257, 269, 299 HRW Photo by Russell Dian
Page 151 Soil Conservation Service
Page 181 HRW Photo by John Running

ISBN 0–03–018561–0

7890123456 032 987654321

CONTENTS

v

1 NUMBERS TO 999

NUMBERS

How many bees?

How many flowers?

The number is the same.

1. Write the numeral.

   a. How many crayons are in this box?

   b. How many crayons are in this box?

   c. How many crayons are in this box?

2. Which have the same number?

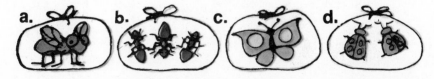

a.   b.   c.   d.

Write a numeral to tell how many.

1.   2.   3.

4.   5.   6.

Which have the same number?

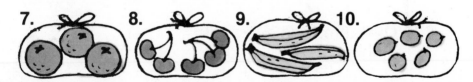

7.   8.   9.   10.

ACTIVITY

How many of each do you see in your classroom?
Count and write how many.

_____ erasers   _____ chairs   _____ clocks

1

COMPARING NUMBERS

We compare numbers.

7 is greater than 5	5 is less than 7
7 > 5	5 < 7
> means **is greater than**	< means **is less than**

1. Compare. Use > or <.

   a. 4 ⬚ 3

   b. 3 ⬚ 4

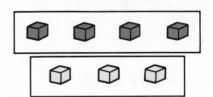

2. Compare. Use >, <, or =.

   a. 2 ⬚ 7   b. 3 ⬚ 0   c. 5 ⬚ 5   d. 9 ⬚ 4

EXERCISES

Compare. Use >, <, or =.

1. 6 ⬚ 4   **2.** 4 ⬚ 6   **3.** 0 ⬚ 1   **4.** 1 ⬚ 0

5. 3 ⬚ 1   **6.** 2 ⬚ 2   **7.** 5 ⬚ 6   **8.** 2 ⬚ 4

9. 5 ⬚ 3   **10.** 7 ⬚ 7   **11.** 9 ⬚ 7   **12.** 3 ⬚ 8

TENS AND ONES

1. Look at the picture.

    a. How many tens?

    b. How many ones?

    c. 2 tens + 3 ones = ___

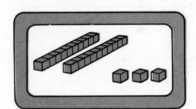

2. Complete.

    a. ___ tens = 30   **b.** 33 = ___ tens + ___ ones

Copy and complete.

1. ___ tens = 50   **2.** 6 tens + 0 ones = ___

3. ___ tens = 70   **4.** 8 tens + 3 ones = ___

5. 6 tens = ___   **6.** 44 = ___ tens + ___ ones

7. 9 tens = ___   **8.** 70 = ___ tens + ___ ones

Keeping Fit

Add.

1. 2 +2		**2.** 0 +1		**3.** 1 +2	
4. 5 +0		**5.** 4 +2		**6.** 2 +3	
7. 3 +2		**8.** 6 +0		**9.** 1 +4	

10. 6 +1	**11.** 7 +1	**12.** 5 +2	**13.** 1 +5	**14.** 8 +0
15. 2 +5	**16.** 4 +4	**17.** 1 +6	**18.** 2 +6	**19.** 4 +3
20. 0 +6	**21.** 3 +5	**22.** 2 +4	**23.** 5 +3	**24.** 0 +7
25. 1 +7	**26.** 3 +3	**27.** 3 +4	**28.** 7 +0	**29.** 6 +2
30. 1 +8	**31.** 3 +6	**32.** 2 +7	**33.** 4 +5	**34.** 6 +3
35. 7 +2	**36.** 0 +5	**37.** 0 +8	**38.** 9 +0	**39.** 2 +1
40. 1 +3	**41.** 5 +1	**42.** 4 +1	**43.** 0 +0	**44.** 5 +4
45. 3 +0	**46.** 8 +1	**47.** 1 +1	**48.** 2 +0	**49.** 0 +9

DENTISTS

1. Bought 5 tubes of
    toothpaste.
    Used 3 tubes.
    How many tubes are left?

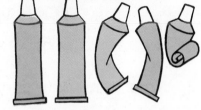

2. 6 bottles of green
    mouthwash.
    2 bottles of red
    mouthwash.
    How many bottles in all?

3. Bob has 3 toothbrushes.
    Mary has 4 toothbrushes.
    How many toothbrushes
    in all?

4. 4 children waiting.
    1 sees the dentist.
    How many still waiting?

EXPANDED AND STANDARD NUMERALS

Expanded Numerals

    2 tens + 3
      20 + 3

Standard Numeral

      23

1. Complete.

   a. 35 = ___ tens + 5

   b. 35 = ___ + 5

2. Write standard numerals.

   a. 3 tens + 0   **b.** 50 + 2   **c.** 70 + 3

EXERCISES

Write expanded numerals.

Example   28 = 2 tens + 8

1. 13   **2.** 46   **3.** 72   **4.** 80   **5.** 99

Write expanded numerals.

Example   38 = 30 + 8

6. 17   **7.** 33   **8.** 59   **9.** 66   **10.** 74

Write standard numerals.

11. 4 tens + 6   **12.** 20 + 1   **13.** 80 + 3

NUMBER WORDS

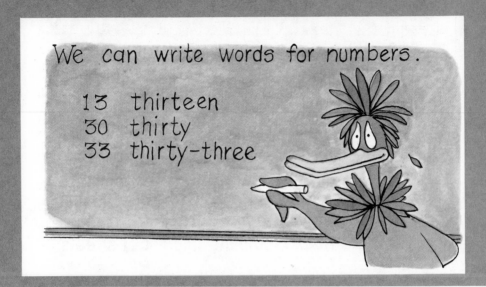

We can write words for numbers.

13 thirteen
30 thirty
33 thirty-three

1. Write standard numerals.

   a. 10 + 2
   twelve

   b. 40 + 2
   forty-two

   c. 9 tens
   ninety

   ___

   ___

   ___

2. Write standard numerals.

   a. Fifty

   b. Sixteen

   c. Eighty-one

Write standard numerals.

1. Seventy

2. Eleven

3. Sixty-six

4. Seventeen

5. Fifteen

6. Eighteen

7. Fourteen

8. Twenty-one

9. Thirteen

10. Eighty-nine

11. Nineteen

12. Fifty-two

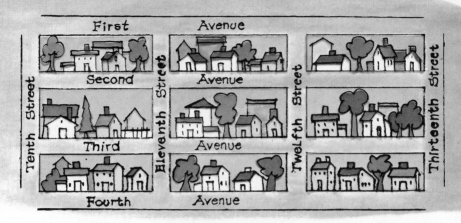

ORDER WORDS

1. Look at the map. Complete this list of streets.

   a. First Street
      Second Street
      ___ Street
      ___ Street
      Fifth Street

   b. Sixth Street
      ___ Street
      Eighth Street
      ___ Street
      ___ Street

2. Which comes before and which comes after?

   a. ___ Seventh ___

   b. ___ Ninth ___

Give the order of these days of the week on a calendar.

Example   Saturday is seventh.

   1. Sunday   **2.** Monday   **3.** Tuesday

   4. Wednesday   **5.** Thursday   **6.** Friday

Which comes before and which comes after?

   7. ___ twelfth ___   ★ **8.** ___ nineteenth ___

8

COMPARING NUMBERS THROUGH 99

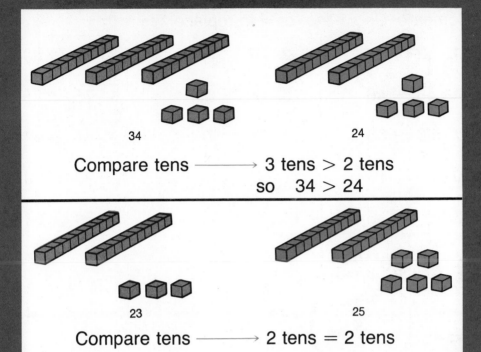

Compare tens ⟶ 3 tens > 2 tens

so   34 > 24

Compare tens ⟶ 2 tens = 2 tens

Compare ones ⟶   3 < 5

so   23 < 25

1. Compare tens. Use > or <.

   a. 15 ▤ 25   **b.** 43 ▤ 23   **c.** 49 ▤ 78
      25 ▤ 15   23 ▤ 43   78 ▤ 49

2. Compare tens. Then compare ones. Use > or <.

   a. 16 ▤ 14   **b.** 34 ▤ 38   **c.** 99 ▤ 96
      14 ▤ 16   38 ▤ 34   96 ▤ 99

3. Compare. Use >, <, or =.

   a. 17 ▤ 27   **b.** 69 ▤ 68   **c.** 58 ▤ 58

   d. 43 ▤ 41   **e.** 76 ▤ 76   **f.** 90 ▤ 81

9

Compare. Use >, <, or = to replace ⫤.

1. 32 ⫤ 42   **2.** 67 ⫤ 57   **3.** 50 ⫤ 50

4. 48 ⫤ 46   **5.** 60 ⫤ 60   **6.** 75 ⫤ 85

7. 56 ⫤ 56   **8.** 69 ⫤ 70   **9.** 44 ⫤ 47

10. 81 ⫤ 80   **11.** 42 ⫤ 37   **12.** 90 ⫤ 89

13. 46 ⫤ 43   **14.** 77 ⫤ 77   **15.** 58 ⫤ 64

Keeping Fit

Subtract.

1. 4 −2	**2.** 1 −1	**3.** 3 −2

4. 4 −3	**5.** 6 −1	**6.** 5 −0

7. 6 −2	**8.** 5 −3	**9.** 5 −1

10. 0 −0	**11.** 5 −2	**12.** 6 −0	**13.** 5 −4	**14.** 7 −1

15. 8 −1	**16.** 7 −2	**17.** 6 −5	**18.** 8 −0	**19.** 7 −5

20. 8 −4	**21.** 7 −6	**22.** 8 −6	**23.** 7 −3	**24.** 6 −6

HUNDREDS

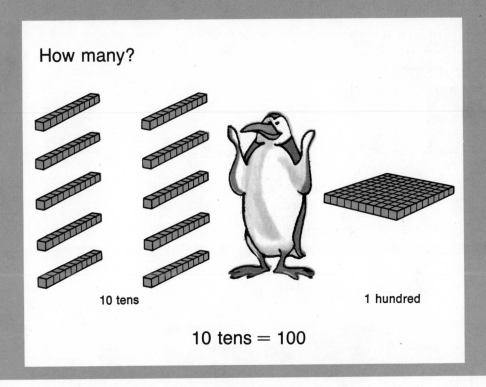

How many?

10 tens

1 hundred

10 tens = 100

1. There are 3 hundreds in 300.
   How many hundreds are in 200? 600? 800?

2. Write the standard numeral for 7 hundreds.

How many hundreds are in each?

1. 400   **2.** 500   **3.** 800   **4.** 900

Write standard numerals.

5. 1 hundred   **6.** 2 hundreds   **7.** 4 hundreds

8. 5 hundreds   **9.** 3 hundreds   **10.** 9 hundreds

How many?

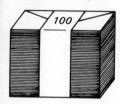 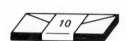 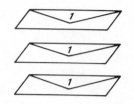

1 hundred + 1 ten + 3

100   +   10   + 3

one hundred thirteen = 113

1. Write standard numerals.

   a. 1 hundred + 2 tens + 0 = ___

   b. 100 + 20 + 0 = ___

2. Complete.

   a. ___ hundreds + 0 tens + 5 = 205

   b. ___ + 0 + 5 = 205

Write standard numerals.

1. 3 hundreds + 3 tens + 3

2. 100 + 40 + 6

3. 2 hundreds + 6 tens + 0

4. 200 + 60 + 0

5. 4 hundreds + 0 tens + 9

6. 400 + 0 + 9

7. 100 + 10 + 9

8. 300 + 70 + 0

9. 400 + 0 + 4

10. 600 + 60 + 5

Write expanded numerals.

Example   245 = 2 hundreds + 4 tens + 5

11. 475   **12.** 357   **13.** 240   **14.** 506

15. 609   **16.** 855   **17.** 172   **18.** 386

Write expanded numerals.

Example   337 = 300 + 30 + 7

19. 173   **20.** 841   **21.** 906   **22.** 210

23. 422   **24.** 834   **25.** 659   **26.** 999

27. 333   **28.** 278   **29.** 196   **30.** 681

Brainteaser

Find the patterns. Copy and complete.

1. 510, 509, ____, ____, ____, 505

2. 46, 44, 42, ____, ____, ____, 34

A digit's place in a numeral tells its value.

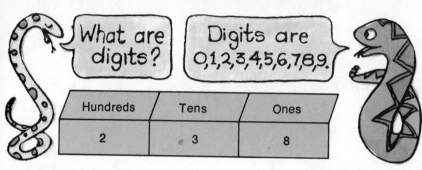

What are digits? Digits are 0,1,2,3,4,5,6,7,8,9.

Hundreds	Tens	Ones
2	3	8

The 3 is in the tens place. Its value is 30.

238 = 2 hundreds + 3 tens + 8

238 =   200   +   30 + 8

1. Look at this place-value chart. Complete.

Hundreds	Tens	Ones
5	2	4

   a. The 5 is in the ___ place. Its value is 500.

   b. The 2 is in the ___ place. Its value is ___.

   c. The 4 is in the ___ place. Its value is ___.

2. What is the value of each underlined digit?

   Example   145   *Answer* 40

   a. 4<u>4</u>0   **b.** 7<u>7</u>7   **c.** 77<u>7</u>   **d.** <u>7</u>77

3. Write standard numerals.

   a. One hundred twenty-eight **b.** Two hundred ten

14

What is the value of each underlined digit?

1. 670<u>0</u>   2. 2<u>6</u>5   3. 80<u>5</u>   4. <u>6</u>66

5. 4<u>8</u>2   6. 659<u>9</u>   7. <u>5</u>68   8. 1<u>7</u>8

Write standard numerals.

9. Two hundred seventy-two

10. Six hundred sixty

11. One hundred one

12. Four hundred thirteen

13. Three hundred four

ACTIVITY

★Copy and complete this puzzle.

a	b			c
d			e	
		f		
	g			

Across

a. One hundred fifty
d. Eighty
e. Ninety
f. Five hundred six
g. Four hundred nineteen

Down

a. One hundred eighty
b. Fifty
c. Two hundred six
e. Nine hundred nine
f. Fifty-one

15

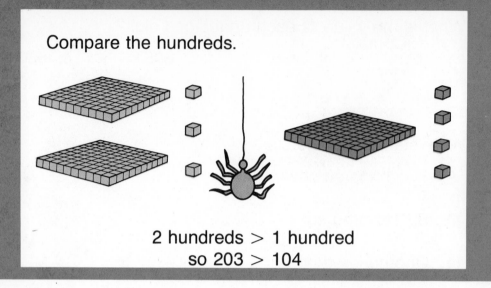

Compare the hundreds.

2 hundreds > 1 hundred
so 203 > 104

1. Compare. Use >, <, or =.

   a. 2 hundreds ≡ 1 hundred
      247 ≡ 134

   b. 6 hundreds ≡ 9 hundreds
      678 ≡ 928

2. Study the pictures. Use >, <, or = to compare.

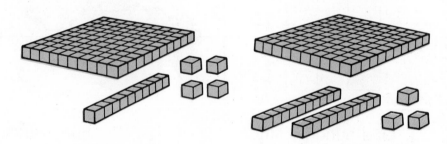

Compare hundreds ——→ 1 hundred = 1 hundred
   Compare tens ——→ 1 ten < 2 tens
            so 114 ≡ 123

16

3. Let's compare 169 and 167. Use >, <, or =.

   a. Compare hundreds.   1 hundred $\equiv$ 1 hundred

   b. Compare tens.   6 tens $\equiv$ 6 tens

   c. Compare ones.   9 $\equiv$ 7

   d. Compare.   so 169 $\equiv$ 167

4. Compare. Use >, <, or =.

   a. 396 $\equiv$ 592   b. 705 $\equiv$ 708   c. 127 $\equiv$ 127

   d. 640 $\equiv$ 619   e. 643 $\equiv$ 650   f. 208 $\equiv$ 207

Compare. Use >, <, or =.

1. 230 $\equiv$ 231   2. 459 $\equiv$ 458   3. 290 $\equiv$ 190

4. 146 $\equiv$ 136   5. 985 $\equiv$ 985   6. 672 $\equiv$ 472

7. 999 $\equiv$ 861   8. 304 $\equiv$ 308   9. 513 $\equiv$ 513

10. 891 $\equiv$ 864   11. 727 $\equiv$ 723   12. 580 $\equiv$ 670

13. 348 $\equiv$ 228   14. 616 $\equiv$ 616   15. 146 $\equiv$ 149

★ Complete the tables.

16.

5 less		5 more
70	75	80
	180	
	295	

17.

10 less		10 more
90	100	110
	350	
	590	

17

TIME: HOUR AND HALF-HOUR

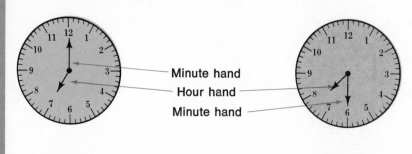

We write time in different ways.

Minute hand

Hour hand

Minute hand

7 o'clock
7:00

30 minutes after 7
half past 7
7:30

1. What times are shown? Complete.

a.

___ o'clock

___:___

b.

___ minutes after ___
half past ___

___:___

2. What times are shown? Complete.

a.

___:___

b.

___:___

c.

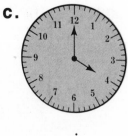

___:___

18

What times are shown? Complete.

1.

:

2.

:

3.

:

What times are shown? Use the ＿:＿ form.

4.

:

5.

:

6.

:

7.

:

8.

:

9.

:

ACTIVITY

This clockface shows 3 o'clock Eastern Time.

Draw three clockfaces and show what time it will be in the Central, Mountain, and Pacific zones.

CHAPTER REVIEW

What is the value of each underlined digit? [14]

1. 1<u>2</u>4   **2.** <u>3</u>25   **3.** 70<u>9</u>   **4.** 89<u>3</u>

Write standard numerals.

5. 7 tens + 6   **6.** 80 + 8
[6]   [6]

7. 6 hundreds + 6 tens + 5   **8.** 900 + 20 + 4
[12]   [12]

9. Nineteen   **10.** Three hundred thirty
[7]   [14]

Write expanded numerals. [6, 12]

Example   47 = 4 tens + 7

11. 34   **12.** 52   **13.** 168   **14.** 209

Write expanded numerals. [6, 12]

Example   23 = 20 + 3

15. 47   **16.** 88   **17.** 251   **18.** 666

Compare. Use >, <, or =. [9, 16]

19. 65 ≡ 62   **20.** 70 ≡ 90   **21.** 58 ≡ 76

22. 234 ≡ 334   **23.** 160 ≡ 161   **24.** 273 ≡ 269

What times are shown? Use the __:__ form. [18]

25.   **26.**   **27.**

      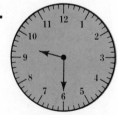

CHAPTER TEST

What is the value of each underlined digit?

1. 2<u>7</u>8   **2.** <u>2</u>15   **3.** 1<u>6</u>3   **4.** <u>4</u>08

Complete.

5. ___ tens + ___ = 66

6. 274 = ___ hundreds + ___ tens + ___

Write standard numerals.

7. 9 tens + 3   **8.** 400 + 60 + 7

9. 3 hundreds + 3 tens + 3   **10.** Twelve

Write expanded numerals.

Example   29 = 20 + 9

11. 37   **12.** 99   **13.** 172   **14.** 203

Compare. Use >, <, or =.

15. 6 ≡ 8   **16.** 60 ≡ 59   **17.** 78 ≡ 78

18. 500 ≡ 300   **19.** 248 ≡ 273   **20.** 489 ≡ 682

What times are shown? Use the ___ : ___ form.

21.    **22.**    **23.**

2 NUMBERS TO 999,999

10 hundreds = 1 thousand
1,000

1. Find the pattern. Copy and complete.

   a. 993, 994, ___, 996, 997, ___, ___, 1,000

   b. 930, 940, ___, ___, ___, 980, ___, 1,000

   c. 300, 400, ___, ___, 700, 800, ___, 1,000

   1 more than 999 is 1,000.
   10 more than 990 is 1,000.
   100 more than 900 is 1,000.

2. The standard numeral for two thousand is 2,000.
   Write standard numerals.

   a. Three thousand   b. Five thousand

22

Find the pattern. Copy and complete.

1. 1,000, 2,000, ___, ___, 5,000

2. 5,000, 6,000, ___, ___, 9,000

Write standard numerals.

3. Six thousand

4. Eight thousand

5. Four thousand

6. Nine thousand

7. Two thousand

8. Seven thousand

Keeping Fit

Copy and complete.

1. ___ ones = 1 ten

2. ___ tens = 1 hundred

Write standard numerals.

3. 300 + 30 + 4

4. 1 hundred + 3 tens + 5

5. 600 + 6

6. 5 hundreds + 8 tens + 0

7. One hundred one

8. One hundred ten

Compare. Use >, <, or =.

9. 18 ≡ 23

10. 99 ≡ 190

11. 223 ≡ 126

12. 888 ≡ 887

13. 500 ≡ 500

14. 999 ≡ 909

15. 66 ≡ 605

16. 103 ≡ 130

17. 803 ≡ 803

23

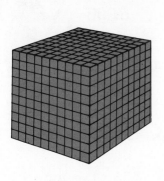 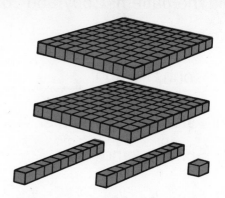

1 thousand + 2 hundreds + 2 tens + 1
1,000 + 200 + 20 + 1 = 1,221
We read 1,221 as:
one thousand, two hundred twenty-one.

1. Read these.

    a. 1,567   **b.** 3,259   **c.** 4,019   **d.** 8,002

2. Find the pattern. Copy and complete.

    a. 1,006,   1,007,   ____,   1,009,   ____,   1,011

    b. 1,016,   1,017,   ____,   1,019,   ____,   1,021

3. Complete.

    a. 1,847 = 1 thousand + 8 hundreds + ___ tens + 7

    b. 1,847 = ___ + 800 + ___ + 7

4. Write standard numerals.

    a. 2 thousands + 7 hundreds + 4 tens + 6

    b. 3,000 + 800 + 20 + 5

Find the pattern. Copy and complete.

1. 1,106,   1,107,   ____   1,109,   ____   1,111

2. 1,996,   1,997,   ____   1,999,   ____   2,001

Complete.

3. 1,762 = 1 thousand + 7 hundreds + ____ tens + 2

4. 3,265 = 3 thousands + ____ hundreds + 6 tens + 5

5. 4,609 = ____ thousands + 6 hundreds + 0 tens + 9

6. 5,488 = 5,000 + 400 + ____ + 8

7. 7,560 = 7,000 + ____ + 60 + 0

8. 8,309 = ____ + 300 + 0 + 9

Write standard numerals.

9. 3 thousands + 1 hundred + 8 tens + 4

10. 6 thousands + 9 hundreds + 7 tens + 0

11. 7 thousands + 7 hundreds + 0 tens + 3

12. 9 thousands + 0 hundreds + 2 tens + 9

13. 1,000 + 100 + 30 + 4

14. 3,000 + 500 + 60 + 1

15. 5,000 + 600 + 70 + 7

25

PLACE VALUE

A digit's value depends on its place.

Thousands	Hundreds	Tens	Ones
6 ,	4	2	5

The 6 is in the thousands place.
Its value is 6,000.
6,425 = 6 thousands + 4 hundreds + 2 tens + 5
6,425 = 6,000 + 400 + 20 + 5
        Six thousand, four hundred twenty-five

1. Complete by using this place-value chart.

Thousands	Hundreds	Tens	Ones
1 ,	2	3	6

   a. The 2 is in the ___ place. Its value is ___.

   b. The 1 is in the ___ place. Its value is ___.

2. What is the value of each underlined digit?

   Example   1,2̲36   *Answer*   1,000

   a. 2,2̲10   b. 3,69̲4   c. 6̲,811

3. Write standard numerals.

   a. Two thousand, nine hundred seven

   b. Three thousand, sixty-eight

   c. Four thousand, one

26

What is the value of each underlined digit?

Example   2,4<u>7</u>8   *Answer* 2,000

1. 1,68<u>3</u>   2. 3,2<u>9</u>0   3. 5,<u>6</u>08   4. <u>6</u>,024

5. 9,<u>8</u>41   6. 7,7<u>7</u>7   7. 7,<u>7</u>77   8. <u>7</u>,777

9. 7,77<u>7</u>   10. 4,<u>0</u>19   11. 9,2<u>3</u>5   12. 1,04<u>7</u>

Write standard numerals.

13. Two thousand, two

14. Two thousand, twenty

15. Two thousand, two hundred

16. Three thousand, one hundred six

17. Three thousand, one hundred sixty

Complete.

18. 10 less than 1,000 = ___

19. 100 less than 1,000 = ___

ACTIVITY

Make a pocket chart like the one shown below.
Use straws to show a number on your chart.
Ask a partner to write the numeral you have shown.

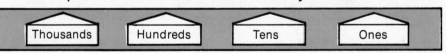

| Thousands | Hundreds | Tens | Ones |

Which number is greater?

Compare thousands → 1 thousand = 1 thousand
Compare hundreds → 2 hundreds > 1 hundred
so 1,200 > 1,100

1. Compare 5,382 and 5,346. Use >, or <, or =.

   a. 5 thousands ≡ 5 thousands

   b. 3 hundreds ≡ 3 hundreds

   c. 8 tens ≡ 4 tens

   d. so, 5,382 ≡ 5,346

2. Compare. Use >, <, or =.

   a. 2,763 ≡ 2,569   **b.** 3,816 ≡ 3,816

EXERCISES

Copy and use >, <, or =.

1. 6,304 ≡ 4,308   2. 3,470 ≡ 3,470

3. 7,231 ≡ 7,271   4. 5,640 ≡ 5,641

Add or subtract.

Keeping Fit

1.   4
   +4

2.   0
   +9

3.   3
   +5

4.   5
   +2

5.   1
   +7

6.   8
   +1

7.   7
   +2

8.   6
   +3

9.   8
   −4

10.   9
   −9

11.   8
   −5

12.   7
   −2

13.   9
   −1

14.   1
   +8

15.   9
   +0

16.   2
   +6

17.   3
   +4

18.   3
   +6

19.   8
   −7

20.   9
   −2

21.   9
   −3

22.   8
   −6

23.   9
   −8

24.   2
   +7

25.   3
   +5

26.   5
   +4

27.   0
   +8

28.   4
   +5

29.   9
   −0

30.   9
   −7

31.   8
   −5

32.   9
   −4

33.   9
   −5

34.   7
   −3

Brainteaser

Solve the case of the missing digits.

  8 ▇
− ▇ 5
‾‾‾‾‾
  2 3

  ▇ 7
− 2 ▇
‾‾‾‾‾
  1 3

  7 ▇
− ▇ 5
‾‾‾‾‾
  4 2

29

TEN THOUSANDS

How many tickets?

10 One Thousands | 1 Ten Thousand

1. Find the pattern. Copy and complete.

9,994, 9,995, ____ , 9,997, ____ , ____ , 10,000

1 more than 9,999 is 10,000.

2. Look at this place-value chart.

Ten Thousands	One Thousands	Hundreds	Tens	Ones
2	5	3	6	8

The 2 is in the ten thousands place.
Its value is 20,000.

What is the value of each underlined digit?

a. 2̲3,145   b. 7̲6,091   c. 62,49̲2   d. 85,00̲2

3. We read 48,672 as forty-eight thousand, six hundred seventy-two.

Read these.

a. 40,000   **b.** 80,000   **c.** 94,282

d. 78,200   **e.** 61,030   **f.** 53,004

EXERCISES

Find the pattern. Copy and complete.

1. 4,000, 5,000, _____, 7,000, _____ , _____ , 10,000

2. 9,940, 9,950, _____, _____ , 9,980, _____ , 10,000

What is the value of each underlined digit?

Example   2̲8,160   *Answer*   20,000

3. 1̲9,235   **4.** 37,9̲83   **5.** 6̲3,120

6. 48,075̲   **7.** 32,0̲70   **8.** 6̲0,112

9. 44̲,600   **10.** 53,201̲   **11.** 76,12̲2

12. 25,3̲48   **13.** 86̲,010   **14.** 9̲4,200

★ Complete.

15. 1 less than 10,000 = ___

16. 10 less than 10,000 = ___

17. 100 less than 10,000 = ___

18. 1,000 less than 10,000 = ___

31

HUNDRED THOUSANDS

Hundred thousands are to the left of ten thousands.

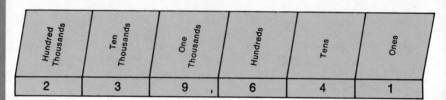

The 2 is in the hundred thousands place.
Its value is 200,000.

1. Find the pattern. Copy and complete.

   a. 99,991, 99,992, _____ , _____ , 99,995

   b. 99,996, 99,997, _____ , _____ , 100,000

2. What is the value of each underlined digit?

   a. 2̲34,167   **b.** 148,2̲21   **c.** 396,2̲15

   d. 57̲8,125   **e.** 6̲19,824   **f.** 635,4̲02

3. Commas help us read large numbers.
   They group the digits into **periods**. Name the
   periods. How many places are in each period?

Periods	Thousands			Ones		
Places	Hundred Thousands	Ten Thousands	One Thousands	Hundreds	Tens	Ones
	3	7	1 ,	4	2	0

4. We read 371,420 as three hundred seventy-one
   thousand, four hundred twenty.
   The digits 3, 7, and 1 are in the thousands period.
   What digits are in the ones period?

5. In which period are the underlined digits?

    Example   634,<u>101</u>   *Answer* Ones

    a. 148,<u>362</u>   **b.** 234,<u>770</u>   **c.** <u>895</u>,302

6. Read these.

    a. 157,622   **b.** 594,103   **c.** 620,004

    d. 400,125   **e.** 715,850   **f.** 984,017

EXERCISES

What is the value of each underlined digit?

1. <u>1</u>23,324   **2.** 346,2<u>7</u>1   **3.** 5<u>2</u>7,180

4. <u>7</u>77,412   **5.** 7<u>7</u>7,190   **6.** 77<u>7</u>,605

7. 376,89<u>5</u>   **8.** 493,<u>8</u>51   **9.** 850,4<u>1</u>4

In which period are the underlined digits?

10. <u>172</u>,205   **11.** 269,<u>073</u>   **12.** <u>408</u>,195

13. 645,<u>317</u>   **14.** <u>854</u>,110   **15.** 967,<u>005</u>

Find the pattern. Copy and complete.

16. 99,960, 99,970, _____ , _____ , 100,000

17. 99,600, _____ , 99,800, _____ , 100,000

18. 96,000, 97,000, _____ , _____ , 100,000

★ Complete:

19. 1 greater than 999,999 is _____ .

FLOW CHARTS

A flow chart gives steps on how to do something. This flow chart shows how to open a door with a key.

```
┌──────────────────────┐
│        Start.        │
└──────────────────────┘
            │
            ▼
┌──────────────────────┐
│   Put the key in     │
│    the keyhole.      │
└──────────────────────┘
            │
            ▼
┌──────────────────────┐
│     Turn the key.    │
└──────────────────────┘
            │
            ▼
┌──────────────────────┐
│   Turn the doorknob. │
└──────────────────────┘
            │
            ▼
┌──────────────────────┐
│    Open the door.    │
└──────────────────────┘
            │
            ▼
┌──────────────────────┐
│        Stop.         │
└──────────────────────┘
```

1. Draw the shape that says to start.

2. Draw the shape that says to stop.

3. Draw the shape that gives a step other than start or stop.

4. Put these steps in order to show how to put on socks and sneakers. Draw a flow chart with these steps.
   (a) tie the sneakers
   (b) put on the socks
   (c) stop
   (d) put on the sneakers
   (e) start

★ **5.** Draw a flow chart on how to get into a car.

34

ROOFERS

1. A roof is being put on a new house. There are 2 men and 2 women roofers. How many roofers in all?

   a. What question is being asked? How many roofers in all?
   b. What do we know? There are 2 men and 2 women.

Read each problem. Then, **a)** tell what question is being asked and **b)** tell what we know.

2. Alice worked 4 hours in the morning. She worked 4 hours in the afternoon. How many hours in all?

3. Tenth Street has 6 houses in all. There are 2 new houses. How many are not new?

4. There are 3 big trees on the street. There are 2 small trees. How many trees in all?

VALUE OF COINS

penny	nickel	dime	quarter
1c	5c	10c	25c

1. What is the value in cents?

Example   2 dimes = 20¢

a. 2 dimes and 4 pennies

b. 3 dimes and 1 nickel

2.

1 half dollar

is the same as

50 pennies
10 nickels
5 dimes
2 quarters

What is the value in cents?

a. 1 half dollar and 2 nickels

b. 1 half dollar and 3 dimes

3. Which is worth more?

a. 3 dimes or 1 quarter

b. 48 pennies or 1 half dollar

What is the value in cents?

1. 1 nickel and 2 pennies

2. 2 nickels

3. 1 dime and 1 nickel

4. 3 nickels

5. 1 quarter and 1 nickel

6. 4 dimes

7. 1 half dollar and 1 dime

8. 6 dimes

Which is worth more?

9. 4 dimes
   or 35 pennies

10. 1 quarter
    or 4 nickels

11. 1 half dollar
    or 6 dimes

12. 1 quarter
    or 3 dimes

ACTIVITY

Use construction paper to make 10 pennies, 4 quarters, 5 dimes, 10 nickels, and 2 half dollars.

Now, show the coins you would need to buy each item here.

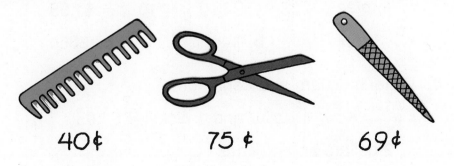

40¢   75 ¢   69¢

1 dollar = 100¢   5 dollars = 500¢
$1.00 $5.00

1. Complete.

a. $1.25 = ___ dollar and ___ cents

b. $1.25 = ___ cents + ___ cents or ___ ¢

2. How many cents?

a. $3.00   **b.** $1.34   **c.** $2.09

3. Write in dollars and cents form.

Examples   38¢ = $.38   105¢ = $1.05

a. 307¢   **b.** 14¢   **c.** 236¢

4. Write in dollars and cents form.

Example   1 dollar and 1 nickel = $1.05

a. 2 dollars and 4 dimes

b. 3 dollars and 2 pennies

How many cents?

1. $3.00 **2.** $3.80 **3.** $4.00 **4.** $.75

5. $5.17 **6.** $.98 **7.** $7.02 **8.** $9.99

Complete.

9. $1.18 = ___ dollar and ___ cents

10. $2.34 = ___ dollars and ___ cents

11. $4.02 = ___ dollars and ___ cents

12. $5.20 = ___ dollars and ___ cents

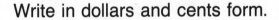

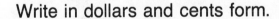

Write in dollars and cents form.

13. 1 dollar and 1 dime

14. 3 dollars and 2 nickels

Write in dollars and cents form.

15. 105¢ **16.** 110¢ **17.** 25¢ **18.** 350¢

19. 21¢ **20.** 501¢ **21.** 728¢ **22.** 910¢

Brainteaser

Rewrite the letters to spell money words.

1. mide **2.** retrauq

3. nnype **4.** radoll

5. ckelni **6.** flha raldol

39

There are 5 minutes between numerals.

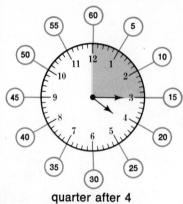

quarter after 4
15 minutes after 4
4:15

quarter to 5
15 minutes to 5
4:45

1. Write two other ways to tell the time.

45 minutes after 1
1:45

2. What times are shown? Complete.

a

5 minutes after 9
:05

b.

5 minutes to 8
7:___

40

What times are shown? Complete.

1.

5 minutes after ___

___ : ___

2.

___ minutes to ___
quarter to ___

___ : ___

What times are shown? Use the ___ : ___ form.

3.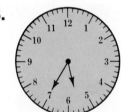

4.

5.

6.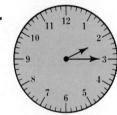

7.

8.

9.

10.

11.

★**12.** How many minutes are there between 12:45 and 25 minutes after 1?

41

TELLING TIME IN MINUTES

Each space between marks shows 1 minute for the minute hand. There are 60 minutes in an hour.

12 minutes after 8
8:12

14 minutes to 4
3:46

1. What times are shown? Complete.

a.

___ minutes after ___

___:___

b.

___ minutes to ___

___:___

2. What times are shown? Use the ___:___ form.

a.

b.

c.

42

3. Look at this clock.

    a. What time is shown?

    b. What time will it be in an hour?

    c. What time was it an hour ago?

What times are shown? Use the __:__ form.

1.

2.

3.

What time will it be in two hours?

4.

5.

6.

What time was it an hour ago?

7.

8.

9.

★ Solve this problem.

10. Sue eats lunch at 12:25. She returns to class at 1:00. How long does Sue have to eat her lunch?

43

CHAPTER REVIEW

Write standard numerals. [24, 26]

1. 1 thousand + 0 hundreds + 2 tens + 1

2. 5,000 + 400 + 10 + 5

3. Five thousand, seven hundred eighty-three

Compare. Use >, <, or =. [28]

4. 3,900 ☰ 4,000   5. 3,280 ☰ 3,190

6. 2,149 ☰ 2,149   7. 2,346 ☰ 2,370

8. 1,165 ☰ 1,418   9. 5,480 ☰ 5,469

What is the value of each underlined digit?

10. 4,781   11. 12,845   12. 672,401
[26]   [30]   [32]

Complete. [36, 38]

13. 3 dimes and 9 pennies = ___ ¢

14. $4.08 = ___ ¢

15. $3.98 = ___ dollars and ___ cents

What times are shown? Use the _:_ form. [40, 42]

16. 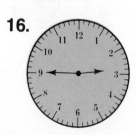   17.

44

CHAPTER TEST

Write standard numerals.

1. 7 thousands + 0 hundreds + 4 tens + 1

2. 5,000 + 300 + 90 + 0

3. Six thousand, five hundred ninety-one

Compare. Use >, <, or =.

4. 999 ≡ 1,000

5. 6,000 ≡ 4,000

6. 1,745 ≡ 1,649

7. 6,025 ≡ 6,023

8. 3,209 ≡ 3,210

9. 9,099 ≡ 9,499

What is the value of each underlined digit?

10. 1,368

11. 17,435

12. 426,150

Complete.

13. $2.49 = 2 dollars and ____ cents

14. $3.82 = ____ cents

15. 2 quarters and 1 nickel = ____ cents

What times are shown? Use the __:__ form.

16.

17.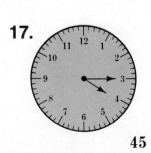

45

3 ADDING • SUBTRACTING

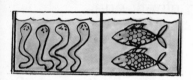

4 + 2 = 6

addend   addend   sum

1. Look at the picture.

   a. How many turtles?

   b. How many frogs?

   c. How many in all?

   d. 1 + 5 = ___

2. Add.

   a. 8 + 1   **b.** 1 + 9   **c.** 0 + 5   **d.** 9 + 0

EXERCISES

Add.

1. 3 + 7   **2.** 6 + 0   **3.** 4 + 6   **4.** 0 + 7

5. 5 + 5   **6.** 8 + 2   **7.** 6 + 4   **8.** 0 + 8

46

VERTICAL ADDITION

4 cars parked.   4 ←addend
3 cars coming.   + 3 ←addend
How many in all?   7 ←sum

1. Look at the addition below.

a. Name the addends.

b. Name the sum.

4
+ 1

2. Add.

a.	**b.**	**c.**	**d.**
0	1	0	9
+7	+8	+9	+1

Add.

1.	**2.**	**3.**	**4.**	**5.**
7	1	8	3	4
+0	+6	+0	+7	+6

6.	**7.**	**8.**	**9.**	**10.**
7	0	2	5	1
+3	+8	+8	+5	+7

ORDER OF ADDENDS

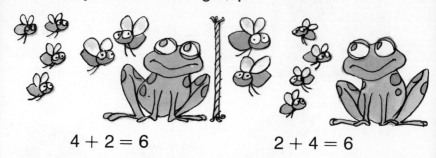

How many flies in each group?

$4 + 2 = 6$ $2 + 4 = 6$

Changing the order of the addends does not change the sum. $4 + 2 = 2 + 4$
This is the **order property of addition.**

1. Look at these sentences.

   a. Find each sum. $5 + 2 =$ ____

   b. Compare the sums. $2 + 5 =$ ____

2. Make true. $5 + 2 = \square + 5$

EXERCISES

Make true sentences.

1. $0 + 5 =$ ____   **2.** $4 + 3 =$ ____   **3.** $6 + 2 =$ ____
   $5 + 0 =$ ____ $3 + 4 =$ ____ $2 + 6 =$ ____

4. $0 + 5 = \square + 0$ **5.** $4 + 3 = 3 + \square$

6. $6 + 2 = 2 + \square$ **7.** $2 + 8 = \square + 2$

48

ADDITION ON THE NUMBER LINE

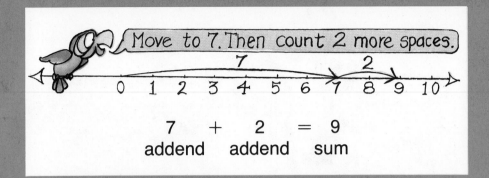

Move to 7. Then count 2 more spaces.

$$7 + 2 = 9$$
addend   addend   sum

1. Study the number line.

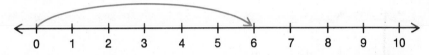

a. What is the first addend?

b. What is the second addend?

c. What is the sum?

2. Complete the addition sentence. $6 + 4 = \underline{\hspace{1em}}$

EXERCISES

Add. Use the number line to help you.

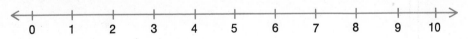

1. $8 + 1$ **2.** $7 + 2$ **3.** $9 + 0$ **4.** $8 + 2$

5. $6 + 3$ **6.** $7 + 3$ **7.** $5 + 4$ **8.** $5 + 5$

9. $\begin{array}{r} 3 \\ +6 \\ \hline \end{array}$ **10.** $\begin{array}{r} 3 \\ +7 \\ \hline \end{array}$ **11.** $\begin{array}{r} 1 \\ +9 \\ \hline \end{array}$ **12.** $\begin{array}{r} 2 \\ +8 \\ \hline \end{array}$ **13.** $\begin{array}{r} 4 \\ +5 \\ \hline \end{array}$

SUBTRACTION

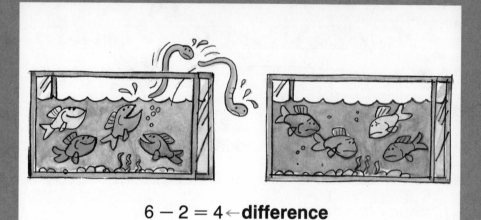

$6 - 2 = 4 \leftarrow$ **difference**

1. Look at the picture.

    a. How many frogs in all?

    b. How many jump away?

    c. How many are left?

    d. $5 - 4 = $ ___

2. Subtract.

    a. $6 - 3$ **b.** $6 - 0$ **c.** $9 - 0$ **d.** $10 - 2$

EXERCISES

Subtract.

1. $7 - 7$ **2.** $6 - 1$ **3.** $7 - 2$ **4.** $9 - 3$

5. $7 - 1$ **6.** $8 - 0$ **7.** $8 - 4$ **8.** $10 - 5$

9. $10 - 1$ **10.** $10 - 8$ **11.** $10 - 3$ **12.** $10 - 4$

VERTICAL SUBTRACTION

7 cars. 3 drive away. How many are left?

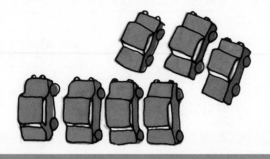

```
   7
 − 3
 ‾‾‾
   4 ←difference
```

1. Subtract to find the difference.

```
   5
 − 1
 ‾‾‾
```

2. Subtract.

a.	**b.**	**c.**	**d.**
9	9	6	10
− 9	− 1	− 6	− 9

Subtract.

1.	**2.**	**3.**	**4.**	**5.**
7	7	8	7	8
− 0	− 6	− 0	− 4	− 6

6.	**7.**	**8.**	**9.**	**10.**
9	8	6	10	10
− 3	− 8	− 4	− 5	− 7

11.	**12.**	**13.**	**14.**	**15.**
10	10	10	10	10
− 8	− 6	− 2	− 4	− 1

SUBTRACTION ON THE NUMBER LINE

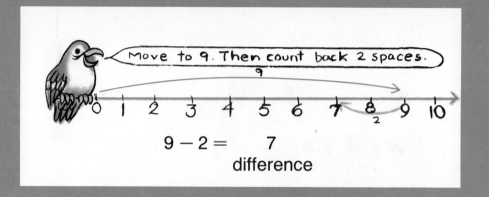

Move to 9. Then count back 2 spaces.

$9 - 2 =$ 7

difference

1. Study the number line.

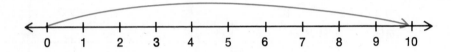

a. What number is shown first?

b. How many spaces are counted back?

c. What is the difference?

2. Complete: $10 - 4 = $ ___ .

Subtract. Use the number line to help you.

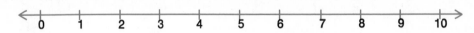

1. $9 - 1$　　**2.** $9 - 2$　　**3.** $10 - 1$　　**4.** $10 - 2$

5. $9 - 4$　　**6.** $10 - 3$　　**7.** $10 - 5$　　**8.** $10 - 6$

9.　 9　　**10.**　 10　　**11.**　 9　　**12.**　 10　　**13.**　 10
　　-6　　　　-7　　　　-5　　　　-8　　　　-7

MISSING ADDENDS

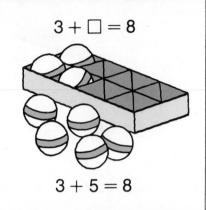

$3 + \square = 8$

$3 + 5 = 8$

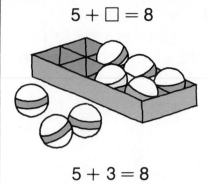

$5 + \square = 8$

$5 + 3 = 8$

1. Look at the picture.

   a. How many have stamps?

   b. How many need stamps?

   c. How many stamps in all?

   d. Complete. $7 + \square = 8$

2. Make true sentences.

   a. $3 + \square = 7$ b. $\square + 5 = 9$ c. $\square + 8 = 8$

EXERCISES

Make true sentences.

1. $2 + \square = 9$ 2. $8 + \square = 8$ 3. $\square + 5 = 10$

4. $\square + 2 = 10$ 5. $\square + 9 = 9$ 6. $3 + \square = 9$

7. $5 + \square = 9$ 8. $3 + \square = 10$ 9. $\square + 4 = 10$

MISSING ADDENDS AND DIFFERENCES

9 boys on a team.
5 boys are ready to play.
How many more boys needed?

We can find a missing addend by writing a related subtraction sentence.

Addition Sentence
$5 + \square = 9$
↑
missing addend

Related Subtraction Sentence
$9 - 5 = \square$
↑
difference

1. Make true sentences to solve the problem.

   a. $2 + \square = 6$ 6 children in a reading group.

   b. $6 - 2 = \square$ 2 have chairs.
   How many more chairs needed?

2. Make true sentences.

   a. $4 + \square = 6$ b. $\square + 3 = 7$ c. $3 + \square = 6$
      $6 - 4 = \square$ $7 - 3 = \square$ $6 - 3 = \square$

EXERCISES

Make true sentences.

1. $5 + \square = 7$ 2. $3 + \square = 8$ 3. $6 + \square = 9$
   $7 - 5 = \square$ $8 - 3 = \square$ $9 - 6 = \square$

4. $\square + 7 = 9$ 5. $\square + 6 = 8$ 6. $\square + 9 = 10$
   $9 - 7 = \square$ $8 - 6 = \square$ $10 - 9 = \square$

54

WRITING RELATED SENTENCES

We can write 4 **related sentences** about this picture.

Related Sentences
$$2 + 3 = 5$$
$$3 + 2 = 5$$
$$5 - 3 = 2$$
$$5 - 2 = 3$$

1. Write 4 related sentences for this picture.

a. ___ + ___ = ___   **c.** ___ − ___ = ___

b. ___ + ___ = ___   **d.** ___ − ___ = ___

2. Make true related sentences.

a. $\square + 4 = 9$ $9 - 4 = \square$ **b.** $3 + 3 = \square$
    $\triangle + 5 = 9$ $9 - 5 = \triangle$ $\square - 3 = 3$

EXERCISES

Write 4 related sentences.

1. $3 + 7 =$ ___   ___ − ___ = ___
     ___ + ___ = ___   ___ − ___ = ___

Make true related sentences.

2. $4 + 4 = \square$ **3.** $9 - 2 = \square$ **4.** $\square + 6 = 10$
    $\square - 4 = 4$ $9 - 7 = \square$ $10 - 6 = \square$

CHOOSING NUMBER SENTENCES

Jan had 5 mice. She took 2 to school.
How many are left at home?

Need to find	We know	How to find
How many are left?	5 mice in all. 2 taken away.	Subtract

Which sentence fits the problem?

$5 + 2 = \triangle$ $(5 - 2 = \square)$ $5 - 3 = \triangledown$

---

1. There are 4 guppies in one bowl.
   There are 3 goldfish in another bowl.
   How many fish in all?

   a. How do we find how many in all?

   b. Which number sentence fits the problem?
      $4 - 3 = \square$ $4 + 2 = \triangle$ $4 + 3 = \triangledown$

2. Sue has 6 puppies. She has only 2 bones.
   How many more puppies than bones?

   a. What must we find?

   b. Which number sentence fits the problem?
      $6 + 2 = \square$ $6 - 2 = \triangledown$ $6 - 4 = \triangle$

56

3. The pet store has 6 parakeets. They have only 4 cages. How many more cages are needed so each parakeet will have one?

Which two number sentences fit the problem?

$4 + \square = 6$ $6 + 4 = \triangle$ $6 - 4 = \square$

EXERCISES

Choose number sentences to fit the problems.

1. A pet shop has 7 parrots. There are only 3 cages. How many more parrots than cages are there?

$7 - 4 = \triangle$ $7 + 3 = \square$ $7 - 3 = \nabla$

2. Jim had 3 balls and 5 kittens. How many more balls are needed so each kitten will have one?

$5 - 3 = \square$ $3 + \square = 5$ $5 + 3 = \triangle$

3. 3 birds.
5 more came.
How many in all?

$3 + 5 = \square$ $5 - 3 = \nabla$ $3 + \triangle = 5$

4. Have 3 fish.
Want 8 in all.
How many needed?

$3 + \triangle = 8$ $3 + 8 = \square$ $8 - 3 = \triangle$

5. Had 3 dogs.
4 puppies born.
How many dogs now?

$3 + 4 = \nabla$ $3 + \triangle = 4$ $4 - 3 = \square$

WRITING NUMBER SENTENCES

We can write number sentences for story problems.

2 plain cookies.
7 nut cookies.
How many in all?

 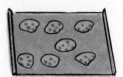

Number Sentence

2	+	7	=	9
plain		nut		cookies
cookies		cookies		in all

1. Solve the number sentences.

a. 5 white rabbits.
   3 brown rabbits.
   How many in all?
   $5 + 3 = \square$

b. 8 rabbits.
   7 carrots.
   How many more rabbits?
   $8 - 7 = \square$

c. Box holds 6 crayons when full.
   2 crayons in the box.
   How many more needed to fill it?
   $2 + \square = 6 \qquad 6 - 2 = \square$

2. Write a number sentence. Solve it.

5 birds.
3 fly away.
How many are left?

Write a number sentence for each. Solve it.

1. 6 boys.
   2 girls.
   How many in all?

2. 9 balloons.
   2 pop.
   How many are left?

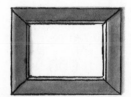

3. 7 pictures.
   5 frames.
   How many more pic-
   tures than frames?

4. 3 ants.
   5 flies.
   How many in all?

5. 8 children.
   4 chairs.
   How many more chairs
   needed?

ACTIVITY

Find a picture in a magazine or newspaper.
Cut it out and paste it on a chart.
Write a mini-problem about your picture.
Write the number sentence. Have a partner
solve it.

Keeping Fit

Compare, Use >, <, or =.

1. 4,138 ▤ 4,129

2. 6,190 ▤ 6,280

3. 9,480 ▤ 9,479

In which period are the underlined digits?

4. 8,704   **5.** 43,062   **6.** 9,894   **7.** 306,175

Write standard numerals.

8. 3 thousands + 6 hundreds + 0 tens + 7

9. 8,000 + 800 + 70 + 9

10. Five thousand, sixty-eight

What is the value of each underlined digit?

11. 3,087   **12.** 5,926   **13.** 17,306   **14.** 135,219

What times are shown? Use the __:__ form.

15.    **16.**    **17.**

18.    **19.**    **20.**

$$(2 + 4) + 3$$
$$6 + 3$$
$$9$$

$$2 + (4 + 3)$$
$$2 + 7$$
$$9$$

Changing the grouping of the addends does not change the sum. $(2 + 4) + 3 = 2 + (4 + 3)$ This is the **grouping property of addition.**

1. Complete.

a. $2 + (3 + 1)$
$2 +$ ___
___

b. $(2 + 3) + 1$
___ $+ 1$
___

2. Complete: $2 + (3 + 1) = (2 + \square) + 1$.

Complete.

1. $(1 + 2) + 4 = 1 + (2 + \square)$

2. $(3 + 2) + 3 = 3 + (\square + 3)$

3. $4 + (3 + 2) = (\square + 3) + 2$

4. $5 + (2 + 3) = (5 + \square) + 3$

5. $(2 + 6) + 1 = \square + (6 + 1)$

61

SUMS 11 AND 12

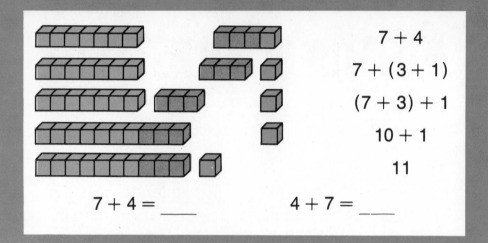

$7 + 4$

$7 + (3 + 1)$

$(7 + 3) + 1$

$10 + 1$

11

$7 + 4 =$ ____ $4 + 7 =$ ____

1. Study the steps. Complete.

 $9 + 3$

   a. Rename 3. $9 + ($ ____ $+ 2)$

   b. Regroup. $(9 +$ ____ $) + 2$

   c. Add $9 + 1$.   ____ $+ 2$

   d. Find the sum.   ____

2. Add.

a.	**b.**	**c.**	**d.**	**e.**
8	9	3	4	2
+4	+2	+9	+8	+9

EXERCISES

Add.

1.	**2.**	**3.**	**4.**	**5.**
7	9	8	5	4
+5	+3	+3	+6	+7

SUBTRACTING FROM 11 AND 12

We can add.

So we can subtract.

Addition Sentences

$7 + 4 = 11$

$4 + 7 = 11$

Related Subtraction Sentences

$11 - 4 = 7$

$11 - 7 = 4$ differences

1. Find the differences.

a. $9 + 2 = 11$
$11 - 2 = \underline{\quad}$
$11 - 9 = \underline{\quad}$

b.
$\begin{array}{r} 8 \\ +4 \\ \hline 12 \end{array}$
$\begin{array}{r} 12 \\ -4 \\ \hline \end{array}$
$\begin{array}{r} 12 \\ -8 \\ \hline \end{array}$

2. Make true related sentences.

a. $5 + \square = 11$
$11 - 5 = \square$

b. $\square + 9 = 11$
$11 - 9 = \square$

c. $6 + \triangle = 12$
$12 - 6 = \triangle$

EXERCISES

Make true related sentences.

1. $6 + \square = 11$
$11 - 6 = \square$

2. $\triangle + 3 = 12$
$12 - 3 = \triangle$

3. $7 + \square = 12$
$12 - 7 = \square$

Subtract.

4. $\begin{array}{r} 10 \\ -2 \\ \hline \end{array}$

5. $\begin{array}{r} 11 \\ -4 \\ \hline \end{array}$

6. $\begin{array}{r} 12 \\ -5 \\ \hline \end{array}$

7. $\begin{array}{r} 11 \\ -3 \\ \hline \end{array}$

8. $\begin{array}{r} 12 \\ -4 \\ \hline \end{array}$

9. $\begin{array}{r} 11 \\ -7 \\ \hline \end{array}$

10. $\begin{array}{r} 12 \\ -8 \\ \hline \end{array}$

11. $\begin{array}{r} 11 \\ -8 \\ \hline \end{array}$

12. $\begin{array}{r} 11 \\ -5 \\ \hline \end{array}$

13. $\begin{array}{r} 12 \\ -9 \\ \hline \end{array}$

63

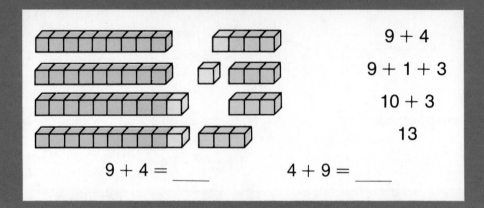

$9 + 4$

$9 + 1 + 3$

$10 + 3$

13

$9 + 4 =$ _____ $4 + 9 =$ _____

1. Study the steps. Complete.

$8 + 6$

a. Rename 6. $8 + ($ _____ $+ 4)$

b. Regroup. $(8 +$ _____ $) + 4$

c. Add $8 + 2$.   _____ $+ 4$

d. Find the sum.   _____

2. Add.

a.	**b.**	**c.**	**d.**	**e.**
7	8	7	9	9
$+6$	$+7$	$+7$	$+6$	$+5$

EXERCISES

Add.

1.	**2.**	**3.**	**4.**	**5.**
9	6	6	5	6
$+4$	$+8$	$+9$	$+8$	$+7$

6.	**7.**	**8.**	**9.**	**10.**
8	5	7	8	7
$+7$	$+9$	$+8$	$+6$	$+7$

64

SUBTRACTING FROM 13, 14, AND 15

We can add.

We can subtract.

Addition Sentence
$7 + 6 = 13$

Related Subtraction Sentences
$13 - 6 = 7$
$13 - 7 = 6$ differences

1. Find the differences.

a. $9 + 4 = 13$
$13 - 4 = \underline{\quad}$
$13 - 9 = \underline{\quad}$

b.
$\begin{array}{r} 9 \\ +5 \\ \hline 14 \end{array}$
$\begin{array}{r} 14 \\ -5 \\ \hline \end{array}$
$\begin{array}{r} 14 \\ -9 \\ \hline \end{array}$

2. Make true related sentences.

a. $8 + \square = 15$
$15 - 8 = \square$

b. $\square + 6 = 14$
$14 - 6 = \square$

c. $7 + \square = 13$
$13 - 7 = \square$

EXERCISES

Make true related sentences.

1. $9 + \triangle = 15$
$15 - 9 = \triangle$

2. $\square + 5 = 13$
$13 - 5 = \square$

3. $7 + \square = 14$
$14 - 7 = \square$

Subtract.

4.
$\begin{array}{r} 13 \\ -\ 8 \\ \hline \end{array}$

5.
$\begin{array}{r} 15 \\ -\ 9 \\ \hline \end{array}$

6.
$\begin{array}{r} 14 \\ -\ 8 \\ \hline \end{array}$

7.
$\begin{array}{r} 13 \\ -\ 4 \\ \hline \end{array}$

8.
$\begin{array}{r} 15 \\ -\ 8 \\ \hline \end{array}$

Check Up

Add.

1.	6 +5	**2.**	4 +8	**3.**	9 +3	**4.**	3 +8
5.	5 +8	**6.**	9 +5	**7.**	8 +7	**8.**	6 +8

Subtract.

9.	12 − 9	**10.**	12 − 7	**11.**	11 − 4
12.	14 − 6	**13.**	15 − 8	**14.**	13 − 7

15.	14 − 8	**16.**	15 − 9

Add or subtract.

17.	3 +9	**18.**	8 +3	**19.**	12 − 6	**20.**	12 − 4	**21.**	11 − 8
22.	7 +7	**23.**	14 − 9	**24.**	4 +9	**25.**	8 +6	**26.**	13 − 6
27.	14 − 9	**28.**	9 +6	**29.**	15 − 7	**30.**	7 +8	**31.**	5 +9

Brainteaser

Copy the triangle. Find the missing numbers to make sums of 10 on each side. Use numbers from 1–6 once.

⑤

○   ○

○   ○   ①

REAL ESTATE AGENTS

Solve these problems.

1. 3 houses sold in June.
4 houses sold in July.
How many sold in all?

June   July

SOLD   SOLD

2. 5 new houses.
4 old houses.
How many in all?

3. 8 houses for sale.
5 sales agents.
How many more houses
than agents?

4. 4 new houses.
3 are sold.
How many are left?

SUMS 16, 17, and 18

$$8 + 8 = 16$$

$$9 + 9 = 18$$

1. Complete.

a.   9 + 7

    9 + ____ + 6

    ____ + 6

    ____

b.   9 + 8

    9 + ____ + 7

    ____ + 7

    ____

2. Add.

a.   9   7
     +7   +9

b.   9   8
     +8   +9

EXERCISES

Add.

1.   9   **2.**   7   **3.**   9   **4.**   8   **5.**   9
   +8   +9   +9   +9   +7

Solve these problems.

6. 8 orange balls.
9 yellow balls.
How many in all?

7. 9 blue birds.
9 red birds.
How many in all?

SUBTRACTING FROM 16, 17, AND 18

We can add.

We can subtract.

Addition Sentences
$$8 + 8 = 16$$
$$9 + 9 = 18$$

Related Subtraction Sentences
$$16 - 8 = 8$$
$$18 - 9 = 9$$

1. Find the differences.

a. $9 + 8 = 17$
$17 - 9 = \underline{\hphantom{00}}$
$17 - 8 = \underline{\hphantom{00}}$

b.
```
   9      16      16
 + 7    - 9     - 7
 ───    ────    ────
  16
```

2. Make true related sentences.

a. $9 + \square = 18$
$18 - 9 = \square$

b. $\square + 8 = 17$
$17 - 8 = \square$

c. $8 + \square = 16$
$16 - 8 = \square$

EXERCISES

Make true related sentences.

1. $\square + 7 = 16$
$16 - 7 = \square$

2. $9 + \square = 17$
$17 - 9 = \square$

3. $7 + \square = 16$
$16 - 7 = \square$

Subtract.

4.
```
  17
- 9
────
```

5.
```
  16
- 7
────
```

6.
```
  18
- 9
────
```

7.
```
  16
- 9
────
```

8.
```
  17
- 8
────
```

ADDITION TABLE

An Addition Table helps us to find facts.

+	0	1	2	3	4	5	6	7	8	9
0	0	1	2	3	4	5	6	7	8	9
1	1	2	3	4	5	6	7	8	9	10
2	2	3	4	5	6	7	8	9	10	11
3	3	4	5	6	7	8	9	10	11	12
4	4	5	6	7	8	9	10	11	12	13
5	5	6	7	8	9	10	11	12	13	14
6	6	7	8	9	10	11	12	13	14	15
7	7	8	9	10	11	12	13	14	15	16
8	8	9	10	11	12	13	14	15	16	17
9	9	10	11	12	13	14	15	16	17	18

1. Let's find $5 + 7$.

   (a) Find 5 on pink.
   (b) Find 7 on blue.
   (c) Follow the yellow path from 5 on pink until it is under 7 on blue.

What is $5 + 7$?

2. Let's find $12 - 7$.

   (a) Find 7 on blue.
   (b) Find 12 under 7.
   (c) Move left to 5 on pink.

What is $12 - 7$?

EXERCISES

Add or subtract. Use the table to check.

1. $8 + 6$ 2. $7 + 9$ 3. $17 - 8$ 4. $16 - 9$

5. $15 - 7$ 6. $9 + 6$ 7. $8 + 8$ 8. $13 - 7$

DIFFERENT KINDS OF NUMBER SENTENCES

I know how to compare.

6 + 3 ≡ 9	6 + 3 ≡ 8	6 + 3 ≡ 10
9 = 9	9 > 8	9 < 10
so 6 + 3 = 9	so 6 + 3 > 8	so 6 + 3 < 10

1. Make true sentences. Use >, <, or =.

   a. 9 − 3 ? 5   **b.** 9 − 3 ? 7   **c.** 9 − 3 ? 6

     .6 ≡ 5   6 ≡ 7   6 ≡ 6

   9 − 3 ≡ 5   9 − 3 ≡ 7   9 − 3 ≡ 6

2. Make true sentences. Use >, <, or =.

   a. 4 + 5 ≡ 9   **b.** 8 + 1 ≡ 10   **c.** 12 − 3 ≡ 7

EXERCISES

Make true sentences. Use >, <, or =.

1. 4 + 7 ≡ 9   2. 8 + 2 ≡ 10   3. 12 − 5 ≡ 7

4. 2 + 7 ≡ 8   5. 12 − 3 ≡ 8   6. 8 + 6 ≡ 13

7. 9 − 4 ≡ 6   8. 6 + 4 ≡ 11   9. 7 + 8 ≡ 16

10. 5 + 9 ≡ 14   11. 15 − 8 ≡ 6   12. 8 + 9 ≡ 18

13. 2 + 7 ≡ 11   14. 13 − 6 ≡ 7   15. 9 + 4 ≡ 12

FUNCTION MACHINE

A function machine follows a rule.
The rule in A is add 4.

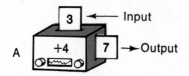 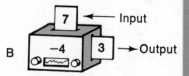

1. Look at function machine B above.

   a. What is the rule?

   b. What is the output?

   c. Find the input.

2. Find the missing numbers.

   a. 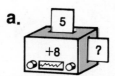 b.  c.

Find the missing numbers.

1.   2.   3.

4.   5.  6.

72

INPUT-OUTPUT TABLES

Tables can show Inputs and Outputs.

Add 3	
Input	*Output*
1	4
3	6
	7
8	

Think

$(1 + 3 = 4)$
$(3 + 3 = 6)$
$(4 + 3 = 7)$
$(8 + 3 = 11)$

Add 3	
Input	*Output*
1	4
3	6
4	7
8	11

1. Let's find the rule for this table.

   a. What was done to 7 to get 1?

   b. What was done to 9 to get 3?

   c. What is the rule?

Input	Output
7	1
9	3
12	6

2. Copy and complete by finding the rules.

   a.

Input	Output
3	2
6	5
9	8
11	

   b.

Input	Output
0	7
4	11
5	12
	14

EXERCISES

Copy and complete each table.

1.

Input	Output
8	0
9	1
11	3
14	

2.

Input	Output
0	4
3	7
4	
	9

CHAPTER REVIEW

Complete. [48, 61]

1. $7 + 2 = \square + 7$

2. $(3 + 7) + 5 = 3 + (\square + 5)$

Make true sentences.

3. $\square + 8 = 8$　　　**4.** $9 + \square = 14$　　　**5.** $\triangle + 7 = 12$
$8 - 8 = \square$　　　　　$14 - 9 = \square$　　　　　$12 - 7 = \triangle$

6. Write a related subtraction sentence for $8 + 1 = 9$.
[55]

Make true sentences. Use $>$, $<$, or $=$. [71]

7. $3 + 5 \equiv 8$　　　**8.** $7 + 5 \equiv 10$　　　**9.** $14 - 8 \equiv 9$

Add or subtract.

| **10.** [47] | 3 $+5$ | **11.** [51] | 9 -4 | **12.** [69] | 16 $- 9$ | **13.** [51] | 4 -4 | **14.** [51] | 9 -8 |

| **15.** [64] | 8 $+5$ | **16.** [47] | 6 $+2$ | **17.** [69] | 17 $- 8$ | **18.** [64] | 6 $+9$ | **19.** [68] | 8 $+9$ |

Write a number sentence for this problem. Solve it. [67]

20. 7 red candies. 9 green candies. How many in all?

Complete and copy by finding the rules. [73]

21.

Input	Output
9	3
10	4
12	6
13	

22.

Input	Output
2	5
3	6
5	8
	10

CHAPTER TEST

Complete.

1. $6 + 7 = \square + 6$

2. $(3 + 4) + 1 = 3 + (4 + \square)$

Make true sentences.

3. $9 + \square = 9$
$9 - 9 = \square$

4. $\triangle + 9 = 12$
$12 - 9 = \triangle$

5. $9 + \square = 17$
$17 - 9 = \square$

6. Write a related subtraction sentence for $7 + 1 = 8$.

Make true sentences. Use $>$, $<$, or $=$.

7. $6 + 4 \equiv 12$

8. $13 - 9 \equiv 4$

9. $11 - 4 \equiv 5$

Add or subtract.

10. $\begin{array}{r} 5 \\ +6 \\ \hline \end{array}$

11. $\begin{array}{r} 6 \\ +8 \\ \hline \end{array}$

12. $\begin{array}{r} 9 \\ +5 \\ \hline \end{array}$

13. $\begin{array}{r} 12 \\ -4 \\ \hline \end{array}$

14. $\begin{array}{r} 13 \\ -7 \\ \hline \end{array}$

15. $\begin{array}{r} 5 \\ +8 \\ \hline \end{array}$

16. $\begin{array}{r} 9 \\ +9 \\ \hline \end{array}$

17. $\begin{array}{r} 7 \\ +8 \\ \hline \end{array}$

18. $\begin{array}{r} 14 \\ -6 \\ \hline \end{array}$

19. $\begin{array}{r} 16 \\ -7 \\ \hline \end{array}$

Write a number sentence for this problem. Solve it.

20. 14 broken chairs. 5 fixed. How many still broken?

Copy and complete by finding the rules.

21.

Input	Output
1	8
3	10
5	12
6	

22.

Input	Output
9	4
10	5
12	7
	8

4 ADDING

ONE ADDEND GREATER THAN TEN

12 pink balloons.
6 green balloons.
How many in all?

$$\begin{array}{r} 12 \\ + \ 6 \\ \hline \end{array}$$

Expanded Form

$$\begin{array}{r} 12 \rightarrow 1 \text{ ten} + 2 \\ + \ 6 \rightarrow \phantom{1 \text{ ten} +} 6 \\ \hline 1 \text{ ten} + 8 = 18 \end{array}$$

Short Form

ADD ONES

$$\begin{array}{r} 12 \\ + \ 6 \\ \hline 8 \end{array}$$

ADD TENS

$$\begin{array}{r} 12 \\ + \ 6 \\ \hline 18 \end{array}$$

1. Complete.

$$\begin{array}{r} 75 \rightarrow 7 \text{ tens} + 5 \\ + \ 3 \rightarrow \phantom{7 \text{ tens}} + 3 \\ \hline \underline{} \text{ tens} + \underline{} = \underline{} \end{array}$$

$$\begin{array}{r} 75 \\ + \ 3 \\ \hline 8 \end{array}$$

2. The ones are the same. Add.

$$\begin{array}{r} 3 \\ +6 \\ \hline \end{array}\qquad \begin{array}{r} 13 \\ + \ 6 \\ \hline \end{array}\qquad \begin{array}{r} 23 \\ + \ 6 \\ \hline \end{array}\qquad \begin{array}{r} 33 \\ + \ 6 \\ \hline \end{array}\qquad \begin{array}{r} 43 \\ + \ 6 \\ \hline \end{array}\qquad \begin{array}{r} 53 \\ + \ 6 \\ \hline \end{array}$$

3. Add.

a. $\begin{array}{r} 23 \\ + \ 4 \\ \hline \end{array}$ **b.** $\begin{array}{r} 35 \\ + \ 2 \\ \hline \end{array}$ **c.** $\begin{array}{r} 44 \\ + \ 4 \\ \hline \end{array}$ **d.** $\begin{array}{r} 60 \\ + \ 5 \\ \hline \end{array}$

76

Add.

1. 20 + 7	**2.** 40 + 9	**3.** 13 + 5	**4.** 17 + 2
5. 14 + 5	**6.** 16 + 2	**7.** 24 + 3	**8.** 31 + 5
9. 11 + 8	**10.** 30 + 6	**11.** 65 + 3	**12.** 94 + 4
13. 13 + 3	**14.** 28 + 1	**15.** 40 + 2	**16.** 75 + 4
17. 21 + 5	**18.** 52 + 7	**19.** 90 + 8	**20.** 86 + 3

Solve these problems.

21. 13 kittens. 6 cats. How many animals in all?

22. 24 red marbles. 4 green marbles. How many in all?

THREE ADDENDS IN COLUMN FORM

Compare the sums.

Add down

4
5 ↓ 9
+3
―――
12

Add up

4
5 ↑ 8
+3
―――
12

The sums are the same.

1. Add down. Then add up.

   a.
   2
   3 ↓ 5
   +4
   ―――

   2
   3 ↑ 7
   +4
   ―――

   b.
   4
   1 ↓
   +2
   ―――

   4
   1 ↑
   +2
   ―――

2. Add down. Then add up.

   a.
   2
   9 ↓ 11
   +5
   ―――

   2
   9 ↑ 14
   +5
   ―――

   b.
   8
   3 ↓
   +7
   ―――

   8
   3 ↑
   +7
   ―――

Add down or add up.

1.
1
4
+2
―――

2.
4
2
+4
―――

3.
6
1
+2
―――

4.
1
5
+4
―――

5.
7
0
+2
―――

6.
7
8
+4
―――

7.
3
9
+7
―――

8.
8
6
+4
―――

9.
7
9
+2
―――

10.
6
8
+5
―――

78

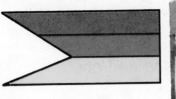  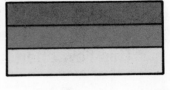

Race Time

Add.

1. 3 4	**2.** 2 2	**3.** 2 4	**4.** 3 2	**5.** 7 0	**6.** 3 3
7. 6 2	**8.** 4 0	**9.** 4 5	**10.** 3 6	**11.** 4 4	**12.** 1 8
13. 2 7	**14.** 5 3	**15.** 6 3	**16.** 1 9	**17.** 1 4	**18.** 8 4
19. 3 7	**20.** 7 8	**21.** 5 5	**22.** 4 7	**23.** 9 3	**24.** 5 0
25. 6 4	**26.** 5 2	**27.** 9 1	**28.** 2 8	**29.** 6 5	**30.** 3 1
31. 9 6	**32.** 8 8	**33.** 0 2	**34.** 7 5	**35.** 3 8	**36.** 9 8
37. 7 7	**38.** 9 2	**39.** 8 9	**40.** 6 9	**41.** 9 9	**42.** 7 4
43. 6 6	**44.** 8 5	**45.** 5 6	**46.** 8 6	**47.** 9 7	**48.** 7 5
49. 8 7	**50.** 9 5	**51.** 5 1	**52.** 6 7	**53.** 9 4	**54.** 9 8

ADDING TENS AND ONES

This flow chart shows how to add tens and ones.

Example

```
Start.
  ↓
Add ones.
  ↓
Add tens.
  ↓
Stop.
```

```
  24
+ 12
   6
```

```
  24
+ 12
  36
```

1. Complete.

   a. $60 \rightarrow$ 6 tens   60
       $+30 \rightarrow$ 3 tens $+30$
            9 tens = ___

   b. $35 \rightarrow$ 3 tens + 5   35
       $+43 \rightarrow$ 4 tens + 3 $+43$
         ___ tens + ___ = ___

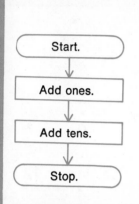

2. We can use the order property to check addition. Add down. Then add up to check.

   a.   78 ↓   78 ↑   b.   36 ↓   36 ↑
      $+\ 60$ ↓ $+60$ $+92$ ↓ $+92$
       138

3. Add and check.

   a.   47   b.   65   c.   48   d.   79
     $+82$ $+34$ $+91$ $+40$

80

Add.

1. 40 + 20	**2.** 30 + 27	**3.** 25 + 54	**4.** 75 + 20
5. 84 + 14	**6.** 77 + 11	**7.** 51 + 47	**8.** 34 + 64
9. 25 + 74	**10.** 40 + 40	**11.** 85 + 10	**12.** 20 + 69
13. 41 + 27	**14.** 53 + 16	**15.** 74 + 22	**16.** 82 + 11
17. 72 + 30	**18.** 61 + 57	**19.** 53 + 74	**20.** 80 + 59

Solve these mini-problems.

21. 50 pink tickets.
30 blue tickets.
How many in all?

22. 56 girls.
23 boys.
How many children?

Brainteaser

What number am I?

1. I am a number 1 less than 999.

2. I am a number 10 less than 999.

3. I am a number 100 less than 999.

ADDING HUNDREDS, TENS, AND ONES

Add in two ways to find the sum.

Expanded Form

$234 \rightarrow$ 2 hundreds + 3 tens + 4
$+352 \rightarrow$ 3 hundreds + 5 tens + 2
5 hundreds + 8 tens + 6 = 586

Short Form

ADD ONES	ADD TENS	ADD HUNDREDS
234	234	234
+352	+352	+352
6	86	586

1. Complete.

a. $500 \rightarrow$ 5 hundreds   500
$+200 \rightarrow$ 2 hundreds $+200$
7 hundreds = __

b. $306 \rightarrow$ 3 hundreds + 0 tens + 6   306
$+452 \rightarrow$ 4 hundreds + 5 tens + 2 $+452$
__ hundreds + __ tens + __ = __

2. Add down. Then add up to check.

a. 460↓   460↑   **b.** 156↓   156↑
$+830$↓ $+830$↑ $+630$↓ $+630$↑

3. Add.

a. 134   **b.** 204   **c.** 318   **d.** 709
$+\ \ 3$ $+\ 12$ $+141$ $+410$

Add.

1.	125 + 4	**2.**	231 + 8	**3.**	302 + 7	**4.**	430 + 54
5.	523 + 35	**6.**	605 + 73	**7.**	600 +200	**8.**	300 +400
9.	700 +200	**10.**	420 +360	**11.**	660 +320	**12.**	328 +271
13.	345 +521	**14.**	492 +507	**15.**	205 +504	**16.**	643 +345
17.	750 +219	**18.**	319 +720	**19.**	804 +403	**20.**	863 +536

★ Make true sentences. Use >, <, or =.

21. $756 + 512 \equiv 514 + 674$

22. $360 + 739 \equiv 643 + 432$

23. $672 + 317 \equiv 426 + 563$

Solve these mini-problems.

24. 265 red roses.
204 yellow roses.
How many in all?

25. 435 butterflies.
352 bees.
How many in all?

RENAMING ONES

Sometimes adding ones gives us a number greater than 9. Then we need to rename ones. Here are two ways:

Expanded Form

$$14 \longrightarrow 1 \text{ ten} + 4$$
$$+\ 9 \longrightarrow \phantom{1 \text{ ten} +} 9$$
$$1 \text{ ten} + 13$$
$$1 \text{ ten} + 1 \text{ ten} + 3$$
$$2 \text{ tens} + 3$$
$$23$$

Short Form

ADD ONES
1

$$14$$
$$+\ 9$$
$$3$$

ADD TENS
1

$$14$$
$$+\ 9$$
$$23$$

1. Complete.

$$19 \rightarrow \quad \overset{1}{1} \ \text{ten} \ + 9$$
$$+\ 3 \rightarrow \phantom{1 \ \text{ten} \ +} 3$$
$$\underline{} \ \text{tens} + 2 = \underline{}$$

2. Add using the expanded form.

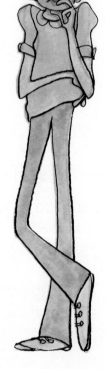

a. $36 \rightarrow \underline{}$ tens + $\underline{}$
   $+\ 4 \rightarrow \phantom{\underline{} \text{tens} +} 4$
   $\underline{}$ tens + $\underline{} = \underline{}$

b. $28 \rightarrow \underline{}$ tens + $\underline{}$
   $+\ 9 \rightarrow \phantom{\underline{} \text{tens} +} 9$
   $\underline{}$ tens + $\underline{} = \underline{}$

c. $47 \rightarrow \underline{}$ tens + $\underline{}$
   $+\ 5 \rightarrow \phantom{\underline{} \text{tens} +} 5$
   $\underline{}$ tens + $\underline{} = \underline{}$

84

3. Add. Use the short form.

a. 19
+ 4

b. 25
+ 5

c. 37
+ 6

d. 83
+ 9

e. 67
+ 4

f. 48
+ 6

g. 22
+ 8

h. 39
+ 5

Add. Use the short form.

1. 18
+ 5

2. 37
+ 8

3. 29
+ 6

4. 43
+ 9

5. 29
+ 4

6. 14
+ 9

7. 76
+ 7

8. 58
+ 8

9. 35
+ 9

10. 86
+ 6

11. 49
+ 7

12. 65
+ 6

13. 85
+ 9

14. 68
+ 7

15. 84
+ 6

16. 56
+ 5

17. 73
+ 8

18. 82
+ 9

19. 41
+ 9

20. 27
+ 6

Brainteaser

Steven's clock strikes the hours. At 1:00 it strikes once. At 2:00 it strikes two times, and so on. How many times did Steven's clock strike in one day?

ADDING FOUR NUMBERS

What's the total score?

Add down		Add up	
3 ↓		3	
5 ↓ 8 ↓		5	↑ 21
7	15	7 ↑ 16	
+9		+9	
24		24	

Think: Think:
3 + 5 = 8   9 + 7 = 16
8 + 7 = 15   16 + 5 = 21
15 + 9 = __   21 + 3 = __

Add down. Then add up.

1. 9 ↓ 13   9 ↑
    4 ↓   4 ↑ 11
  +7   +7

2. 2 ↓ 9   2
    7 ↓   7
    9   9 ↑ 14
  +5   +5

EXERCISES

Add down. Then add up.

	1.	**2.**	**3.**	**4.**	**5.**
	5	9	6	8	8
	8	4	9	8	7
	+7	+8	+7	+7	+8

	6.	**7.**	**8.**	**9.**	★**10.**
	1	2	3	4	5
	7	6	7	5	8
	9	8	6	9	8
	+8	+6	+8	+8	+9

COOKS AND CHEFS

Write number sentences. Do not solve.

1. 9 men chefs.
7 women chefs.
How many in all?

2. 17 people eating.
8 leave.
How many are left?

3. 13 pies.
8 cakes.
How many more
pies?

4. 16 cooks.
7 white caps.
How many more caps
needed?

5. 36 hamburgers.
20 cheeseburgers.
How many in all?

6. 35 apple pies.
24 cherry pies.
How many pies?

7. 125 yellow chairs.
200 black chairs.
How many chairs?

8. 210 grown-ups.
78 children.
How many people?

9. 104 big plates.
93 little plates.
How many in all?

★**10.** ▽ chocolate cookies.
△ oatmeal cookies.
How many in all?

TENS AND ONES—RENAMING

37 bicycles.
25 wagons.
How many in all?

Expanded Form

$$37 \rightarrow \overset{1}{3} \text{ tens} + 7$$
$$+25 \rightarrow 2 \text{ tens} + 5$$
$$6 \text{ tens} + 2 = 62$$

Short Form

ADD ONES

$$\begin{array}{r} \overset{1}{3}7 \\ +25 \\ \hline 2 \end{array}$$

ADD TENS

$$\begin{array}{r} \overset{1}{3}7 \\ +25 \\ \hline 62 \end{array}$$

1. Complete to find 56 + 39.

   a. Add ones. 6 + 9 = ___

   b. Rename 15.
       15 = ___ ten + ___

   $$56 \rightarrow \overset{1}{5} \text{ tens} + 6$$
   $$+39 \rightarrow 3 \text{ tens} + 9$$
   $$9 \text{ tens} + 5$$

   c. Add tens. 1 + 5 + 3 = ___

   d. What is the sum?

2. Complete.

   $$38 \rightarrow \overset{1}{3} \text{ tens} + 8$$
   $$+45 \rightarrow 4 \text{ tens} + 5$$
   $$\underline{\quad} \text{ tens} + 3 = \underline{\quad}$$

   $$\begin{array}{r} \overset{1}{38} \\ +45 \\ \hline 3 \end{array}$$

3. Add.

   a. $\begin{array}{r} 27 \\ +16 \\ \hline \end{array}$
   b. $\begin{array}{r} 35 \\ +29 \\ \hline \end{array}$
   c. $\begin{array}{r} 58 \\ +27 \\ \hline \end{array}$
   d. $\begin{array}{r} 89 \\ +19 \\ \hline \end{array}$

88

Add.

1.	45 + 15	**2.**	27 + 35	**3.**	35 + 38	**4.**	29 + 47
5.	26 + 65	**6.**	53 + 29	**7.**	37 + 58	**8.**	48 + 42
9.	46 + 57	**10.**	65 + 48	**11.**	48 + 79	**12.**	76 + 78

ACTIVITY

Across

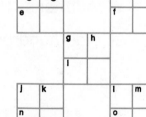

a.	18 + 17	c.	49 + 14	e.	28 + 8
f.	10 + 10	g.	49 + 17	i.	12 + 9
j.	20 + 27	l.	69 + 18	n.	17 + 28
o.	49 + 29				

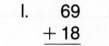

Down

a.	20 + 13	b.	29 + 27	c.	23 + 39	d.	15 + 15	g.	14 + 48
h.	54 + 7	j.	15 + 29	k.	36 + 39	l.	59 + 28	m.	38 + 40

89

We can find 425 + 238 this way:

Short Form

ADD ONES
1
425
+238
3

ADD TENS
1
425
+238
63

ADD HUNDREDS
1
425
+238
663

1. Let's find 247 + 326. Complete.

   a. Add ones. 7 + 6 = ___

   b. Rename 13.
      13 = ___ ten + ___

   c. Add tens. 1 + 4 + 2 = ___

   d. Add hundreds. 2 + 3 = ___

1
247
+ 326
573

2. Add.

   a. 419
      + 3

   b. 238
      + 24

   c. 127
      +248

   d. 307
      +725

EXERCISES

Add.

1. 167
   + 8

2. 309
   + 4

3. 614
   + 76

4. 805
   + 69

5. 279
   +416

6. 548
   +129

7. 309
   +375

8. 609
   +807

RENAMING

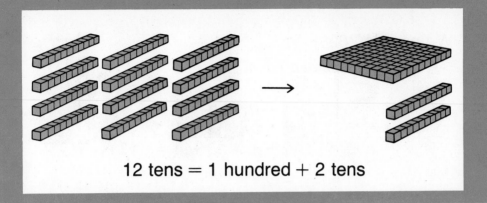

12 tens = 1 hundred + 2 tens

1. We can rename tens. Complete.

10 tens = 1 hundred
20 tens = 2 hundreds
30 tens = ___ hundreds

2. Complete.

29 tens = 20 tens + ___ tens
so, 29 tens = ___ hundreds + ___ tens

Complete.

1. 50 tens = 5 hundreds + ___ tens

2. 15 tens = 1 hundred + ___ tens

3. 27 tens = ___ hundreds + 7 tens

4. 24 tens = ___ hundreds + 4 tens

5. 16 tens = ___ hundred + ___ tens

91

TENS GREATER THAN 9

We can do 762 + 51.

Expanded Form

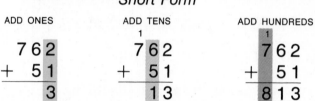

$$762 \rightarrow \overset{1}{7} \text{ hundreds} + 6 \text{ tens} + 2$$
$$+ \ 51 \rightarrow \qquad\qquad\quad 5 \text{ tens} + 1$$
$$\overline{8 \text{ hundreds} + 1 \text{ ten} + 3 = 813}$$

Short Form

ADD ONES	ADD TENS	ADD HUNDREDS
	1	1
7 6 2	7 6 2	7 6 2
+ 5 1	+ 5 1	+ 5 1
3	1 3	8 1 3

1. Complete to find 453 + 95.

$$453 \rightarrow \overset{1}{4} \text{ hundreds} + 5 \text{ tens} + 3$$
$$+ \ 95 \rightarrow \qquad\qquad\qquad 9 \text{ tens} + 5$$
$$\underline{\quad} \text{ hundreds} + 4 \text{ tens} + 8 = \underline{\quad}$$

2. Complete.

   a. Add ones. 4 + 0 = ____

   b. Add tens. 8 + 7 = ____

   c. Rename 15 tens.
      15 tens = ____ hundred + ____ tens

   d. Add hundreds. 1 + 6 + 5 = ____

   $$\overset{1}{684}$$
   $$+ 570$$
   $$\overline{1254}$$

3. Add.

a.	157	b.	234	c.	320	d.	548
	+ 82		+ 71		+ 194		+ 460

Add.

1.	326 + 82	**2.**	241 + 68	**3.**	674 + 43	**4.**	122 + 85

5.	288 + 51	**6.**	666 + 72	**7.**	685 +181	**8.**	347 +361

9.	167 +271	**10.**	324 +184	**11.**	235 +294	**12.**	586 +183

13.	340 +378	**14.**	278 +571	**15.**	699 +250	**16.**	197 +782

17.	246 +793	**18.**	892 +263	**19.**	845 +472	**20.**	947 +481

Solve these mini-problems.

21. 165 blue pens.
142 black pens.
How many pens?

22. 208 red pencils.
170 green pencils.
How many pencils?

23. 344 pink crayons.
462 blue crayons.
How many crayons?

24. 120 red rulers.
186 white rulers.
How many rulers?

Brainteaser

Solve these cases of missing digits.

1. 2■
+ 8
■0

2. ■6
+ 8
6■

3. 68
+ ■
■5

4. ■■
+ 8
97

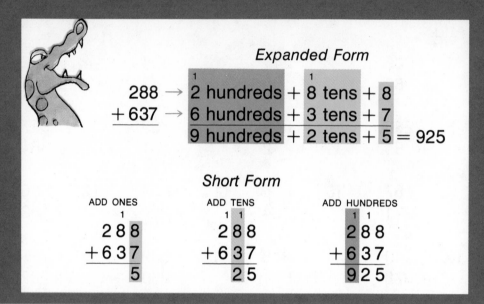

Expanded Form

$$288 \rightarrow \overset{1}{2} \text{ hundreds} + \overset{1}{8} \text{ tens} + 8$$
$$+637 \rightarrow 6 \text{ hundreds} + 3 \text{ tens} + 7$$
$$9 \text{ hundreds} + 2 \text{ tens} + 5 = 925$$

Short Form

ADD ONES	ADD TENS	ADD HUNDREDS
1	1 1	1 1
2 8 8	2 8 8	2 8 8
+ 6 3 7	+ 6 3 7	+ 6 3 7
5	2 5	9 2 5

1. Complete to find $546 + 296$.

$$546 \rightarrow 5 \text{ hundreds} + \overset{1}{4} \text{ tens} + 6$$
$$+296 \rightarrow 2 \text{ hundreds} + 9 \text{ tens} + 6$$
$$\underline{} \text{ hundreds} + \underline{} \text{ tens} + 2 = \underline{}$$

2. Look at $345 + 459$. Complete.

    a. Add ones. $5 + 9 = \underline{}$

    b. Add tens. $1 + 4 + 5 = \underline{}$

    c. Rename 10 tens.
       10 tens = $\underline{}$ hundred + 0 tens

    d. Complete the addition.

$$\overset{1\ 1}{345}$$
$$+459$$
$$\overline{04}$$

3. Add.

    a. $\begin{array}{r} 589 \\ +29 \\ \hline \end{array}$ **b.** $\begin{array}{r} 246 \\ +497 \\ \hline \end{array}$ **c.** $\begin{array}{r} 602 \\ +399 \\ \hline \end{array}$ **d.** $\begin{array}{r} 849 \\ +186 \\ \hline \end{array}$

1.	159 + 61	**2.**	397 + 34	**3.**	186 + 14	**4.**	248 + 98
5.	659 + 165	**6.**	369 + 379	**7.**	539 + 296	**8.**	327 + 587
9.	139 + 678	**10.**	258 + 686	**11.**	756 + 196	**12.**	488 + 447
13.	796 + 306	**14.**	453 + 859	**15.**	762 + 798	**16.**	847 + 879

Solve these problems.

17. There are 69 boys' bikes and 57 girls' bikes parked in the bike stand. How many bikes in all?

18. There are 207 boys and 286 girls at Bryant School. How many children are in the school?

★ **19.** A library has 2 bookcases each with 183 books, and 4 bookcases each with 246 books. How many books are in these 6 bookcases?

ACTIVITY

1. Find out how many girls there are in your school.

2. Find out how many boys there are in your school.

3. Now, write your own story problem.

95

COLUMN ADDITION

How many minutes did Carla practice this week?

Days	Number of Minutes
Monday	35
Tuesday	28
Wednesday	34

ADD ONES
```
  1
  3 5
  2 8
+ 3 4
    7
```

ADD TENS
```
  1
  3 5
  2 8
+ 3 4
  9 7
```

1. Complete.

   a. Add ones and rename.
   $(9 + 6) + 8 =$ ___
   $23 =$ ___ tens + ___

   b. Add tens. $2 + 1 + 4 + 5 =$ ___

   ```
     2
    19
    46
  + 58
   123
   ```

2. Complete.

   a. Add ones. $4 + 6 + 2 =$ ___
   Rename. $12 =$ ___ ten + ___ ones

   b. Add tens. $1 + 9 + 8 + 6 =$ ___
   Rename. 24 tens = ___ hundreds + ___ tens

   ```
     2 1
    394
     86
  + 462
    942
   ```

   c. Add hundreds. $2 + 3 + 4 =$ ___

96

3. Add.

	a.		**b.**		**c.**		**d.**
	23		36		43		104
	12		40		25		386
	+ 34		+ 22		+ 41		+ 203

1.	**2.**	**3.**	**4.**
43	35	56	78
14	23	37	24
+ 25	+ 32	+ 65	+ 65

5.	**6.**	**7.**	**8.**
14	20	234	347
20	16	328	108
+ 43	+ 42	+ 416	+ 534

9.	**10.**	**11.**	**12.**
322	138	472	276
470	241	152	490
+ 144	+ 590	+ 272	+ 132

Keeping Fit

How many cents?

1. 1 quarter

2. 1 quarter and 2 dimes

3. 1 half dollar

4. 1 half dollar and 1 quarter

5. 1 dollar

6. 2 dimes and 1 nickel

Rewrite in dollars and cents form.

7. 150¢   **8.** 205¢   **9.** 360¢   **10.** 485¢

11. 640¢   **12.** 525¢   **13.** 410¢   **14.** 730¢

Check Up

Add.

1.   7
     4
  +6

2.   8
     5
  +9

3.   6
     9
  +5

4.   14
  + 3

5.   53
  +36

6.   527
  +862

7.   18
  + 4

8.   27
  +69

9.   68
  +79

10.   324
  + 39

11.   746
  +236

12.   581
  + 148

13.   873
  +676

14.   961
  +366

15.   364
  + 78

16.   479
  +226

17.   647
  + 193

18.   498
  +858

19.   22
     4
  + 31

20.   43
    16
  + 25

21.   145
    260
  + 127

22.   247
    401
  +984

Brainteaser

1. Place the numbers in 4 new rows, so that each row and column has a sum of 10.

```
1  1  1  1
2  2  2  2
3  3  3  3
4  4  4  4
```

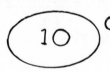

2. Added together, we make 25.
Take one from the other.
Now you have 9.
What numbers are we?

98

ADDING DOLLARS AND CENTS

How much did Jane spend for these gifts?

$2.68
$5.26

$$\begin{array}{r} 1 \\ \$2.68 \\ +\ 5.26 \\ \hline \$7.94 \end{array}$$

1. Complete.

Blouse cost $5.67.
Shirt cost $3.59.
How much in all?

$$\begin{array}{r} 1\ 1 \\ \$5.67 \\ +\ 3.59 \\ \hline 6 \end{array}$$

2. Add.

a. $3.56
   + 1.76

b. $4.02
   + .88

c. $6.98
   + .12

d. $7.97
   + 1.14

EXERCISES

Add.

1. $1.05
  + 1.14

2. $1.36
  + 2.02

3. $2.43
  + 1.37

4. $2.36
  + .58

5. $1.60
  + 3.70

6. $3.57
  + .90

7. $4.86
  + 1.29

8. $2.75
  + 4.78

Solve these mini-problems.

9. $3.25 for a book.
$1.29 for a pen.
How much in all?

★ **10.** $2.75 in piggy bank.
50¢ is put in.
How much in all?

99

STREET POLLUTION

Street pollution causes problems.

1. Mr. Keller had a flat tire because of a nail on the road. He paid $4.25 to have the tire changed and $2.50 to have the tire fixed. How much did street pollution cost him?

2. Bob slipped on a banana peel. He hurt his arm. It cost $4.57 for medicine and $1.86 for a sling. How much did Bob's parents have to spend?

3. Bob could not mow two lawns that week. He would have earned $3.90 for one lawn and $4.25 for another. How much did Bob lose?

4. Two women had to pick up leaflets in the street. One was paid $4.50 and the other was paid $2.75. How much did it cost to pick up the leaflets?

5. Dust made Jane sick. She could not babysit. She would have earned $3.50 on Saturday and $5.50 on Sunday. How much did Jane lose?

Complete.

1. $6 + 3 = 3 + \square$

2. $5 + (2 + 6) = (5 + \square) + 6$

3. $(10 + 4) + 9 = 10 + (4 + \square)$

Add.

4.	5.	6.	7.	8.
4 +8	6 +8	5 +3	8 +9	6 +4

9.	10.	11.	12.	13.
8 +8	4 +7	6 +6	5 +8	9 +9

Subtract.

14.	15.	16.	17.	18.
12 − 7	14 − 8	17 − 9	15 − 8	12 − 6

19.	20.	21.	22.	23.
13 − 5	16 − 9	10 − 6	11 − 3	18 − 9

What times are shown? Use the __:__ form.

24.

25.

26.

27.

28.

29.

101

CHAPTER REVIEW

Add.

1. 75 [76] $+\ 4$	**2.** 16 [80] $+70$	**3.** 54 [80] $+25$	**4.** 163 [82] $+625$
5. 631 [82] $+128$	**6.** 37 [84] $+\ 8$	**7.** 17 [88] $+57$	**8.** 48 [88] $+38$
9. 706 [90] $+108$	**10.** 327 [90] $+\ 45$	**11.** 822 [90] $+\ 9$	**12.** 525 [90] $+636$
13. 442 [92] $+295$	**14.** 270 [92] $+251$	**15.** 847 [92] $+161$	**16.** 749 [92] $+270$
17. 187 [94] $+426$	**18.** 274 [94] $+586$	**19.** 716 [94] $+287$	**20.** 655 [94] $+786$
21. $1.38 [99] $+2.47$	**22.** $1.72 [99] $+6.14$	**23.** $3.28 [99] $+2.64$	**24.** $4.98 [99] $+4.86$
25. 2 [78] 4 $+3$	**26.** 8 [78] 6 $+7$	**27.** 6 [78] 0 $+3$	**28.** 27 [96] 11 $+49$
29. 245 [96] 23 $+601$	**30.** 537 [96] 162 $+250$	**31.** 426 [96] 214 $+145$	**32.** 717 [96] 184 $+324$

Solve these mini-problems. [90, 96]

33. 205 girls.
268 boys.
How many children?

34. 12 red marbles.
23 green marbles.
17 yellow marbles.
How many in all?

CHAPTER TEST

Add.

1. 94
   + 4

2. 20
   +63

3. 720
   +359

4. 58
   + 8

5. 85
   +36

6. 419
   + 2

7. 452
   + 91

8. 263
   +384

9. 619
   +296

10. 386
    +428

11. $6.25
    + 1.38

12. $2.57
    +2.94

13. 4
    3
    +2

14. 9
    6
    +4

15. 7
    9
    +5

16. 16
    20
    +53

17. 27
    31
    +49

18. 537
    162
    + 50

19. 425
    349
    +228

20. 187
    519
    +355

Solve these mini-problems.

21. 128 cars in a lot.
    37 more come.
    How many in all?

22. 15 gumdrops.
    28 jelly beans.
    How many candies?

ACTIVITY

Look in a newspaper. Find the cost of each grocery item.

Write each amount and find the total cost.

5 SUBTRACTING

SUBTRACTING TENS AND ONES

18 balloons.
6 pop.
How many are left?

$$\begin{array}{r} 18 \\ -\ 6 \\ \hline 12 \end{array}$$

Expanded Form

$$\begin{array}{r} 18 \rightarrow \\ -\ 6 \rightarrow \\ \hline \end{array} \begin{array}{l} 1 \text{ ten} + 8 \\ 6 \\ \hline 1 \text{ ten} + 2 = 12 \end{array}$$

Short Form

SUBTRACT ONES

$$\begin{array}{r} 18 \\ -\ 6 \\ \hline 2 \end{array}$$

SUBTRACT TENS

$$\begin{array}{r} 18 \\ -\ 6 \\ \hline 12 \end{array}$$

1. Complete.

a.
$$\begin{array}{r} 70 \rightarrow \\ -30 \rightarrow \\ \hline \end{array} \begin{array}{l} 7 \text{ tens} \\ 3 \text{ tens} \\ \hline 4 \text{ tens} = \underline{} \end{array}$$

$$\begin{array}{r} 70 \\ -30 \\ \hline \end{array}$$

b.
$$\begin{array}{r} 96 \rightarrow \\ -23 \rightarrow \\ \hline \end{array} \begin{array}{l} 9 \text{ tens} + 6 \\ 2 \text{ tens} + 3 \\ \hline 7 \text{ tens} + 3 = \underline{} \end{array}$$

$$\begin{array}{r} 96 \\ -23 \\ \hline \end{array}$$

2. Subtract.

a.
$$\begin{array}{r} 50 \\ -20 \\ \hline \end{array}$$

b.
$$\begin{array}{r} 97 \\ -\ 3 \\ \hline \end{array}$$

c.
$$\begin{array}{r} 78 \\ -74 \\ \hline \end{array}$$

d.
$$\begin{array}{r} 53 \\ -43 \\ \hline \end{array}$$

104

Subtract. Use the short form.

1. 36 − 6	**2.** 48 − 7	**3.** 87 − 5	**4.** 79 − 4

5. 40 − 30   **6.** 62 − 40   **7.** 67 − 63   **8.** 85 − 84

9. 22 − 11   **10.** 38 − 27   **11.** 58 − 34   **12.** 66 − 20

13. 42 − 30   **14.** 68 − 35   **15.** 74 − 41   **16.** 86 − 53

Solve these mini-problems.

17. 78 children.
35 boys.
How many girls?

★ **18.** 87 marbles.
44 lost.
32 won.
How many now?

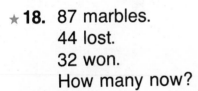

Brainteaser

What number am I?

1. I am a number 1 less than 1,000.

2. I am a number 10 less than 1,000.

3. I am a number 100 less than 1,000.

CHECKING SUBTRACTION

We can check subtraction by adding.

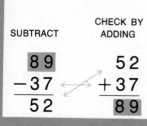

SUBTRACT	CHECK BY ADDING
89	52
− 37	+ 37
52	89

1. Add to check. Is the subtraction correct?

```
  97        73
- 25       + 25
  73
```

2. Subtract.

a. 29
      − 23

b. 47
      − 7

c. 70
      − 20

d. 89
      − 12

EXERCISES

Subtract and check.

1. 26
      − 3

2. 77
      − 7

3. 57
      − 25

4. 69
      − 64

5. 94
      − 63

6. 63
      − 43

7. 78
      − 44

8. 80
      − 50

9. 65
      − 53

10. 56
       − 43

11. 85
       − 72

12. 79
       − 36

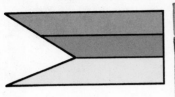

Race Time

Subtract.

1. 8 <u>0</u>	**2.** 7 <u>5</u>	**3.** 3 <u>2</u>	**4.** 4 <u>2</u>	**5.** 7 <u>0</u>	**6.** 9 <u>2</u>
7. 7 <u>3</u>	**8.** 7 <u>2</u>	**9.** 6 <u>3</u>	**10.** 2 <u>2</u>	**11.** 6 <u>0</u>	**12.** 8 <u>4</u>
13. 9 <u>7</u>	**14.** 8 <u>5</u>	**15.** 8 <u>3</u>	**16.** 9 <u>3</u>	**17.** 10 <u>9</u>	**18.** 9 <u>5</u>
19. 6 <u>2</u>	**20.** 0 <u>0</u>	**21.** 8 <u>1</u>	**22.** 10 <u>4</u>	**23.** 6 <u>4</u>	**24.** 14 <u>9</u>
25. 10 <u>8</u>	**26.** 13 <u>4</u>	**27.** 12 <u>8</u>	**28.** 11 <u>5</u>	**29.** 10 <u>2</u>	**30.** 14 <u>8</u>
31. 17 <u>9</u>	**32.** 16 <u>8</u>	**33.** 11 <u>2</u>	**34.** 17 <u>8</u>	**35.** 14 <u>7</u>	**36.** 13 <u>9</u>
37. 12 <u>4</u>	**38.** 15 <u>9</u>	**39.** 12 <u>3</u>	**40.** 11 <u>4</u>	**41.** 12 <u>9</u>	**42.** 13 <u>5</u>
43. 11 <u>7</u>	**44.** 16 <u>7</u>	**45.** 13 <u>7</u>	**46.** 11 <u>6</u>	**47.** 15 <u>7</u>	**48.** 15 <u>6</u>
49. 16 <u>9</u>	**50.** 15 <u>8</u>	**51.** 14 <u>6</u>	**52.** 14 <u>5</u>	**53.** 8 <u>2</u>	**54.** 18 <u>9</u>

HUNDREDS, TENS, AND ONES

We can subtract large numbers.

Expanded Form

$356 \rightarrow$ 3 hundreds + 5 tens + 6
$-142 \rightarrow$ 1 hundred + 4 tens + 2
2 hundreds + 1 ten + 4 = 214

Short Form

SUBTRACT ONES	SUBTRACT TENS	SUBTRACT HUNDREDS
356	356	356
−142	−142	−142
4	14	214

1. Complete.

a.
$900 \rightarrow$ 9 hundreds
$-500 \rightarrow$ 5 hundreds
4 hundreds = ___

b.
$787 \rightarrow$ 7 hundreds + 8 tens + 7
$-352 \rightarrow$ 3 hundreds + 5 tens + 2
___ hundreds + ___ tens + 5 = ___

2. Copy and complete.

a.	b.	c.	d.
649	567	935	798
− 326	− 463	− 624	− 576
23	04	1	2

3. Subtract. Use the short form.

a.	b.	c.	d.
800	735	420	358
− 600	− 4	− 10	− 127

108

Subtract. Use the short form.

1.	175 − 3	**2.**	138 − 37	**3.**	386 − 81	**4.**	470 −230
5.	666 −665	**6.**	129 −120	**7.**	280 −130	**8.**	604 −502
9.	709 −504	**10.**	988 −345	**11.**	969 −219	**12.**	907 −403
13.	780 −360	**14.**	599 −271	**15.**	677 −177	**16.**	893 −373

★ **17.** Make a flow chart to show how to subtract hundreds, tens, and ones.

Solve these mini-problems.

18. 196 sheets of paper.
65 are used.
How many are left?

19. 596 library books.
330 are old.
How many are new?

★ **20.** 688 pages in a book.
Read 240 pages.
Read another 142.
How many pages left?

★ **21.** 85 books on a shelf.
32 are removed.
12 returned.
How many on the shelf?

109

Keeping Fit

Compare. Use >, <, or =.

1. 6,300 ≣ 6,800

2. 5,260 ≣ 3,987

3. 9,028 ≣ 9,028

Make true sentences. Use >, <, or =.

4. 4 + 8 ≣ 14

5. 7 + 9 ≣ 16

6. 13 − 9 ≣ 5

7. 16 − 8 ≣ 3

Add.

8. 8
+ 6

9. 6
+ 5

10. 5
+ 7

11. 3
+ 8

12. 9
+ 9

Subtract.

13. 15
− 9

14. 17
− 9

15. 13
− 5

16. 12
− 6

17. 17
− 8

What times are shown? Use the __:__ form.

18.

19.

What time will it be in 2 hours?

20.

21.

110

RENAMING TENS

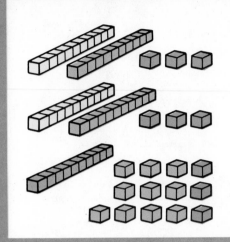

$23 = 2 \text{ tens} + 3$
$= 1 \text{ ten} + 1 \text{ ten} + 3$
$= 1 \text{ ten} + 13$

1. Complete.

$56 = 5 \text{ tens} + 6$
$= 4 \text{ tens} + \underline{} \text{ ten} + \underline{}$
$= 4 \text{ tens} + \underline{}$

2. Complete.

a. $90 = \underline{} \text{ tens} + 10$ **b.** $34 = \underline{} \text{ tens} + 14$

EXERCISES

Complete.

1. $40 = 3 \text{ tens} + \underline{}$ **2.** $53 = 4 \text{ tens} + \underline{}$

3. $65 = \underline{} \text{ tens} + 15$ **4.** $71 = \underline{} \text{ tens} + 11$

5. $85 = 7 \text{ tens} + \underline{}$ **6.** $93 = 8 \text{ tens} + \underline{}$

7. $62 = 5 \text{ tens} + \underline{}$ **8.** $80 = \underline{} \text{ tens} + 10$

111

Look at 23 − 5.

Expanded Form

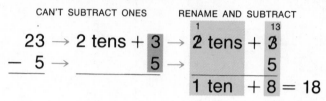

CAN'T SUBTRACT ONES   RENAME AND SUBTRACT

$$23 \rightarrow 2 \text{ tens} + 3 \rightarrow \overset{1}{2} \text{ tens} + \overset{13}{\cancel{3}}$$
$$- 5 \rightarrow \qquad\quad 5 \rightarrow \qquad\qquad 5$$
$$\qquad\qquad\qquad\qquad\qquad 1 \text{ ten} + 8 = 18$$

Short Form

CAN'T SUBTRACT ONES	RENAME	SUBTRACT ONES	SUBTRACT TENS
	1 13	1 13	1 13
2 3	2 3	2 3	2 3
− 5	− 5	− 5	− 5
		8	1 8

1. Complete to find 32 − 7.

a. Rename 32.
32 = 2 tens + ___

b. Subtract ones.
12 − 7 = ___

$$32 \rightarrow \overset{2}{\cancel{3}} \text{ tens} + \overset{12}{2}$$
$$- 7 \rightarrow \qquad\qquad 7$$
$$\qquad\qquad 2 \text{ tens} + 5 = 25$$

c. How many tens?

2. Complete to find 67 − 8.

$$67 \rightarrow \overset{5}{\cancel{6}} \text{ tens} + \overset{17}{7}$$
$$- 8 \rightarrow \qquad\qquad 8$$
$$\qquad\quad \underline{\quad} \text{ tens} + \underline{\quad} = \underline{\quad}$$

$$\overset{5\ 17}{\cancel{6}\cancel{7}}$$
$$- \quad 8$$

3. Subtract. Use the short form.

a. 28
− 9

b. 74
− 8

c. 90
− 2

d. 82
− 7

112

Subtract. Use the short form.

1. 82
    − 3

2. 63
    − 7

3. 36
    − 8

4. 42
    − 6

5. 56
    − 9

6. 91
    − 7

7. 43
    − 4

8. 53
    − 6

9. 35
    − 9

10. 86
    − 8

11. 22
    − 9

12. 71
    − 4

13. 74
    − 5

14. 45
    − 8

15. 35
    − 6

16. 52
    − 9

17. 34
    − 8

18. 56
    − 7

19. 70
    − 4

20. 64
    − 7

21. 41
    − 9

22. 20
    − 8

23. 94
    − 7

24. 85
    − 8

25. 72
    − 8

26. 83
    − 4

27. 60
    − 7

28. 98
    − 9

Solve these mini-problems.

29. 24 sea shells.
    8 broken.
    How many sea shells
    not broken?

30. 32 fish.
    5 eaten.
    How many are left?

TENS AND ONES: RENAMING

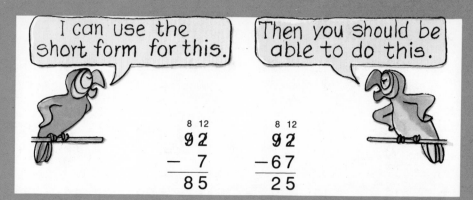

1. Complete to find 87 − 49.

$$87 \rightarrow \overset{7}{\cancel{8}}\text{ tens} + \overset{17}{\cancel{7}}$$
$$-49 \rightarrow 4\text{ tens} + 9$$
$$\underline{}\text{ tens} + \underline{} = \underline{}$$

$$\overset{7\ 17}{\cancel{8}\cancel{7}}$$
$$-49$$

2. Subtract. Use the short form.

a.	b.	c.	d.
26	84	74	85
− 19	− 38	− 29	− 28

EXERCISES

Subtract. Use the short form.

1.	2.	3.	4.
46	54	82	95
− 28	− 28	− 47	− 36

5.	6.	7.	8.
45	62	76	87
− 28	− 45	− 49	− 78

9.	10.	11.	12.
40	40	66	93
− 15	− 38	− 37	− 46

114

SUBTRACTING HUNDREDS

Subtracting hundreds is like subtracting tens.

I can rename tens.

```
  5 15
  6 5
- 5 8
───────
    7
```

```
  5 15
3 6 5
-1 5 8
───────
2 0 7
```

1. Complete.

a.
```
  6 14
2 7 4
-   8
───────
```

b.
```
  5 10
3 6 0
-  27
───────
```

c.
```
  6 13
8 7 3
-1 3 9
───────
```

d.
```
  7 11
9 8 1
-4 5 6
───────
```

2. Subtract.

a.
```
  235
- 208
─────
```

b.
```
  450
- 446
─────
```

c.
```
  530
- 126
─────
```

d.
```
  787
- 249
─────
```

EXERCISES

Subtract.

1.
```
  362
-   4
─────
```

2.
```
  432
-  25
─────
```

3.
```
  695
- 279
─────
```

4.
```
  684
- 309
─────
```

5.
```
  892
- 769
─────
```

6.
```
  677
- 548
─────
```

7.
```
  916
- 609
─────
```

8.
```
  996
- 358
─────
```

9.
```
  683
- 258
─────
```

10.
```
  740
- 425
─────
```

11.
```
  582
- 527
─────
```

12.
```
  950
- 943
─────
```

RENAMING HUNDREDS

We can rename 1 hundred as 10 tens.

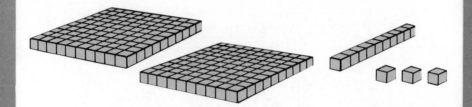

213 = 2 hundreds + 1 ten + 3
= (1 hundred + 1 hundred) + 1 ten + 3
= 1 hundred + (10 tens + 1 ten) + 3
= 1 hundred + 11 tens + 3

1. Complete to rename.

   a. 374 = 3 hundreds + 7 tens + 4
   = (2 hundreds + ___ hundred) + 7 tens + 4
   = 2 hundreds + (___ tens + 7 tens) + 4
   = 2 hundreds + ___ tens + 4

   b. 682 = 6 hundreds + 8 tens + 2
   = ___ hundreds + (10 tens + 8 tens) + 2
   = ___ hundreds + ___ tens + 2

2. Complete to rename.

   a. 240 = 2 hundreds + 4 tens + 0
   = ___ hundred + 14 tens + 0

   b. 451 = 4 hundreds + 5 tens + 1
   = 3 hundreds + ___ tens + 1

   c. 762 = 7 hundreds + 6 tens + 2
   = ___ hundreds + 16 tens + 2

Complete to rename.

1. 853 = 8 hundreds + 5 tens + 3
= ___ hundreds + 15 tens + ___

2. 632 = ___ hundreds + 3 tens + ___
= 5 hundreds + ___ tens + ___

3. 751 = 7 hundreds + ___ tens + 1
= ___ hundreds + 15 tens + ___

4. 946 = 9 hundreds + 4 tens + 6
= ___ hundreds + 14 tens + ___

5. 485 = ___ hundreds + 8 tens + ___
= 3 hundreds + ___ tens + ___

ACTIVITY

1. Make a pocket chart like the one shown below. You will need to make paper strips: 4 red, 10 orange, and 3 yellow.

2. Show 403 on your chart, using only the red and yellow strips.

3. Now replace 1 hundred with 10 orange tens.

4. Complete. Use your chart to help you.
403 = 3 hundreds + ___ tens + ___ ones.

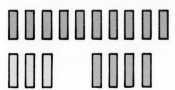

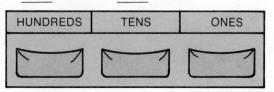

HUNDREDS	TENS	ONES

SUBTRACTING: RENAMING HUNDREDS

Let's find 214 − 62.

Expanded Form

$$\begin{array}{r} \overset{1}{214} \rightarrow \overset{1}{2}\text{ hundreds} + \overset{11}{1}\text{ ten } + 4 \\ -\ 62 \rightarrow \phantom{2\text{ hundreds} + }6\text{ tens} + 2 \\ \hline 1\text{ hundred } + 5\text{ tens} + 2 = 152 \end{array}$$

Short Form

SUBTRACT ONES	CAN'T SUBTRACT TENS	RENAME	SUBTRACT
$\begin{array}{r} 214 \\ -\ 62 \\ \hline 2 \end{array}$	$\begin{array}{r} 214 \\ -\ 62 \\ \hline 2 \end{array}$	$\begin{array}{r} \overset{1\ 11}{2\!1\,4} \\ -\ 62 \\ \hline 2 \end{array}$	$\begin{array}{r} \overset{1\ 11}{2\!1\,4} \\ -\ 62 \\ \hline 152 \end{array}$

1. Complete.

$$\begin{array}{r} 726 \rightarrow \overset{6}{7}\text{ hundreds} + \overset{12}{2}\text{ tens} + 6 \\ -375 \rightarrow 3\text{ hundreds} + 7\text{ tens} + 5 \\ \hline 3\text{ hundreds} + 5\text{ tens} + 1 = 351 \end{array} \qquad \begin{array}{r} \overset{6\ 12}{7\,2\,6} \\ -375 \\ \hline 351 \end{array}$$

a. Subtract ones. $6 - 5 = $ ___

b. Rename. 7 hundreds + 2 tens + 6
___ hundreds + 12 tens + 6

c. Subtract tens. $12 - 7 = $ ___

d. Subtract hundreds. $6 - 3 = $ ___

2. Subtract. Use the short form.

a. $\begin{array}{r} 326 \\ -\ 70 \\ \hline \end{array}$ b. $\begin{array}{r} 670 \\ -190 \\ \hline \end{array}$ c. $\begin{array}{r} 349 \\ -263 \\ \hline \end{array}$ d. $\begin{array}{r} 915 \\ -462 \\ \hline \end{array}$

Subtract. Use the short form.

1. 240 − 80	**2.** 327 − 57	**3.** 568 − 72	**4.** 719 − 63
5. 529 − 335	**6.** 769 − 586	**7.** 956 − 270	**8.** 849 − 678
9. 849 − 799	**10.** 727 − 493	**11.** 618 − 372	**12.** 979 − 197
13. 426 − 334	**14.** 745 − 574	**15.** 878 − 384	**16.** 914 − 682

Solve these mini-problems.

17. Had 538 stones.
Lost 272.
How many left? *266*

★**18.** 352 boys and 375 girls.
485 chairs.
How many more chairs needed?

ACTIVITY

1. Make paper strips for a chart. Show 520.

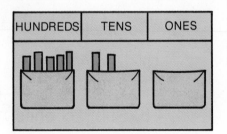

2. Make another 10 orange strips. Replace 1 hundred with 10 tens.

3. Now remove as many paper strips as needed to show 270.

4. Find the difference. You may use your chart to check.

520
− 270

119

We can find $341 - 167$.

Expanded Form

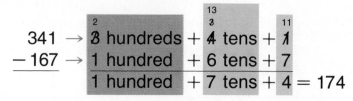

$$
\begin{aligned}
341 &\to \overset{2}{\cancel{3}} \text{ hundreds} + \overset{\overset{13}{\cancel{3}}}{4} \text{ tens} + \overset{11}{\cancel{1}} \\
-167 &\to 1 \text{ hundred } + 6 \text{ tens} + 7 \\
\hline
& 1 \text{ hundred } + 7 \text{ tens} + 4 = 174
\end{aligned}
$$

Short Form

SUBTRACT ONES	SUBTRACT TENS	SUBTRACT HUNDREDS
$\begin{array}{r} {}^{3}\ {}^{11} \\ 34\cancel{1} \\ -167 \\ \hline 4 \end{array}$	$\begin{array}{r} {}^{2}\ {}^{13}_{3}\ {}^{11} \\ \cancel{3}4\cancel{1} \\ -167 \\ \hline 74 \end{array}$	$\begin{array}{r} {}^{2}\ {}^{13}_{3}\ {}^{11} \\ \cancel{3}4\cancel{1} \\ -167 \\ \hline 174 \end{array}$

1. Complete the expanded form to find $462 - 287$.

$$
\begin{aligned}
462 &\to \overset{3}{\cancel{4}} \text{ hundreds} + \overset{\overset{15}{\cancel{5}}}{6} \text{ tens} + \overset{12}{2} \\
-287 &\to 2 \text{ hundreds} + 8 \text{ tens} + 7 \\
\hline
& \underline{} \text{ hundreds} + \underline{} \text{ tens} + \underline{} = \underline{}
\end{aligned}
$$

2. Complete.

a. Rename tens.
6 tens $+ 2 = $ _____ tens $+ 12$

$$\begin{array}{r} {}^{5}\,{}^{12} \\ 4\cancel{6}\cancel{2} \\ -287 \\ \hline 5 \end{array}$$

b. Subtract ones. $12 - 7 = $ _____

c. Rename hundreds.
4 hundreds $+ 5$ tens $+ 12$
$= $ _____ hundreds $+ 15$ tens $+ 12$

$$\begin{array}{r} {}^{15} \\ {}^{3}\,{}^{5}\,{}^{12} \\ 4\cancel{6}\cancel{2} \\ -287 \\ \hline \end{array}$$

d. Subtract tens. $15 - 8 = $ _____

e. Subtract hundreds. $3 - 2 = $ _____

3. Subtract. Use the short form.

a. 212 **b.** 412 **c.** 722 **d.** 853
$-\ 68$ -147 -645 -289

Subtract. Use the short form.

1. 625 **2.** 436 **3.** 635 **4.** 824
$-\ 47$ $-\ 69$ -387 -165

5. 744 **6.** 835 **7.** 914 **8.** 814
-376 -296 -587 -678

9. 634 **10.** 945 **11.** 852 **12.** 936
-578 -687 -796 -488

13. 364 **14.** 521 **15.** 815 **16.** 972
-287 -238 -548 -463

17. 565 **18.** 897 **19.** 786 **20.** 654
-386 -698 -589 -465

Solve these mini-problems.

21. 234 bikes.
146 boys' bikes.
How many girls'
bikes?

22. 125 bells.
68 ringing.
How many not
ringing?

23. 364 apples.
187 red apples.
How many apples
not red?

24. 150 cars.
138 green cars.
How many cars
not green?

ZEROS IN SUBTRACTION

We can find 602 − 135.

CAN'T SUBTRACT ONES   CAN'T RENAME TENS

$$602$$
$$-135$$

$$602$$
$$-135$$

RENAME HUNDREDS   RENAME TENS   SUBTRACT

$$
\begin{array}{r}
^{5}\;^{10}\\
\cancel{6}0\,2\\
-1\,3\,5\\
\end{array}
$$

$$
\begin{array}{r}
^{9}\\
^{5}\;^{\cancel{10}}\;^{12}\\
\cancel{6}\,\cancel{0}\,\cancel{2}\\
-1\,3\,5\\
\end{array}
$$

$$
\begin{array}{r}
^{9}\\
^{5}\;^{\cancel{10}}\;^{12}\\
\cancel{6}\,\cancel{0}\,\cancel{2}\\
-1\,3\,5\\
\hline
4\,6\,7\\
\end{array}
$$

1. Let's practice renaming.

    a. 302 = 3 hundreds + 0 tens + 2
            = 2 hundreds + ___ tens + 2

    b. 500 = 5 hundreds + 0 tens + 0
            = 4 hundreds + 10 tens + 0
            = 4 hundreds + ___ tens + 10

2. Complete to find 800 − 231.

    a. Rename 800.
        800 = 7 hundreds + ___ tens + 0
             = 7 hundreds + 9 tens + ___

$$
\begin{array}{r}
^{9}\\
^{7}\;^{10}\;^{10}\\
\cancel{8}\,\cancel{0}\,\cancel{0}\\
-2\,3\,1\\
\hline
9\\
\end{array}
$$

    b. Subtract ones. 10 − 1 = ___

    c. Complete the subtraction.

3. Subtract.

    a. $\begin{array}{r}600\\-4\\\hline\end{array}$ **b.** $\begin{array}{r}904\\-27\\\hline\end{array}$ **c.** $\begin{array}{r}700\\-578\\\hline\end{array}$ **d.** $\begin{array}{r}306\\-234\\\hline\end{array}$

Subtract.

1.	306 − 8	**2.**	707 − 9	**3.**	300 − 9	**4.**	200 − 8
5.	708 − 29	**6.**	404 − 85	**7.**	602 − 59	**8.**	407 −338
9.	500 −464	**10.**	407 −359	**11.**	705 −697	**12.**	400 −395
13.	706 −152	**14.**	800 −403	**15.**	501 −384	**16.**	908 −729
17.	900 −597	**18.**	603 −256	**19.**	900 −450	**20.**	605 −338
21.	800 −642	**22.**	903 −385	**23.**	608 −349	**24.**	704 −438

Solve these problems.

25. There were 407 ghosts in a house.
One night 348 of them flew away.
How many ghosts were left?

26. There were 304 goblins at a
party. 138 went home.
How many goblins were left?

27. 606 ghosts went to a convention.
269 of them were friendly.
How many ghosts were not friendly?

Subtract.

1.	79 − 4	2.	56 −20	3.	85 −23
4.	843 −512	5.	727 −315	6.	958 −657
7.	22 − 4	8.	63 −54	9.	96 −59
10.	363 − 39	11.	792 −283	12.	654 −638	13.	729 −148
14.	458 −367	15.	968 −284	16.	715 −636	17.	823 −568
18.	956 −458	19.	506 − 38	20.	900 −366	21.	400 −167

Brainteaser

1. Follow these steps.   *Example*

   (a) Choose any 3-digit number.   853
   (b) Reverse the digits in the
       hundreds and ones places.   − 358
   (c) Subtract.   495
   (d) Reverse the digits in the
       hundreds and ones places.   + 594
   (e) Add. What is the sum?

2. Begin with another 3-digit number. Do steps (a) through (e) again. What do you discover?

3. Do it again with another 3-digit number.

124

MAKING CHANGE

Making change is easy.

Notebook cost 30¢.
Gave 2 quarters.
What is the change?

Think:
2 quarters = 50 cents
50¢ − 30¢ = 20¢

1. Solve these mini-problems.

   a. Candy: 12¢.
   Gave 2 dimes.
   What is the change?

   b. Hamburger: 45¢.
   Gave 1 dollar.
   What is the change?

Choose 2 coins to show the change.

	Cost	Paid	Change			
			Quarter	Dime	Nickel	Penny
1.	4¢	1 dime				
2.	14¢	1 quarter				
3.	35¢	2 quarters				
4.	70¢	1 dollar				
5.	24¢	1 half dollar				

	RENAME	SUBTRACT
	9	9
	4 10 10	4 10 10
Toy monkey cost $2.94.	$ 5.0 0	$ 5.0 0
Gave clerk $5.00.	− 2.9 4	− 2.9 4
How much change?		$ 2.0 6

Solve these mini-problems.

1. Had $2.75 in the bank.
   Put in $1.00 more.
   How much money now?

2. Saved $4.83.
   Spent $1.37.
   How much is left?

3. Shirt cost $2.19.
   Hat cost $1.68.
   How much in all?

4. Must pay $3.87.
   Gave clerk $5.00.
   How much change?

5. Had $6.00.
   Spent $2.75.
   How much is left?

6. Have $4.25.
   Got $2.35 more.
   How much in all?

★ 7. Susie bought a toy for $3.10 and a pencil case for $.89. She gave the clerk $5.00. How much change did she get?

126

ROUNDING TO NEAREST TEN

Which guess was closer if there were 43 beads?

43 is nearer to 40 than to 50.
So, 43 rounded to the **nearest ten** is 40.

1. Look at this number line.

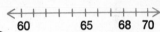

a. Is 68 nearer to 60 or to 70?

b. So, 68 rounded to the nearest ten is ___ .

2. Look at the number line above.

What is the halfway mark between 60 and 70?

We round numbers halfway between tens to the greater ten.   65 is rounded to 70.

EXERCISES

Round to the nearest ten.

1. 21	**2.** 48	**3.** 65	**4.** 57	**5.** 75
6. 92	**7.** 86	**8.** 84	**9.** 71	**10.** 99
11. 26	**12.** 42	**13.** 63	**14.** 77	**15.** 45

ROUNDING TO NEAREST HUNDRED

About how many kilometers to Springville?

236 kilometers.
The tens digit is
less than 5.

2**3**6 is nearer to 200 than to 300.
So, 236 rounded to the **nearest hundred** is 200.

1. Let's round 373 to the nearest hundred.
The tens digit is greater than 5.

Is 373 nearer to 300 or 400?
So, 373 rounded to the nearest hundred is ___ .

2. Look at this number line.

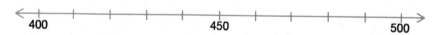

What is the halfway mark between 400 and 500?

We round numbers halfway between hundreds to
the greater hundred.   450 is rounded to 500.

3. Dollars and cents can be rounded to the nearest
dollar. Complete.

a. 112 rounded to the nearest hundred is 100.
So, $1.12 rounded to the nearest dollar is ___ .

b. 591 rounded to the nearest hundred is 600.
So, $5.91 rounded to the nearest dollar is ___ .

c. Round $6.50 to the nearest dollar.

128

Round to the nearest hundred.

1. 218　　**2.** 350　　**3.** 684　　**4.** 727

5. 437　　**6.** 536　　**7.** 780　　**8.** 859

9. 943　　**10.** 658　　**11.** 576　　**12.** 760

Round to the nearest dollar.

13. $1.50　**14.** $5.42　**15.** $5.84　**16.** $6.10

17. $3.98　**18.** $6.19　**19.** $4.10　**20.** $7.50

21. $2.02　**22.** $4.68　**23.** $5.70　**24.** $8.97

Keeping Fit

Add.

1. 69 +89　**2.** 328 +546　**3.** 439 +375　**4.** 748 +597

5. 567 +676　**6.** 972 +648　**7.** 699 +738　**8.** 457 +787

Make true sentences. Use >, <, or =.

9. $6 + 5 \equiv 12$　　**10.** $12 - 4 \equiv 9$　　**11.** $16 - 7 \equiv 9$

12. $17 - 9 \equiv 10$　　**13.** $9 + 5 \equiv 13$　　**14.** $18 - 9 \equiv 9$

Compare. Use > or <.

15. $7,500 \equiv 5,800$　　　　**16.** $6,270 \equiv 5,983$

17. $9,067 \equiv 9,065$　　　　**18.** $5,708 \equiv 5,718$

129

ESTIMATING SUMS AND DIFFERENCES

When we do not need the exact sum, we can estimate.

42 lights on. 26 lights off.
About how many lights in all?

ROUNDED
```
   40
+ 30
  70 estimate
```

EXACT
```
   42
+ 26
  68 exact sum
```

The estimated sum is close to the exact sum.

1. Read this mini-problem.

314 gumdrops.
192 eaten.
About how
many left?

  a. Estimate the difference.
    $300 - 200 = $ ___

  b. Find the exact difference.

2. Estimate these sums and differences.

a.	b.	c.	d.
34 + 58	89 + 75	272 − 158	313 − 124

Estimate these sums and differences.

1.	2.	3.	4.
25 + 32	67 + 21	55 − 24	19 + 23

5.	6.	7.	8.
142 + 167	250 + 375	463 − 115	628 − 273

Estimate the answers.

Example   In one week Bob spent $4.15 for his bus fare and $3.98 for lunch. About how much did he spend that week?

$4.15 is rounded to $4.00
$3.98 is rounded to $4.00
                      $8.00   **Estimate**

Bob spent about $8.00 that week.

1. Ruth bought a bus ticket for $2.50 and lunch for $1.37. About how much did she spend?

2. José had $4.10 in his piggy bank. He took out $1.85 for a bus trip. About how much was left?

3. Sue had $7.32 saved for a trip. She got $2.75 for her birthday. About how much did she have then?

4. Louis's bus ticket cost $4.19. He gave the bus driver $10.00. About how much change did Louis get?

CHAPTER REVIEW

Subtract.

1. 86 [104] − 10	**2.** 98 [104] − 37	**3.** 299 [108] − 89	**4.** 438 [108] − 105
5. 86 [114] − 38	**6.** 50 [114] − 22	**7.** 383 [115] − 5	**8.** 470 [115] − 434
9. 658 [118] − 549	**10.** 526 [118] − 382	**11.** 912 [120] − 473	**12.** 625 [120] − 387
13. 300 [122] − 125	**14.** 704 [122] − 365	**15.** $9.70 [126] − 4.80	**16.** $6.00 [126] − 2.78

Round to the nearest ten. [127]

17. 64 **18.** 38 **19.** 75 **20.** 76 **21.** 92

Round to the nearest hundred. [128]

22. 145 **23.** 237 **24.** 550 **25.** 768

Round to the nearest dollar. [128]

26. $5.13 **27.** $6.49 **28.** $7.50 **29.** $8.83

Estimate the sums and differences. [130]

30. 38 +21	**31.** 80 −47	**32.** 293 +120	**33.** 631 −482

Solve these mini-problems. [126]

34. Mary has $5.00
Has to pay $1.45.
How much change?

35. 68 pencils.
25 pens.
How many more pencils?

CHAPTER TEST

Subtract.

1.	49 − 23	**2.**	148 − 7	**3.**	82 − 46	**4.**	293 − 75

5.	752 − 747	**6.**	647 − 585	**7.**	724 − 365	**8.**	870 − 391

9.	647 − 235	**10.**	487 − 94	**11.**	620 − 337	**12.**	185 − 89

13.	703 − 421	**14.**	800 − 247	**15.**	$3.52 − 2.38	**16.**	$5.00 − 1.98

Round to the nearest ten.

17. 42   **18.** 67   **19.** 85

Round to the nearest hundred.

20. 570   **21.** 650   **22.** 232

Round to the nearest dollar.

23. $2.50   **24.** $6.98   **25.** $1.10

Estimate the sums or differences.

26.	28 + 42	**27.**	592 − 236	**28.**	$1.70 + 3.25	**29.**	$4.15 − 2.83

Solve these mini-problems.

30. 30 rabbits.
28 chickens.
How many more rabbits?

31. Had $4.25.
Spent $1.15.
How much left?

6 MEASUREMENT

WAYS TO MEASURE LENGTH

Hands, arms and feet were once used to measure length.

1. The width of a finger was once a unit of measure.

   a. Which would you measure with your finger?
   a pen   a room   a book

   b. Is the width of everyone's finger the same?

2. A cubit is the length from your elbow to your fingers.

   a. Use your cubit to measure the chalkboard.

   b. Is a cubit the same for everyone?

3. The pace was used to measure longer distances.

   a. Is your pace the same length as your teacher's?

   b. Is everyone's pace the same?

134

1. Measure the length of this page with your finger. How many finger widths did you get?

2. Is your measure the same as your neighbor's?

3. Find the length of your desk with your hand. How many hand widths is your desk?

4. Is the width of a hand a good measure?

5. Use your pace to find the width of your classroom. How many paces did you find?

Keeping Fit

Add.

1.	23 + 5	**2.**	428 + 7	**3.**	231 +524	**4.**	407 +483
5.	725 +238	**6.**	519 +467	**7.**	606 +319	**8.**	325 +587

Subtract.

9.	59 −12	**10.**	98 −26	**11.**	627 −426	**12.**	968 −687
13.	763 −538	**14.**	523 −349	**15.**	800 −672	**16.**	700 −425

135

MEASURING IN CENTIMETERS

A **centimeter (cm)** is a unit of measure. ⊢——⊣ 1 centimeter
Some rulers are marked in centimeters.

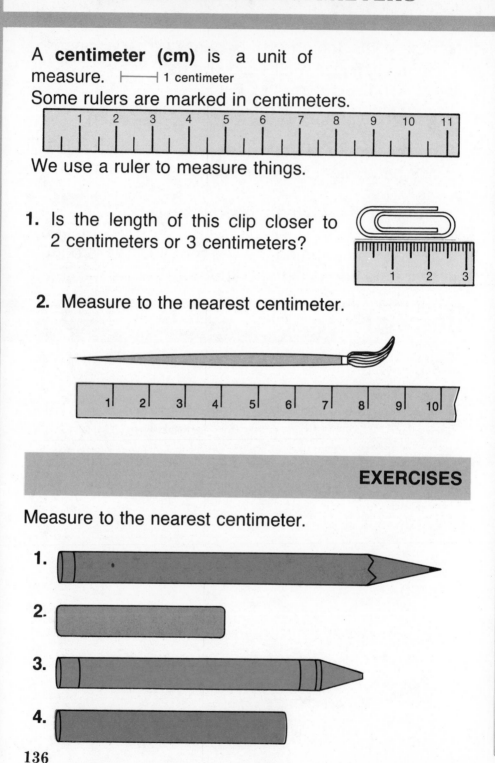

We use a ruler to measure things.

1. Is the length of this clip closer to 2 centimeters or 3 centimeters?

2. Measure to the nearest centimeter.

EXERCISES

Measure to the nearest centimeter.

1.

2.

3.

4.

136

EXTRA INFORMATION

Some problems have extra information.

Lu paid 45¢ for a drink.	45¢
Cara paid 40¢ for a hot dog.	+ 40¢
Dee paid 30¢ for an ice cream. **Extra**	85¢
How much did Cara and Lu spend together?	

Copy the extra information. Solve these mini-problems.

1. Math book—$3.50.
   Spelling book—$2.00.
   Pen—$1.55.
   How much more is the
   math book than the pen?

2. 14 papers.
   24 pencils.
   46 crayons.
   How many things
   to write with?

3. Walked 3 hours Sunday.
   Ran 1 hour Monday.
   Walked 5 hours Tuesday.
   How many hours walked?

4. Ken spent $5.85.
   Len spent $3.20.
   Sue spent $1.50.
   How much more did
   Ken spend than Len?

137

METERS AND CENTIMETERS

1. Follow these steps to make a **meter** stick.

   (a) Mark 10 centimeters on the edge of your paper.
   (b) Cut out the 10 centimeter strip.
   (c) Cut out 9 more like the first one.
   (d) Place 10 strips end to end on the floor.

   How many centimeters are there in all?

   100 centimeters = 1 meter (m)

2. Complete.

   a. 2 m = 1 m + 1 m
   $\qquad$ = 100 cm + 100 cm or ___ cm

   b. 4 m = ___ cm

3. Complete.

   300 cm = 100 cm + 100 cm + 100 cm
   $\qquad$ = 1 m + 1 m + 1 m or ___ m

4. Complete.
   435 cm = 100 cm + 100 cm + 100 cm + 100 cm
   $\qquad\qquad\qquad\qquad\qquad\qquad$ + 35 cm
   $\qquad$ = 1 m + 1 m + 1 m + 1 m + 35 cm
   $\qquad$ = ___ m and ___ cm

5. Which would you use to measure these, a meter or a centimeter?

   a. A school yard $\qquad$ **b.** A pencil

   c. A book $\qquad\qquad\quad$ **d.** A room

138

Complete. Change meters to centimeters.

1.

meters	1	2	3	4	5
centimeters	100	200			

Complete.

2. 8 m = ___ cm

3. 600 cm = ___ m

4. 9 m = ___ cm

5. 700 cm = ___ m

Which would you use to measure these, a meter or a centimeter?

6. A house

7. A farm

8. Scissors

9. A finger

10. A shoe box

11. A comb

ACTIVITY

For each of these activities, complete these three steps:
Step 1   Estimate the length in centimeters or meters.
Step 2   Measure the length in centimeters or meters.
Step 3   Compare your estimate and the actual measurement.

1. Find the width of a driveway in meters.

2. Find the length of a bus in meters.

3. Find the distance from your elbow to the tips of your fingers in centimeters.

4. Find the distance around your wrist in centimeters.

139

MEASURING LIQUIDS

We can measure liquids in **liters**.

2 half liters make 1 liter (L).
2 quarter liters make 1 half liter.

One Liter

Half Liter

Quarter Liter

1. How many half liters are in 2 liters?
   Complete.

   2 liters = 2 half liters + 2 half liters
          = ____ half liters

2. How many quarter liters in one liter? Complete.

   1 liter = 2 half liters
        = 2 quarter liters + 2 quarter liters
        = ____ quarter liters

3. Which is more?

   a. 1 liter or 3 half liters   **b.** 3 liters or 8 half liters

Complete.

1. 3 liters = ____ half liters   2. 2 liters = ____ quarter liters

3. 3 liters = ____ quarter liters   4. 5 half liters = ____ quarter li

Which is more?

5. 3 half liters or 1 liter   6. 9 quarter liters or 2 liters

7. 4 half liters or 5 quarter liters   8. 2 liters or 7 quarter liters

140

MEASURING WEIGHT

Here are weight measures of some familiar objects.

Another unit of weight is the **gram (g).**
This bee weighs about 1 gram.

$$1{,}000 \text{ grams (g)} = 1 \text{ kilogram (kg)}$$

1. How many grams are in 4 kilograms?

   $1 \text{ kg} = 1{,}000 \text{ g}$

   $4 \text{ kg} = 1{,}000 \text{ g} + 1{,}000 \text{ g} + 1{,}000 \text{ g} + 1{,}000 \text{ g}$

   $\qquad = 4{,}000 \text{ g}$

   Complete.

   a. 3 kg = ____ g   **b.** 5 kg = ____ g

2. How many kilograms are in 2,000 grams?

   $1{,}000 \text{ g} = 1 \text{ kg}$

   so $2{,}000 \text{ g} = 2 \text{ kg}$

   Complete.

   a. 6,000 g = ____ kg   **b.** 10,000 g = ____ kg

EXERCISES

Complete.

1. 3,000 g = ____ kg   **2.** 7 kg = ____ g

3. 8,000 g = ____ kg   **4.** 9 kg = ____ g

141

TEMPERATURE

A thermometer mea-
sures temperature in
degrees. Each mark
means 2 degrees. This
thermometer shows
32°.

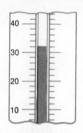

1. We count degrees above and below zero.

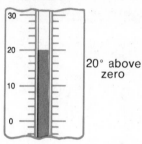
20° above
zero

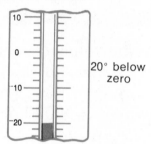
20° below
zero

What temperatures are shown?

a.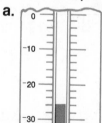

b.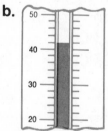

c.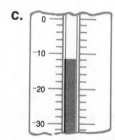

2. When it gets warmer, the liquid in the thermometer
goes up. What happens when it gets colder?

3. The temperature was 13°. It rose 27°. What is the
new temperature?

4. The temperature was 10° below zero. It rose 28°. Follow the steps to find the new temperature.

(a) Put your finger on 10° below zero.

(b) Count by 2's to 28.

What is the new temperature?

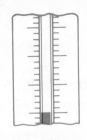

What temperature is shown on each thermometer?

1.

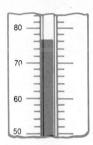

2.

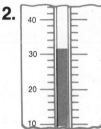

3.

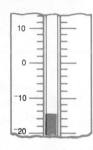

4.

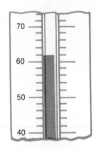

5.

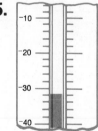

6.

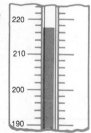

Use this thermometer to solve these mini-problems.

7. Was 20°.
Fell 14°.
Find the new temperature.

8. Was 12° below zero.
Rose 32°.
Find the new temperature.

143

CUSTOMARY MEASUREMENT

An **inch (in.)** is a unit of measure. Some rulers are marked in inches.

1 inch

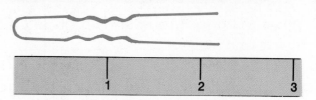

1. Is the length of this hairpin nearer to 2 inches or 3 inches?

The hairpin is 2 inches long to the nearest inch.

2. Measure to the nearest inch.

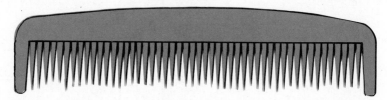

3. Some rulers are marked in half inches. This nail is $2\frac{1}{2}$ inches long to the nearest $\frac{1}{2}$ inch.

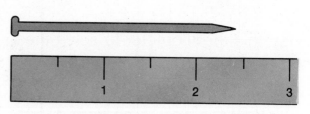

Measure to the nearest $\frac{1}{2}$ inch.

4. Some rulers are marked in quarter inches.

This peanut is $1\frac{1}{4}$ inches to the nearest $\frac{1}{4}$ inch.

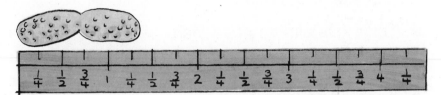

Measure to the nearest $\frac{1}{4}$ inch.

a.  **b.**

Measure to the nearest inch.

1.

2.

3.

Measure to the nearest $\frac{1}{2}$ inch.

4.  **5.**

6.

Measure to the nearest $\frac{1}{4}$ inch.

1.  **2.**

3.  **4.**  145

INCHES, FEET, AND YARDS

1. We can also use the **foot** ruler to measure. Let's make a foot ruler.

   a. Trace this picture of an inch.

   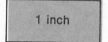

   b. Trace another inch next to it.

   c. Keep doing this until there are 12 inches in all.

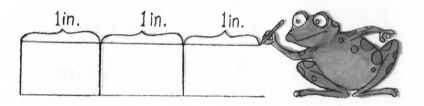

12 inches = 1 foot (ft)

2. Complete.

$$2 \text{ ft} = 1 \text{ ft} + 1 \text{ ft}$$
$$= 12 \text{ in.} + 12 \text{ in. or } \underline{\quad} \text{ in.}$$

3. Tiger put 3 foot rulers end to end.

3 feet = 1 **yard** (yd)

Complete.

$$2 \text{ yd} = 1 \text{ yd} + 1 \text{ yd}$$
$$= 3 \text{ ft} + 3 \text{ ft or } \underline{\quad} \text{ ft}$$

146

4. How many inches are in a yard? Complete.

$$1 \text{ yd} = 1 \text{ ft} + 1 \text{ ft} + 1 \text{ ft}$$
$$= 12 \text{ in.} + 12 \text{ in.} + 12 \text{ in. or } \underline{\quad} \text{ in.}$$

36 inches = 1 yard

5. Look at the machines. They change yards to feet or yards to inches. Complete.

a. 5 yds
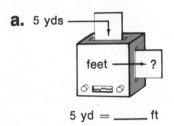
5 yd = _____ ft

b. 3 yds
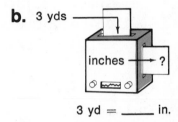
3 yd = _____ in.

EXERCISES

Complete.

1. 4 ft = ___ in.

2. 3 yd = ___ ft

3. 2 yd = ___ in.

4. 6 yd = ___ ft

Solve these problems.

5. The sidewalk at Emerson School is 4 yards wide. How many feet is that?

6. Al's desk is 3 feet wide. How many inches is that?

★**7.** Copy and complete to change feet to yards.

feet	9	12	15	18	21
yards	3	4			

147

GALLONS, QUARTS, AND PINTS

We can measure liquids.
1 **gallon (gal)** = 4 **quarts (qt)**
1 **quart** = 2 **pints (pt)**
1 **pint** = 2 **cups**

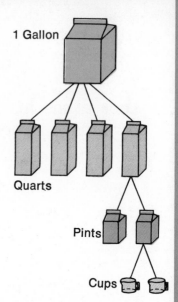

1 Gallon

Quarts

Pints

Cups

1. How many quarts in 2 gallons? Complete.

   1 gal = ___ qt, so 2 gal = 4 × 2 or ___ qt

2. How many cups in 3 pints? Complete.

   1 pt = ___ cups, so 3 pt = 3 × 2 or ___ cups

3. Milk may come in **half-gallon** containers.

   Complete: $\frac{1}{2}$ gal = ___ qt.

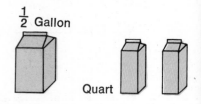

$\frac{1}{2}$ Gallon

Quart

4. Milk may also come in **half-pint** containers.

   Complete: $\frac{1}{2}$ pt = ___ cup.

5. Copy and complete.

Gallons	Quarts	Pints	Cups
1		8	
	8		
	16		

6. Which is more, 1 gal or 3 qt?

1 gal = 4 qt, so 1 gal is more than 3 qt

Which is more?

a. 2 qt or 1 gal of milk

b. 1 pt or 3 cups of cream

EXERCISES

Complete.

1. 6 qt = ___ pt

2. 4 pt = ___ cups

3. 3 gal = ___ qt

4. 3 qt = ___ pt

5. 6 pt = ___ cups

6. 4 gal = ___ qt

Which is more?

7. 4 pints or 1 quart

8. 4 cups or 1 pint

9. 5 quarts or 1 gallon

10. 1 half-gallon or 3 quarts

11. 3 quarts or 1 gallon

12. 3 cups or 1 pint

★**13.** 1 quart or 8 cups

★**14.** 1 gallon or 4 pints

149

POUNDS AND OUNCES

We measure weight in **pounds (lb)**. The oranges weigh 2 pounds. The pears weigh 4 pounds.

1. Each space on this scale shows 1 **ounce (oz)**.

   a. How many spaces are between 0 and 1 pound?

   b. How many ounces are in 1 pound?

   c. How many ounces are between 0 and the red mark?

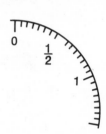

16 ounces = 1 pound   8 ounces = $\frac{1}{2}$ pound

2. Complete.

   a.   1 lb = ___ oz   b. 4 lb = ___ oz
      so 2 lb = 16 + 16 or ___ oz

EXERCISES

Complete.

1. 3 lb = ___ oz   2. 5 lb = ___ oz

3. 6 lb = ___ oz   4. 8 lb = ___ oz

5. 9 lb = ___ oz   ★ 6. $4\frac{1}{2}$ lb = ___ oz

150

SURVEYORS

1. One year there were 60,000 people who worked as surveyors. The next year there were 62,500. How many more surveyors were there the second year?

2. A surveyor measured the distance around a certain plot of land. There were three sides. One side measured 700 meters, one side measured 900 meters and another side measured 1,000 meters. What was the total distance around this land?

3. Ms. Basco is a surveyor for the federal government. One week she worked some days in the office and some days outdoors.

    Monday, office, 8 hours
    Tuesday, outdoors, 10 hours
    Wednesday, outdoors, 8 hours
    Thursday, office, 6 hours
    Friday, outdoors, 8 hours

    How many hours did she work in the office that week? How many hours did she work outdoors that week?

CHAPTER REVIEW

Measure to the nearest centimeter. [136]

1. 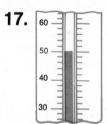 **2.**

Complete.

3. 4 m = ___ cm [138]

4. 800 cm = ___ m [138]

5. 750 cm = ___ m ___ cm [138]

6. 2 m 30 cm = ___ cm [138]

7. 4 L = ___ half liters [140]

8. 10 L = ___ half liters [140]

9. 3 L = ___ quarter liters [140]

10. 6 half liters = ___ L [140]

11. 4 kg = ___ g [141]

12. 7,000 g = ___ kg [141]

13. 5,000 g = ___ kg [141]

14. 8 kg = ___ g [141]

Which is more?

15. 2 liters or 5 half liters [140]

16. 3 kilograms or 2,500 g [141]

What temperature is shown on each thermometer? [142]

17. 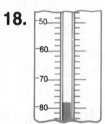 **18.** **19.**

Solve this problem. [137]

20. 25 chickens, 10 ducks, 20 cows. How many chickens and ducks together?

152

CHAPTER TEST

Measure to the nearest centimeter.

1. **2.**

Complete.

3. 3 m = ____ cm   **4.** 900 cm = ____ m

5. 3 L = ____ half liters **6.** 4 liters = ____ quarter liters

7. 5 kg = ____ g   **8.** 9,000 g = ____ kg

Which is more?

9. 2 kilograms or 1,500 grams   **10.** 5 liters or 9 half liters

What temperature is shown on each thermometer?

11.    **12.** 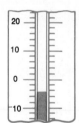   **13.**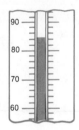

Solve this problem.

14. Book: $5.30. Toy: $3.00. Pen: $4.30. How much more is the pen than the toy?

153

7 MULTIPLICATION AND DIVISION

REPEATED ADDITION

How many?

2 children in each set.
2 + 2 + 2 tells how many in all.
2 + 2 + 2 = 6
   3 twos = 6

1. Complete.

    a. How many fish bowls?

    b. How many fish in each bowl?

    c. How many fish in all?
       4 + 4 = ___

       2 fours = ___

2. Make true sentences.

    a. 2 + 2 + 2 + 2 = 8   **b.**   3 + 3 = 6
                  4 twos = ___   2 threes = ___

    c. 4 + 4 + 4 = ___   **d.** 1 + 1 + 1 + 1 = ___
              3 fours = ___   4 ones = ___

154

Solve these mini-problems.

1. 2 boxes.
5 crayons in each box.
How many crayons in all?

$5 + 5 =$ ___
2 fives = ___

2. 4 baskets.
3 kittens in each.
How many kittens in all?

$3 + 3 + 3 + 3 =$ ___
4 threes = ___

Make true sentences.

3. $3 + 3 + 3 = 9$
3 threes = ___

4. $1 + 1 + 1 + 1 + 1 = 5$
5 ones = ___

5. $2 + 2 = 4$
2 twos = ___

6. $4 + 4 + 4 + 4 = 16$
4 fours = ___

7. $5 + 5 + 5 =$ ___
3 fives = ___

8. $3 + 3 + 3 + 3 + 3 =$ ___
5 threes = ___

9. $1 + 1 + 1 =$ ___
3 ones = ___

10. $0 + 0 + 0 =$ ___
3 zeros = ___

Solve this mini-problem.

★**11.** 10 bags of marbles.
10 marbles in each bag.
How many marbles?

155

MULTIPLICATION SENTENCES

We can write multiplication sentences.

$4 + 4 + 4 = 12$ **Addition Sentence**
3 fours $= 12$
$3 \times 4 = 12$ **Multiplication Sentence**

We read: three times four is equal to twelve.

1. Complete.

   $3 + 3 = 6$
   2 threes $= 6$
   $2 \times 3 = \underline{}$

2. Write a multiplication sentence for each.

   a. $5 + 5 = 10$ **b.** $1 + 1 + 1 + 1 + 1 = 5$

3. Write an addition sentence for each.

   a. $2 \times 4 = 8$ **b.** $3 \times 5 = 15$ **c.** $4 \times 3 = 12$

4. This picture shows an array for $3 \times 2 = 6$.

   a. How many rows?

   b. How many in each row?

   c. How many in all?

5. Write a multiplication sentence for each.

a. 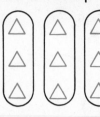 **b.**  **c.**

Complete.

1. $5 + 5 + 5 =$ ___
$\quad\quad 3 \times 5 =$ ___

2. $2 + 2 + 2 + 2 + 2 =$ ___
$\quad\quad\quad\quad 5 \times 2 =$ ___

Write a multiplication sentence for each.

3. $2 + 2 + 2 = 6$ **4.** $5 + 5 + 5 + 5 = 20$

5. $3 + 3 + 3 = 9$ **6.** $4 + 4 + 4 + 4 = 16$

7. $1 + 1 + 1 + 1 = 4$ **8.** $4 + 4 = 8$

Write an addition sentence for each.

9. $3 \times 2 = 6$ **10.** $2 \times 1 = 2$ **11.** $5 \times 2 = 10$

12. $4 \times 5 = 20$ **13.** $5 \times 3 = 15$ ★ **14.** $9 \times 4 = 36$

Write a multiplication sentence for each.

15.   **16.**

ORDER OF FACTORS

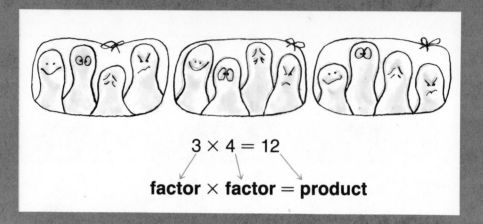

$3 \times 4 = 12$

factor × factor = product

1. Give the factors. Give the products.

    a. $2 \times 4 = 8$ **b.** $4 \times 1 = 4$ **c.** $3 \times 2 = 6$

2. Find the products. Complete.

    a. $3 \times 4 = \underline{\quad}$ **b.** $4 \times 3 = \underline{\quad}$

    c. $3 \times 4 = 4 \times \square$

Changing the order of the factors does not change the product. $3 \times 4 = 4 \times 3$
This is the **order property of multiplication.**

3. Complete.

    a. $2 \times 3 = 6$ **b.** $2 \times 4 = 8$
    $\ 3 \times 2 = \underline{\quad}$ $\ 4 \times 2 = \underline{\quad}$
    $\ 2 \times 3 = 3 \times \square$ $\ 2 \times 4 = \square \times 2$

    c. $3 \times 1 = \square \times 3$ **d.** $3 \times 6 = 6 \times \square$

158

Give the factors.

1. $2 \times 5 = 10$ 2. $4 \times 3 = 12$ 3. $1 \times 5 = 5$

4. $3 \times 3 = 9$ 5. $3 \times 5 = 15$ 6. $2 \times 2 = 4$

Give the products.

7. $4 \times 2 = 8$ 8. $1 \times 3 = 3$ 9. $5 \times 4 = 20$

10. $5 \times 3 = 15$ 11. $3 \times 2 = 6$ 12. $4 \times 4 = 16$

Complete.

13. $3 \times 5 = 15$
    $5 \times 3 = \underline{}$
    $3 \times 5 = \square \times 3$

14. $5 \times 1 = 5$
    $1 \times 5 = \underline{}$
    $5 \times 1 = 1 \times \square$

15. $2 \times 5 = 10$
    $5 \times 2 = \underline{}$
    $2 \times 5 = 5 \times \square$

16. $2 \times 1 = 2$
    $1 \times 2 = \underline{}$
    $2 \times 1 = \square \times 2$

17. $4 \times 5 = 20$
    $5 \times 4 = \underline{}$
    $4 \times 5 = \square \times 4$

18. $2 \times 6 = 12$
    $6 \times 2 = \underline{}$
    $2 \times 6 = 6 \times \square$

Complete.

19. $2 \times 3 = 3 \times \square$ 20. $4 \times 6 = \square \times 4$

21. $5 \times 1 = \square \times 5$ 22. $2 \times 4 = 4 \times \square$

23. $2 \times 5 = 5 \times \square$ ★24. $4 \times 11 = \square \times 4$

★25. $33 \times 45 = \square \times 33$ ★26. $61 \times 87 = 87 \times \square$

159

We know how to count by 2.

So, we know multiplication facts for 2.

2	$1 \times 2 = 2$
4	$2 \times 2 = 4$
6	$3 \times 2 = 6$
8	$4 \times 2 = 8$
10	$5 \times 2 = 10$

1. Find the products.

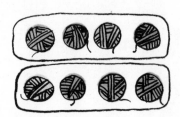
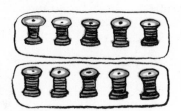

a. $2 \times 4 = \underline{\quad}$

b. $2 \times 5 = \underline{\quad}$

2. Find the products. Complete.

	Addition Sentence	Multiplication Sentence
a.	$3 + 3 = 6$	$2 \times 3 = \underline{\quad}$
b.	$3 + 3 + 3 = 9$	$3 \times 3 = \underline{\quad}$
c.	$3 + 3 + 3 + 3 = 12$	$4 \times 3 = \underline{\quad}$
d.	$3 + 3 + 3 + 3 + 3 = 15$	$5 \times 3 = \underline{\quad}$

3. Make true sentences.

a. $4 \times 2 = \underline{\quad}$
$2 \times 4 = \underline{\quad}$

b. $5 \times 3 = \underline{\quad}$
$3 \times 5 = \underline{\quad}$

c. $2 \times 5 = \underline{\quad}$
$5 \times 2 = \underline{\quad}$

4. We can multiply another way.

$$
\begin{array}{r} 3 \\ \times 4 \\ \hline 12 \end{array}
\qquad
\begin{array}{r} 5 \\ \times 2 \\ \hline 10 \end{array}
\qquad
\begin{array}{r} 4 \\ \times 2 \\ \hline 8 \end{array}
\qquad
\begin{array}{r} 2 \\ \times 4 \\ \hline 8 \end{array}
$$

Multiply.

a. $\begin{array}{r} 2 \\ \times 3 \\ \hline \end{array}$
b. $\begin{array}{r} 5 \\ \times 3 \\ \hline \end{array}$
c. $\begin{array}{r} 2 \\ \times 2 \\ \hline \end{array}$
d. $\begin{array}{r} 3 \\ \times 3 \\ \hline \end{array}$
e. $\begin{array}{r} 3 \\ \times 2 \\ \hline \end{array}$

EXERCISES

Make true sentences.

1. $4 \times 3 = \underline{\quad}$
 $3 \times 4 = \underline{\quad}$

2. $3 \times 2 = \underline{\quad}$
 $2 \times 3 = \underline{\quad}$

3. $3 \times 1 = \underline{\quad}$
 $1 \times 3 = \underline{\quad}$

Multiply.

4. $\begin{array}{r} 2 \\ \times 5 \\ \hline \end{array}$
5. $\begin{array}{r} 4 \\ \times 2 \\ \hline \end{array}$
6. $\begin{array}{r} 3 \\ \times 5 \\ \hline \end{array}$
7. $\begin{array}{r} 3 \\ \times 2 \\ \hline \end{array}$
8. $\begin{array}{r} 2 \\ \times 4 \\ \hline \end{array}$

9. $\begin{array}{r} 3 \\ \times 3 \\ \hline \end{array}$
10. $\begin{array}{r} 4 \\ \times 3 \\ \hline \end{array}$
11. $\begin{array}{r} 3 \\ \times 4 \\ \hline \end{array}$
12. $\begin{array}{r} 5 \\ \times 3 \\ \hline \end{array}$
13. $\begin{array}{r} 2 \\ \times 2 \\ \hline \end{array}$

Solve these mini-problems.

14. 2 boxes.
4 balls in each box.
How many balls in all?
$2 \times 4 = \underline{\quad}$

15. 4 jars.
3 bees in each jar.
How many bees in all?
$4 \times 3 = \underline{\quad}$

161

ONE AS A FACTOR

3 rows	1 row	1 row
1 in each row	2 in the row	1 in the row
$3 \times 1 = 3$	$1 \times 2 = 2$	$1 \times 1 = 1$

1. Complete.

a. $1 \times 1 = 1$
$2 \times 1 = 2$
$3 \times 1 = 3$
$4 \times 1 = \underline{}$
$5 \times 1 = \underline{}$

b. $1 \times 1 = 1$
$1 \times 2 = \underline{}$
$1 \times 3 = \underline{}$
$1 \times 4 = \underline{}$
$1 \times 5 = \underline{}$

When 1 is a factor, the product is the other factor.

2. Multiply.

a. $\begin{array}{r} 1 \\ \times 3 \\ \hline \end{array}$
b. $\begin{array}{r} 4 \\ \times 1 \\ \hline \end{array}$
c. $\begin{array}{r} 1 \\ \times 1 \\ \hline \end{array}$
d. $\begin{array}{r} 1 \\ \times 5 \\ \hline \end{array}$

EXERCISES

Multiply.

1. $\begin{array}{r} 3 \\ \times 1 \\ \hline \end{array}$
2. $\begin{array}{r} 1 \\ \times 2 \\ \hline \end{array}$
3. $\begin{array}{r} 5 \\ \times 1 \\ \hline \end{array}$
4. $\begin{array}{r} 4 \\ \times 4 \\ \hline \end{array}$
5. $\begin{array}{r} 2 \\ \times 1 \\ \hline \end{array}$

6. $\begin{array}{r} 1 \\ \times 4 \\ \hline \end{array}$
7. $\begin{array}{r} 3 \\ \times 2 \\ \hline \end{array}$
8. $\begin{array}{r} 1 \\ \times 1 \\ \hline \end{array}$
9. $\begin{array}{r} 1 \\ \times 3 \\ \hline \end{array}$
★ **10.** $\begin{array}{r} 24 \\ \times 1 \\ \hline \end{array}$

ZERO AS A FACTOR

3 nests.
0 eggs in each nest.
0 eggs in all.
$3 \times 0 = 0$

1. Complete.

a. $0 \times 0 = 0$
   $1 \times 0 = 0$
   $2 \times 0 = 0$
   $3 \times 0 = \underline{}$
   $4 \times 0 = \underline{}$
   $5 \times 0 = \underline{}$

b. $0 \times 0 = 0$
   $0 \times 1 = 0$
   $0 \times 2 = 0$
   $0 \times 3 = \underline{}$
   $0 \times 4 = \underline{}$
   $0 \times 5 = \underline{}$

c. When 0 is one factor, what is the product?

When 0 is one factor, the product is 0.

2. Multiply.

a.   0
   $\times 1$

b.   4
   $\times 0$

c.   0
   $\times 5$

d.   0
   $\times 0$

Multiply.

1.   2
   $\times 0$

2.   0
   $\times 3$

3.   1
   $\times 1$

4.   3
   $\times 1$

5.   3
   $\times 0$

6.   0
   $\times 2$

7.   1
   $\times 0$

8.   0
   $\times 0$

9.   0
   $\times 4$

★ **10.**   35
   $\times 0$

4 cages. 5 birds in each. 20 birds in all.

$$5 + 5 + 5 + 5 = 20$$
$$4 \times 5 = 20$$

$$\begin{array}{r} 5 \\ \times 4 \\ \hline 20 \end{array}$$

1. Find the products.

$4 \times 4 =$ ___ $5 \times 5 =$ ___

2. Copy and complete. Look for patterns.

a. $1 \times 4 =$ ___   **b.** $1 \times 5 =$ ___
$2 \times 4 =$ ___ $2 \times 5 =$ ___
$3 \times 4 =$ ___ $3 \times 5 =$ ___
$4 \times 4 =$ ___ $4 \times 5 =$ ___
$5 \times 4 =$ ___ $5 \times 5 =$ ___

3. Multiply.

a. $\begin{array}{r} 5 \\ \times 3 \\ \hline 15 \end{array}$ $\begin{array}{r} 3 \\ \times 5 \\ \hline \end{array}$ **b.** $\begin{array}{r} 5 \\ \times 2 \\ \hline 10 \end{array}$ $\begin{array}{r} 2 \\ \times 5 \\ \hline \end{array}$ **c.** $\begin{array}{r} 5 \\ \times 4 \\ \hline 20 \end{array}$ $\begin{array}{r} 4 \\ \times 5 \\ \hline \end{array}$

Multiply.

1.	2 × 5	**2.**	3 × 4	**3.**	1 × 5	**4.**	5 × 3	**5.**	4 × 4
6.	4 × 2	**7.**	5 × 4	**8.**	3 × 5	**9.**	0 × 5	**10.**	2 × 4
11.	4 × 0	**12.**	5 × 5	**13.**	4 × 1	**14.**	5 × 2	**15.**	4 × 5

ACTIVITY

Make a multiplication table.

X	0	1	2	3	4	5
0						
1						
2						
3						
4						
5						

Show $4 \times 3 = 12$ on your table.

(a) Find 4 on the left.
(b) Find 3 on the top.
(c) Follow the yellow paths coming from 4 and 3 until they meet in a box.
(d) Write the product 12 in that box.

Complete the table.

Keeping Fit

Compare. Use >, <, or =.

1. 368 ▤ 269   2. 419 ▤ 418

3. 314 ▤ 502   4. 512 ▤ 512

5. 749 ▤ 746   6. 911 ▤ 812

Add.

7.   35
  +24

8.   46
  +38

9.   34
  +72

10.   57
  +68

11. 503
 +274

12. 268
 +419

13. 342
 +596

14. 475
 +288

15. 275
 +329

16. 538
 +179

17. 604
 +158

18. 809
 +447

19.   4
   8
  +9

20. 36
  12
 +25

21. 45
  27
 +56

22. 263
 450
 +142

Subtract.

23.   68
  −20

24.   49
  −19

25.   52
  −38

26.   70
  −23

27. 309
 − 46

28. 487
 − 83

29. 763
 −428

30. 547
 −380

31. 137
 − 54

32. 905
 −623

33. 635
 −278

34. 700
 −354

35. 452
 − 38

36. 695
 −187

37. 860
 −247

38. 950
 −478

MISSING INFORMATION

Some problems do not have enough information.

Bought nails to
hang pictures.
Used 10.
How many are left?

1. Britt bought 4 candy bars. How much did they cost?

   a. What information is missing?

   b. Make up the missing information. Solve the problem.

2. Kathy has 5 pennies in each of her piggy banks. How many pennies has she in all? Solve the problem. If there is not enough information, make it up.

EXERCISES

Solve these problems. If information is missing, make it up.

1. Have 2 dolls. How many doll dresses needed?

2. 3 bags of cookies. Same number of cookies in each bag. How many cookies in all?

3. Walk 4 blocks to school. 2 minutes to walk each block. How many minutes to walk to school?

12 bugs in all.
3 rows, each with the
same number of bugs.
How many in each row?

$3 \times \square = 12$ $3 \times 4 = 12$

↓

missing factor   There are 4 bugs in each row.

1. Find the missing factors to solve.

    a. 20 arrowheads in all.
    4 in each row.
    How many rows?
    $\square \times 4 = 20$

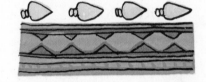

    b. 15 marbles in all.
    5 sacks.
    Same number in each
    sack.
    How many in each
    sack?
    $5 \times \square = 15$

2. Find the missing factors.

    a. $3 \times 5 = 15$ **b.** $1 \times 3 = 3$ **c.** $0 \times 4 = 0$
        $\square \times 5 = 15$ $1 \times \square = 3$ $\square \times 4 = 0$

3. Make true sentences.

    a. $2 \times \square = 8$ **b.** $\square \times 3 = 9$ **c.** $\square \times 3 = 0$

    d. $4 \times \square = 12$ **e.** $5 \times \square = 10$ **f.** $\square \times 2 = 4$

Find the missing factors.

1. $3 \times 4 = 12$ **2.** $2 \times 3 = 6$ **3.** $5 \times 1 = 5$
$3 \times \square = 12$ $\square \times 3 = 6$ $5 \times \square = 5$

Make true sentences.

4. $3 \times \square = 6$ **5.** $2 \times \square = 2$ **6.** $\square \times 3 = 15$

7. $4 \times \square = 0$ **8.** $\square \times 4 = 16$ **9.** $5 \times \square = 25$

10. $4 \times \square = 4$ **11.** $1 \times \square = 1$ **12.** $\square \times 3 = 9$

13. $\square \times 5 = 20$ **14.** $\square \times 3 = 3$ **15.** $\square \times 5 = 10$

16. $\square \times 4 = 12$ **17.** $\square \times 1 = 5$ **18.** $4 \times \square = 8$

Solve these mini-problems.

19. 2 dolls.
10 doll dresses.
Same number of dress-
es for each doll.
How many dresses for
each doll?

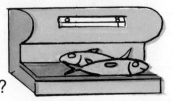

20. 20 children.
4 children in each car.
How many cars?

21. Caught 2 fish.
Weighed 8 kilograms in all.
Each fish weighed the same.
How much did each fish weigh?

169

DIVISION SENTENCES

We can write division sentences for problems.

8 apples in all.
4 in each box.
How many boxes?

$\square \times 4 = 8$ **Multiplication Sentences** $2 \times 4 = 8$
$8 \div 4 = \square$ **Division Sentences** $8 \div 4 = 2$
8 divided by 4 is equal to 2.

factor × factor = product   quotient
  ↓   ↓   ↓   ↓
  2 × 4 = 8   so $8 \div 4 =$ 2

---

1. Find the quotients.

a. $5 \times 2 = 10$ **b.** $3 \times 4 = 12$ **c.** $3 \times 2 = 6$
$10 \div 2 = \square$ $12 \div 4 = \square$ $6 \div 2 = \square$

2. Make true sentences.

a. $\square \times 5 = 15$ **b.** $\square \times 2 = 8$ **c.** $\square \times 3 = 6$
$15 \div 5 = \square$ $8 \div 2 = \square$ $6 \div 3 = \square$

EXERCISES

Make true sentences.

1. $4 \times 5 = 20$ **2.** $4 \times 3 = 12$ **3.** $\square \times 1 = 2$
$20 \div 5 = \square$ $12 \div 3 = \square$ $2 \div 1 = \square$

4. $\square \times 4 = 8$ **5.** $\square \times 4 = 16$ **6.** $\square \times 2 = 10$
$8 \div 4 = \square$ $16 \div 4 = \square$ $10 \div 2 = \square$

RELATED SENTENCES

Multiplication and division are related.
Look at this array.

Related Sentences

$2 \times 3 = 6$ $6 \div 3 = 2$

$3 \times 2 = 6$ $6 \div 2 = 3$

1. Write two related division sentences for each.

    Example $2 \times 4 = 8$ Answer $8 \div 4 = 2;$
                                                 $8 \div 2 = 4$

    a. $3 \times 5 = 15$ **b.** $4 \times 3 = 12$ **c.** $2 \times 4 = 8$

2. Write the related division sentence for $3 \times 3 = 9$.

3. Write two related multiplication sentences for each.

    Example $6 \div 3 = 2$ Answer $2 \times 3 = 6;$
                                               $3 \times 2 = 6$

    a. $12 \div 3 = 4$ **b.** $10 \div 2 = 5$ **c.** $3 \div 1 = 3$

4. Write the related multiplication sentence for $4 \div 2 = 2$.

5. We may use a related multiplication sentence to find a quotient.

    Example $8 \div 2 = \square$ Think $\square \times 2 = 8$
               so $4 \times 2 = 8$ and $8 \div 2 = 4$

    Divide. Use the multiplication sentence to check.

    a. $15 \div 3 = \square$ **b.** $6 \div 2 = \triangle$ **c.** $9 \div 3 = \square$
         $\square \times 3 = 15$ $2 \times \triangle = 6$ $\square \times 3 = 9$

171

Write two related division sentences for each.

1. $3 \times 2 = 6$　　**2.** $4 \times 5 = 20$　　**3.** $5 \times 3 = 15$

Write two related multiplication sentences for each.

4. $12 \div 4 = 3$　　**5.** $20 \div 4 = 5$　　**6.** $4 \div 1 = 4$

Divide. Use the multiplication sentence to check.

7. $6 \div 2 = \square$
　　$\square \times 2 = 6$

8. $3 \div 1 = \triangle$
　　$1 \times \triangle = 3$

9. $8 \div 2 = \square$
　　$\square \times 2 = 8$

10. $10 \div 2 = \triangle$
　　$2 \times \triangle = 10$

11. $15 \div 3 = \square$
　　$\square \times 3 = 15$

12. $2 \div 2 = \triangledown$
　　$2 \times \triangledown = 2$

Divide.

13. $4 \div 2$　　**14.** $4 \div 1$　　**15.** $20 \div 4$　　**16.** $12 \div 3$

17. $8 \div 2$　　**18.** $5 \div 5$　　**19.** $6 \div 3$　　**20.** $9 \div 3$

21. $15 \div 5$　　**22.** $2 \div 1$　　**23.** $1 \div 1$　　**24.** $3 \div 3$

Solve these problems.

25. 12 candles in all.
4 candles in each box.
How many boxes?

26. 10 boys in all. 2 cars.
Same number in each car.
How many boys in each car?

★**27.** Mr. Collins has 36 apple trees. There are 12 trees in each row. How many rows are there?

REPEATED SUBTRACTION

12 cookies in all.
4 cookies for each plate.
How many plates needed?

$$12 \div 4 = \underline{\qquad}$$

We may subtract to
find the quotient.

```
   12
 −  4   1 four
  ───
    8
 −  4   1 four
  ───
    4
 −  4   1 four
  ───
    0
```

3 fours in 12
$$12 \div 4 = 3$$

1. Complete.

   a. ___ fives in 10

   b. $10 \div 5 = $ ___

2. Find each quotient. Use repeated subtraction.

   a. $15 \div 3$ **b.** $8 \div 2$ **c.** $20 \div 4$

EXERCISES

Find each quotient. Use repeated subtraction.

1. $25 \div 5$ **2.** $9 \div 3$ **3.** $10 \div 2$ **4.** $24 \div 3$

5. $18 \div 2$ **6.** $8 \div 4$ **7.** $12 \div 4$ ★**8.** $84 \div 21$

173

We can multiply by 4 and by 5. We can divide by 4 and by 5.

$$4 \times 5 = 20 \qquad 20 \div 5 = 4$$
$$5 \times 4 = 20 \qquad 20 \div 4 = 5$$

1. Count by fives to 25.

   a. 5, 10, ___ , ___ , ___

   b. How many fives in 25?

   c. $25 \div 5 =$ ___

2. Count by fours to 16.

   a. 4, 8, ___ , ___

   b. How many fours in 16?

   c. $16 \div 4 =$ ___

3. Divide. Use the multiplication sentences to check.

   a. $10 \div 5 = \square$ **b.** $12 \div 4 = \square$ **c.** $4 \div 4 = \square$
       $\square \times 5 = 10$ $\square \times 4 = 12$ $4 \times \square = 4$

4. Divide.

   a. $8 \div 4$ **b.** $15 \div 5$ **c.** $5 \div 1$

Divide. Use the multiplication sentences to check.

1. $15 \div 3 = \square$ **2.** $25 \div 5 = \square$ **3.** $16 \div 4 = \square$
$\square \times 3 = 15$ $\square \times 5 = 25$ $4 \times \square = 16$

Divide.

4. $2 \div 2$ **5.** $12 \div 3$ **6.** $5 \div 5$ **7.** $20 \div 4$

8. $10 \div 5$ **9.** $8 \div 2$ **10.** $4 \div 1$ **11.** $20 \div 5$

12. $16 \div 4$ **13.** $10 \div 2$ **14.** $5 \div 1$ **15.** $8 \div 4$

16. $12 \div 4$ **17.** $3 \div 3$ **18.** $15 \div 5$ **19.** $4 \div 4$

Solve these problems.

20. Amy picked 20 apples. She put 5 apples in each basket. How many baskets did she use?

21. Ann used 16 cups at a party. She put 4 on each table. How many tables were there?

Brainteaser

This is a magic square. Place each of the digits 1, 2, 3, 4, 5, 6, 7, 8, 9, so their sums are 15 in all directions.

Write expanded numerals.

Example   25 = 2 tens + 5

1. 48   **2.** 76   **3.** 33

4. 117   **5.** 680   **6.** 302

Find the pattern. Copy and complete.

7. 21, 24, 27, ___ , ___ , ___ , ___ , ___ ___

8. 224, 228, 232, ___ , ___ , ___ , ___

9. 270, 275, 280, ___ , ___ , ___ , ___

Write in dollars and cents form.

10. 107¢   **11.** 239¢   **12.** 457¢   **13.** 860¢

14. 396¢   **15.** 597¢   **16.** 930¢   **17.** 998¢

Measure to the nearest centimeter.

18.

19.

20.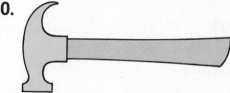

CLEAN-UP DAY

Mr. Lee's class went to the park to pick up trash.

1. There were 25 children. Five children rode in each car. How many cars were needed?

2. The boys and girls played a game of "picking up cans". The girls won. They found 75 cans. How many more cans did the girls find than the boys?

3. The boys found 128 paper cups and 64 bottles. The girls found 157 paper cups. How many paper cups did the children find in all?

4. Jill found 5 bottles. Jo found 3 times as many bottles as Jill. How many bottles did Jo find?

5. The children found 142 bottles. The boys found 64 bottles. How many bottles did the girls find?

6. The girls found 376 pieces of paper. The boys found 298 pieces of paper. How many pieces of paper did the children find in all?

177

MINUTES LATER AND EARLIER

Awoke at 7:15. Ate 10 minutes later. What time was that?

7:15

7:25

1. What time will it be in 20 minutes? Complete.

a.

:32

b.

10:___

c.

___:___

2. Frank came to school at 8:53. Ann was there 10 minutes before Frank. What time did Ann get to school?

3. What time was it 20 minutes ago? Complete.

a.

:10

b.

9:___

c.

___:___

178

What time will it be in a half hour?

1.    **2.**    **3.**

What time will it be in 15 minutes?

4.    **5.**    **6.**

What time was it 20 minutes ago?

7.    **8.**    **9.**

ACTIVITY

What time did you arrive home yesterday?

Copy this clock.
Show the time you
got home.

Write the time
you got home.

Thirty days hath November,
April, June, and September.
February hath twenty-eight alone,
And all the rest have thirty-one.

1. The poem tells the number of days in each month.

    a. How many months are in a year?

    b. Which month has the fewest days?

    c. Which months have the most days?

2. Look at the calendar for March.

    a. How many days are in a week?

    b. How many days are in 2 weeks?

    c. On what day is the first of March?

March						
S	M	T	W	Th.	F	S
		1	2	3	4	5
6	7	8	9	10	11	12
13	14	15	16	17	18	19
20	21	22	23	24	25	26
27	28	29	30	31		

    d. On what day is the fourth of March?

    e. What will be the date one week from March 4?

ACTIVITY
Make a calendar for this month.
Write the month and the year.
Ring each date you are in school.

180

NEWSPAPER REPORTERS

1. Miss Stacy is a reporter for her town's daily newspaper. She is waiting at the train station to interview a state senator. Four trains arrive at the station each hour. How many trains will arrive in 3 hours?

2. Miss Stacy uses a recorder at her interviews. Each tape for the recorder will run for 2 hours. How many hours of interviews can she record with 3 tapes?

3. A reporter worked 7 hours on Monday, 8 hours on Wednesday, and 9 hours on Friday on one story. How many hours did he work on that story?

4. A reporter bought 5 pencils on her way to an interview. Each pencil cost 5 cents. How much did the pencils cost in all?

5. Miss Stacy travels about 3 hours every day to cover her stories. How many hours does she spend traveling in 5 days?

CHAPTER REVIEW

1. Write an addition sentence for $3 \times 4 = 12$.
[156]

2. Write the related division sentence for $3 \times 3 = 9$.
[171]

3. Write two related multiplication sentences for
[171] $6 \div 2 = 3$.

Make true sentences. [168, 158]

4. $2 \times \square = 4$ **5.** $\square \times 5 = 0$ **6.** $3 \times 2 = \square \times 3$

Multiply.

7. 1	**8.** 4	**9.** 0	**10.** 5	**11.** 3
[162]$\times 2$	[164]$\times 5$	[163]$\times 0$	[164]$\times 5$	[160]$\times 4$

12. 3	**13.** 4	**14.** 1	**15.** 5	**16.** 4
[160]$\times 3$	[163]$\times 0$	[162]$\times 1$	[160]$\times 3$	[164]$\times 4$

Divide. [171, 174]

17. $20 \div 5$ **18.** $5 \div 5$ **19.** $2 \div 1$ **20.** $15 \div 5$

21. $16 \div 4$ **22.** $9 \div 3$ **23.** $8 \div 2$ **24.** $3 \div 3$

25. What time will it be [178] in 20 minutes?

26. What time was it 15 [178] minutes ago?

Solve these mini-problems.

27. 3 candy bars.
[177] 4 cents each.
     How much in all?

28. 20 hats in all.
[177] 4 in each box.
     How many boxes?

182

CHAPTER TEST

1. Write an addition sentence for $5 \times 2 = 10$.

2. Write the related division sentence for $2 \times 2 = 4$.

3. Write two related multiplication sentences for $8 \div 4 = 2$.

Make true sentences.

4. $3 \times \square = 9$　　5. $4 \times \square = 0$　　6. $4 \times 3 = 3 \times \square$

Multiply.

7. $\begin{array}{r} 0 \\ \times 3 \\ \hline \end{array}$　　8. $\begin{array}{r} 5 \\ \times 4 \\ \hline \end{array}$　　9. $\begin{array}{r} 2 \\ \times 1 \\ \hline \end{array}$　　10. $\begin{array}{r} 1 \\ \times 1 \\ \hline \end{array}$　　11. $\begin{array}{r} 5 \\ \times 3 \\ \hline \end{array}$

12. $\begin{array}{r} 2 \\ \times 5 \\ \hline \end{array}$　　13. $\begin{array}{r} 0 \\ \times 2 \\ \hline \end{array}$　　14. $\begin{array}{r} 2 \\ \times 4 \\ \hline \end{array}$　　15. $\begin{array}{r} 3 \\ \times 2 \\ \hline \end{array}$　　16. $\begin{array}{r} 1 \\ \times 5 \\ \hline \end{array}$

Divide.

17. $10 \div 2$　　18. $3 \div 1$　　19. $6 \div 2$　　20. $2 \div 2$

21. $12 \div 4$　　22. $25 \div 5$　　23. $12 \div 3$　　24. $5 \div 1$

25. What time will it be in 10 minutes?

26. What time was it 20 minutes ago?

Solve these mini-problems.

27. 5 balloons.
3 cents each.
How much in all?

28. 12 balls.
4 balls for each child.
How many children?

183

8 MULTIPLICATION AND DIVISION

RENAMING A FACTOR

Another name for 4 is 3 + 1.

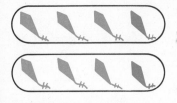

2 rows
4 in each row
8 in all
2 × 4 = 8

2 rows
3 + 1 in each row
8 in all
2 × (3 + 1) = 8

2 × 4 = 2 × (3 + 1)

1. Complete.

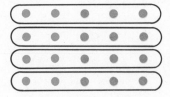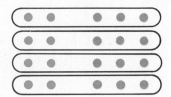

4 × 5 = 4 × (2 + □)

2. Complete.

a. 3 × 5 = 3 × (4 + □)

b. 2 × 3 = 2 × (□ + 1)

184

Complete.

1.

$$2 \times 5 = 2 \times (3 + \square)$$

2.

$$5 \times 4 = 5 \times (\square + 2)$$

Complete.

3. $4 \times 3 = 4 \times (2 + \square)$

4. $3 \times 2 = 3 \times (\square + 1)$

5. $2 \times 4 = 2 \times (1 + \square)$

6. $4 \times 5 = 4 \times (\square + 1)$

7. $5 \times 3 = 5 \times (\square + 2)$

8. $4 \times 4 = 4 \times (3 + \square)$

We may think about 2 × 5 in these ways.

2 × (4 + 1)	(2 × 4) + (2 × 1)
2 × 5	8 + 2
10	10

$$2 \times (4 + 1) = (2 \times 4) + (2 \times 1)$$
Multiplication-Addition Property

1. We may use the multiplication-addition property to find new facts. Copy and complete.

   a. $\qquad$ 2 × 8
   $\qquad$ 2 × (5 + 3)
   $\qquad$ (2 × 5) + (2 × 3)
   $\qquad$ 10 + ___
   $\qquad$ ___

   b. $\qquad$ 2 × 6
   $\qquad$ 2 × (4 + 2)
   $\qquad$ (2 × 4) + (2 × 2)
   $\qquad$ 8 + ___
   $\qquad$ ___

2. Multiply.

   a. 2 $\quad$ 9
   $\quad$ ×9 $\quad$ ×2
   $\quad$ 18

   b. 2 $\quad$ 7
   $\quad$ ×7 $\quad$ ×2
   $\quad$ 14

   c. 2 $\quad$ 8
   $\quad$ ×8 $\quad$ ×2
   $\quad$ 16

3. Make true sentences.

   a. □ × 2 = 12
   $\quad$ 12 ÷ 2 = □

   b. □ × 2 = 16
   $\quad$ 16 ÷ 2 = □

   c. □ × 9 = 18
   $\quad$ 18 ÷ 9 = □

186

Multiply.

1. 7 ×2	**2.** 2 ×7	**3.** 5 ×2	**4.** 8 ×2	**5.** 6 ×2
6. 2 ×9	**7.** 2 ×1	**8.** 0 ×2	**9.** 2 ×2	**10.** 4 ×2
11. 1 ×2	**12.** 3 ×2	**13.** 9 ×2	**14.** 2 ×8	**15.** 2 ×6
16. 2 ×4	**17.** 2 ×5	**18.** 2 ×0	**19.** 2 ×7	**20.** 2 ×3

Divide.

21. 16 ÷ 2   **22.** 10 ÷ 5   **23.** 14 ÷ 7

24. 12 ÷ 6   **25.** 4 ÷ 2   **26.** 8 ÷ 2

27. 18 ÷ 2   **28.** 10 ÷ 2   **29.** 14 ÷ 2

30. 12 ÷ 2   **31.** 8 ÷ 4   **32.** 6 ÷ 2

Brainteaser

Mr. Dan, a very old man,
When asked his age,
Said with a frown,
"The year I was born
is the same upside down."
How old is Mr. Dan?

EVEN AND ODD

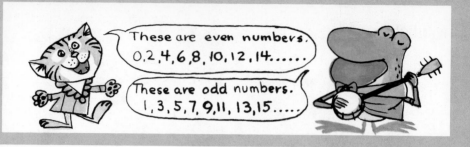

These are even numbers.
0,2,4,6,8,10,12,14......

These are odd numbers.
1,3,5,7,9,11,13,15.....

1. Find the pattern. Copy and complete.

   a. 10, 12, 14, ___ , ___ , ___ , ___ , ___

   b. 9, 11, 13, ___ , ___ , ___ , ___ , ___

2. Multiply.

   a. 2×0 **b.** 3×2 **c.** 2×6 **d.** 5×2

When 2 is one factor, the product is an even number.

EXERCISES

Which are even numbers? Which are odd numbers?

1. 19   **2.** 0   **3.** 7   **4.** 23   **5.** 38

6. 14   **7.** 41   **8.** 6   **9.** 32   **10.** 25

Name the next five even numbers.

11. 40, 42, 44, ___ , ___ , ___ , ___ , ___

Name the next five odd numbers.

12. 25, 27, 29, ___ , ___ , ___ , ___ , ___

188

HOBBIES ARE FUN

Some problems have extra information. Copy the extra information and solve. Some problems have information missing. Make up the missing information and solve.

1. Ed has 2 pages of stamps. How many stamps has he?

2. Joan has 20 toy cars and 10 toy trucks. She put 4 cars in each box. How many boxes of cars does she have?

3. Donna has flags from 9 countries. She has 2 flags from each country. How many flags does she have?

4. Gino made 16 bird houses and 4 model planes. He made 2 bird houses each day. For how many days did he make bird houses?

5. Sam has 5 books of coins. Each book has 4 pages. How many pages of coins does Sam have in all?

6. Ann painted 3 pictures each day. How many pictures did Ann paint in all?

WORKING WITH 3

Here are two ways to find 3 × 8.

$$3 \times 8$$
$$3 \times (5 + 3)$$
$$(3 \times 5) + (3 \times 3)$$
$$15 \quad + \quad 9$$
$$24$$

$$8 + 8 + 8 = 24$$
so, $3 \times 8 = 24$

1. Copy and complete.

a.
$$3 \times 7$$
$$3 \times (5 + 2)$$
$$(3 \times 5) + (3 \times 2)$$
$$15 \quad + \quad \underline{\quad}$$
$$\underline{\quad}$$

b.
$$3 \times 9$$
$$3 \times (4 + 5)$$
$$(3 \times 4) + (3 \times \underline{\quad})$$
$$\underline{\quad} \quad + \quad \underline{\quad}$$
$$\underline{\quad}$$

2. Make true sentences.

a. $6 + 6 + 6 =$ _____
   $3 \times 6 =$ _____

b. $5 + 5 + 5 =$ _____
   $3 \times 5 =$ _____

3. Multiply.

a.
$$\begin{array}{cc} 3 & 8 \\ \times 8 & \times 3 \\ \hline 24 & \end{array}$$

b.
$$\begin{array}{cc} 3 & 9 \\ \times 9 & \times 3 \\ \hline 27 & \end{array}$$

c.
$$\begin{array}{cc} 3 & 7 \\ \times 7 & \times 3 \\ \hline 21 & \end{array}$$

4. Make true sentences.

a. $\square \times 3 = 21$
   $21 \div 3 = \square$

b. $3 \times \square = 18$
   $18 \div 3 = \square$

c. $\square \times 3 = 24$
   $24 \div 3 = \square$

Multiply.

1.	4 × 3	**2.**	2 × 8	**3.**	7 × 3	**4.**	2 × 5	**5.**	3 × 0
6.	3 × 8	**7.**	6 × 2	**8.**	9 × 3	**9.**	1 × 3	**10.**	3 × 6
11.	9 × 2	**12.**	3 × 7	**13.**	8 × 3	**14.**	7 × 2	**15.**	6 × 3
16.	3 × 3	**17.**	5 × 3	**18.**	3 × 9	**19.**	2 × 9	**20.**	3 × 4

Divide.

21. $12 \div 6$ **22.** $24 \div 3$ **23.** $18 \div 3$ **24.** $12 \div 3$

25. $27 \div 9$ **26.** $3 \div 1$ **27.** $14 \div 7$ **28.** $18 \div 2$

29. $21 \div 3$ **30.** $3 \div 3$ **31.** $18 \div 6$ **32.** $15 \div 3$

33. $6 \div 3$ **34.** $15 \div 5$ **35.** $21 \div 7$ **36.** $27 \div 3$

Solve these mini-problems.

37. 16 chicks in all.
2 chicks in each box.
How many boxes?

38. 3 cartons.
6 eggs in each carton.
How many eggs in all?

191

4 cakes.
6 candles on
each cake.
How many can-
dles in all?

$$4 \times 6$$
$$4 \times (5 + 1)$$
$$(4 \times 5) + (4 \times 1)$$
$$20 \quad + \quad 4$$
$$24$$

There are 24 candles in all.

1. Copy and complete.

a.
$$4 \times 8$$
$$4 \times (5 + 3)$$
$$(4 \times 5) + (4 \times \underline{\quad})$$
$$20 \quad + \quad \underline{\quad}$$
$$\underline{\quad}$$

b.
$$4 \times 7$$
$$4 \times (2 + 5)$$
$$(4 \times 2) + (4 \times 5)$$
$$\underline{\quad} \quad + \quad \underline{\quad}$$
$$\underline{\quad}$$

2. Multiply.

a.
$$\begin{array}{cc} 4 & 8 \\ \times 8 & \times 4 \\ \hline 32 & \end{array}$$

b.
$$\begin{array}{cc} 4 & 7 \\ \times 7 & \times 4 \\ \hline 28 & \end{array}$$

c.
$$\begin{array}{cc} 4 & 9 \\ \times 9 & \times 4 \\ \hline 36 & \end{array}$$

3. Make true sentences.

a. $\square \times 4 = 28$
$28 \div 4 = \square$

b. $\square \times 6 = 24$
$24 \div 6 = \square$

c. $4 \times \square = 20$
$20 \div 4 = \square$

d. $4 \times \square = 36$
$36 \div 4 = \square$

e. $\square \times 8 = 32$
$32 \div 8 = \square$

f. $7 \times \square = 28$
$28 \div 7 = \square$

192

Multiply.

1.	3	**2.**	7	**3.**	4	**4.**	5	**5.**	4
	× 4		× 4		× 9		× 4		× 1

6.	9	**7.**	8	**8.**	4	**9.**	4	**10.**	6
	× 4		× 4		× 2		× 4		× 4

11.	4	**12.**	0	**13.**	4	**14.**	4	**15.**	4
	× 6		× 4		× 8		× 3		× 7

Divide.

16. 28 ÷ 4   **17.** 20 ÷ 4   **18.** 24 ÷ 6   **19.** 12 ÷ 4

20. 36 ÷ 4   **21.** 4 ÷ 4   **22.** 32 ÷ 4   **23.** 16 ÷ 4

24. 24 ÷ 4   **25.** 28 ÷ 7   **26.** 4 ÷ 1   **27.** 36 ÷ 9

Copy and complete the chart. Factors are in yellow. Products are in blue.

28.  **29.** 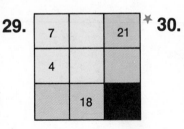 **30.**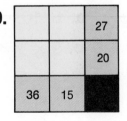

Solve these mini-problems.

31. 4 pads.
6 pages in each pad.
How many pages in all?

32. 12 gum drops.
4 gum drops for each child.
How many children?

193

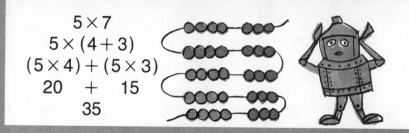

5×7
$5 \times (4 + 3)$
$(5 \times 4) + (5 \times 3)$
$20 \ \ + \ \ 15$
35

1. Copy and complete.

a.
5×6
$5 \times (4 + 2)$
$(5 \times 4) + (5 \times \underline{\quad})$
$20 \ \ + \ \ \underline{\quad}$

$\underline{\quad}$

b.
5×8
$5 \times (5 + 3)$
$(5 \times 5) + (5 \times \underline{\quad})$
$\underline{\quad} \ \ + \ \ \underline{\quad}$

$\underline{\quad}$

2. Count by fives to find 9×5.

a. 5, 10, ___, 20, ___, ___, 35, ___, ___

b. $9 \times 5 = \underline{\quad}$

3. Multiply.

a.
$\begin{array}{cc} 5 & 7 \\ \times 7 & \times 5 \\ \hline \end{array}$

b.
$\begin{array}{cc} 5 & 8 \\ \times 8 & \times 5 \\ \hline \end{array}$

c.
$\begin{array}{cc} 5 & 9 \\ \times 9 & \times 5 \\ \hline \end{array}$

4. Make true sentences.

a. $5 \times \square = 30$
$30 \div 5 = \square$

b. $\square \times 9 = 45$
$45 \div 9 = \square$

c. $5 \times \square = 35$
$35 \div 5 = \square$

194

5. Here are two ways to show division.

$$18 \div 6 = 3 \qquad 6\overline{)18}^{\,3}$$

Divide.

a. $3\overline{)6}$ **b.** $5\overline{)40}$ **c.** $7\overline{)35}$ **d.** $4\overline{)28}$

Multiply.

1. $\begin{array}{r} 5 \\ \times 7 \\ \hline \end{array}$	**2.** $\begin{array}{r} 6 \\ \times 5 \\ \hline \end{array}$	**3.** $\begin{array}{r} 4 \\ \times 5 \\ \hline \end{array}$	**4.** $\begin{array}{r} 8 \\ \times 5 \\ \hline \end{array}$	**5.** $\begin{array}{r} 5 \\ \times 1 \\ \hline \end{array}$
6. $\begin{array}{r} 9 \\ \times 5 \\ \hline \end{array}$	**7.** $\begin{array}{r} 5 \\ \times 2 \\ \hline \end{array}$	**8.** $\begin{array}{r} 5 \\ \times 9 \\ \hline \end{array}$	**9.** $\begin{array}{r} 0 \\ \times 5 \\ \hline \end{array}$	**10.** $\begin{array}{r} 7 \\ \times 5 \\ \hline \end{array}$
11. $\begin{array}{r} 5 \\ \times 3 \\ \hline \end{array}$	**12.** $\begin{array}{r} 5 \\ \times 8 \\ \hline \end{array}$	**13.** $\begin{array}{r} 5 \\ \times 4 \\ \hline \end{array}$	**14.** $\begin{array}{r} 5 \\ \times 6 \\ \hline \end{array}$	**15.** $\begin{array}{r} 5 \\ \times 5 \\ \hline \end{array}$

Divide.

16. $9\overline{)45}$ **17.** $4\overline{)20}$ **18.** $8\overline{)40}$ **19.** $5\overline{)5}$

20. $5\overline{)25}$ **21.** $5\overline{)30}$ **22.** $3\overline{)15}$ **23.** $7\overline{)35}$

24. $5\overline{)35}$ **25.** $5\overline{)10}$ **26.** $5\overline{)20}$ **27.** $6\overline{)30}$

Solve these mini-problems.

28. 40 boys.
5 boys on each team.
How many teams?

29. Bought 7 cookies.
Each cookie costs 5¢.
How much spent in all?

195

X	0	1	2	3	4	5	6	7	8	9
0	0	0	0	0	0	0	0	0	0	0
1	0	1	2	3	4	5	6	7	8	9
2	0	2	4	6	8	10				
3	0	3	6	9	12	15				
4	0	4	8	12	16	20				
5	0	5	10	15	20	25				
6	0	6								
7	0	7								
8	0	8								
9	0	9								

Now you also know the facts for the pink parts.

1. Let's look at 3 × 8.

    a. Name the first factor.

    b. Name the second factor.

    c. Name the product.

$3 \times 8 = 24$

2. Copy the table. Then fill in the pink parts. You will use this table later.

EXERCISES

Multiply. Use the table if you need help.

1.	9	2.	7	3.	2	4.	6	5.	5
	×4		×5		×8		×4		×9

6.	8	7.	9	8.	7	9.	8	10.	4
	×5		×3		×4		×3		×8

Add.

1.	64	2.	392	3.	467
	+ 47		+ 46		+ 397

4.	507	5.	676	6.	557
	+ 295		+ 362		+ 76

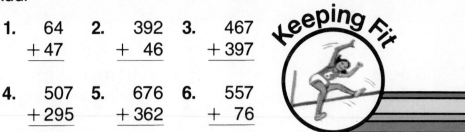

Keeping Fit

Subtract.

7.	432	8.	500	9.	974	10.	96
	− 280		− 72		− 786		− 48

11.	804	12.	510	13.	$7.75	14.	$5.00
	− 526		− 339		− .86		− 1.98

Multiply.

15.	4	16.	2	17.	1	18.	5	19.	1
	× 4		× 3		× 2		× 3		× 1

20.	2	21.	4	22.	3	23.	0	24.	3
	× 2		× 5		× 3		× 5		× 4

25.	5	26.	0	27.	2	28.	3	29.	5
	× 2		× 0		× 4		× 1		× 5

Divide.

30. $12 \div 3$ **31.** $8 \div 4$ **32.** $4 \div 1$

33. $10 \div 2$ **34.** $15 \div 5$ **35.** $25 \div 5$

36. $16 \div 4$ **37.** $3 \div 3$ **38.** $6 \div 2$

39. $20 \div 4$ **40.** $10 \div 5$ **41.** $15 \div 3$

197

WORKING WITH 6

6 weeks.
7 days in each week.
How many days in all?

6×7
$6 \times (5 + 2)$
$(6 \times 5) + (6 \times 2)$
$30 \quad + \quad 12$
42

1. **Copy and complete.**

   a. 6×8
   $6 \times (5 + 3)$
   $(6 \times 5) + (6 \times \underline{\quad})$
   $30 \quad + \quad \underline{\quad}$
   $\underline{\quad}$

   b. 6×6
   $6 \times (5 + \underline{\quad})$
   $(6 \times 5) + (6 \times \underline{\quad})$
   $\underline{\quad} \quad + \quad \underline{\quad}$
   $\underline{\quad}$

2. **Find the products.**

   a. $6 \times 9 = \underline{\quad}$
   $9 \times 6 = \underline{\quad}$

   b. $6 \times 8 = \underline{\quad}$
   $8 \times 6 = \underline{\quad}$

   c. $6 \times 7 = \underline{\quad}$
   $7 \times 6 = \underline{\quad}$

3. **Make true sentences.**

   a. $\square \times 6 = 36$
   $36 \div 6 = \square$

   b. $6 \times \square = 42$
   $42 \div 6 = \square$

   c. $\square \times 6 = 30$
   $30 \div 6 = \square$

   d. $6 \times \square = 48$
   $48 \div 6 = \square$

   e. $\square \times 4 = 24$
   $24 \div 4 = \square$

   f. $\square \times 6 = 54$
   $54 \div 6 = \square$

4. **Multiply.**

   a. $\begin{array}{r} 6 \\ \times 8 \\ \hline \end{array}$

   b. $\begin{array}{r} 7 \\ \times 6 \\ \hline \end{array}$

   c. $\begin{array}{r} 6 \\ \times 6 \\ \hline \end{array}$

   d. $\begin{array}{r} 9 \\ \times 6 \\ \hline \end{array}$

5. **Divide.**

   a. $9 \overline{)54}$

   b. $6 \overline{)48}$

   c. $7 \overline{)42}$

   d. $6 \overline{)36}$

198

Multiply.

1. 3 × 6	**2.** 6 × 8	**3.** 9 × 4	**4.** 6 × 5	**5.** 7 × 4
6. 6 × 9	**7.** 8 × 5	**8.** 7 × 6	**9.** 6 × 0	**10.** 6 × 1
11. 5 × 7	**12.** 0 × 6	**13.** 8 × 4	**14.** 9 × 6	**15.** 6 × 7

Divide.

16. 7)42   **17.** 6)12   **18.** 9)45   **19.** 2)12

20. 6)6   **21.** 6)24   **22.** 7)28   **23.** 6)48

24. 6)36   **25.** 8)40   **26.** 6)42   **27.** 7)35

28. 8)48   **29.** 6)30   **30.** 3)18   **31.** 9)54

Solve these mini-problems.

32. Baked 36 cookies.
Each child ate 4 cookies.
How many children?

33. Sold 6 books each day.
Worked 3 days.
How many books sold?

★ **34.** Candles cost 8¢ each.
Bought 6 candles.
How much change from $1.00?

199

How many legs in all?

$$7 \times 8$$
$$7 \times (5 + 3)$$
$$(7 \times 5) + (7 \times 3)$$
$$35 \quad + \quad 21$$
$$56$$

1. Copy and complete.

a.
$$7 \times 7$$
$$7 \times (4 + 3)$$
$$(7 \times 4) + (7 \times \underline{\quad})$$
$$28 \quad + \quad \underline{\quad}$$
$$\underline{\quad}$$

b.
$$7 \times 9$$
$$7 \times (5 + \underline{\quad})$$
$$(7 \times 5) + (7 \times \underline{\quad})$$
$$\underline{\quad} \quad + \quad \underline{\quad}$$
$$\underline{\quad}$$

2. Multiply.

a. $\begin{array}{r} 7 \\ \times 8 \\ \hline \end{array}$ $\begin{array}{r} 8 \\ \times 7 \\ \hline \end{array}$

b. $\begin{array}{r} 7 \\ \times 9 \\ \hline \end{array}$ $\begin{array}{r} 9 \\ \times 7 \\ \hline \end{array}$

c. $\begin{array}{r} 7 \\ \times 7 \\ \hline \end{array}$

3. Make true sentences.

a. $7 \times \square = 49$
$49 \div 7 = \square$

b. $\square \times 7 = 56$
$56 \div 7 = \square$

c. $\square \times 9 = 63$
$63 \div 9 = \square$

4. Divide.

a. $8\overline{)56}$ **b.** $7\overline{)42}$ **c.** $9\overline{)63}$ **d.** $7\overline{)49}$

200

Multiply.

1. 7 $\times 9$	**2.** 5 $\times 7$	**3.** 8 $\times 7$	**4.** 7 $\times 1$	**5.** 7 $\times 7$
6. 0 $\times 7$	**7.** 7 $\times 6$	**8.** 3 $\times 7$	**9.** 9 $\times 7$	**10.** 1 $\times 7$
11. 4 $\times 7$	**12.** 6 $\times 7$	**13.** 7 $\times 3$	**14.** 7 $\times 2$	**15.** 7 $\times 8$
16. 2 $\times 7$	**17.** 7 $\times 4$	**18.** 7 $\times 5$	**19.** 7 $\times 9$	**20.** 7 $\times 0$

Divide.

21. $7\overline{)56}$ **22.** $6\overline{)42}$ **23.** $8\overline{)48}$ **24.** $7\overline{)35}$

25. $4\overline{)28}$ **26.** $7\overline{)49}$ **27.** $9\overline{)54}$ **28.** $3\overline{)21}$

29. $9\overline{)63}$ **30.** $7\overline{)7}$ **31.** $8\overline{)56}$ **32.** $9\overline{)36}$

ACTIVITY

Copy and complete the wheels.

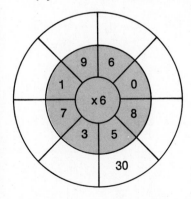

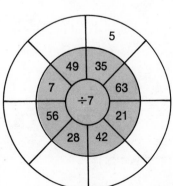

WORKING WITH 8 AND 9

8 boxes.
9 pens in each box.
How many in all?

$$8 \times 9$$
$$8 \times (5 + 4)$$
$$(8 \times 5) + (8 \times 4)$$
$$40 \quad + \quad 32$$
$$72$$

1. Copy and complete.

   a. 8×8
            $8 \times (5 + \underline{\quad})$
      $(8 \times 5) + (8 \times \underline{\quad})$
         $40 \quad + \quad \underline{\quad}$
              $\underline{\quad\quad}$

   b. 9×9
            $9 \times (5 + \underline{\quad})$
      $(9 \times 5) + (9 \times \underline{\quad})$
       $\underline{\quad} \quad + \quad \underline{\quad}$
            $\underline{\quad\quad}$

2. Multiply.

   a.   9   **b.**   8   **c.**   9
      $\times 8$ $\times 8$ $\times 9$

   d.   9   **e.**   7   **f.**   9
      $\times 6$ $\times 8$ $\times 7$

3. Make true sentences.

   a. $\square \times 8 = 72$ **b.** $\square \times 8 = 64$ **c.** $\square \times 9 = 81$
      $72 \div 8 = \square$ $64 \div 8 = \square$ $81 \div 9 = \square$

4. Divide.

   a. $8\overline{)72}$ **b.** $9\overline{)54}$ **c.** $8\overline{)64}$ **d.** $9\overline{)81}$

   e. $9\overline{)63}$ **f.** $8\overline{)56}$ **g.** $9\overline{)72}$ **h.** $8\overline{)48}$

Multiply.

1. 7
    ×9

2. 9
    ×8

3. 8
    ×7

4. 8
    ×3

5. 6
    ×9

6. 7
    ×8

7. 9
    ×5

8. 6
    ×8

9. 8
    ×4

10. 9
    ×3

11. 9
    ×9

12. 8
    ×9

13. 9
    ×6

14. 5
    ×9

15. 9
    ×7

16. 8
    ×8

17. Complete your multiplication table.

Divide.

18. 8)56

19. 9)81

20. 6)63

21. 8)8

22. 9)45

23. 8)24

24. 9)27

25. 8)64

26. 9)54

27. 8)72

28. 9)36

29. 8)48

30. 8)32

31. 9)9

32. 8)40

33. 9)72

Solve these mini-problems.

34. 4 crates.
    8 cans in each
    crate.
    How many cans
    in all?

35. 81 crayons.
    9 girls.
    Each girl gets the same
    number of crayons.
    How many crayons each?

FINDING QUOTIENTS

A multiplication table can help us find quotients.

X	0	1	2	3	4	5	6	7	8	9
0	0	0	0	0	0	0	0	0	0	0
1	0	1	2	3	4	5	6	7	8	9
2	0	2	4	6	8	10	12	14	16	18
3	0	3	6	9	12	15	18	21	24	27
4	0	4	8	12	16	20	24	28	32	36
5	0	5	10	15	20	25	30	35	40	45
6	0	6	12	18	24	30	36	42	48	54
7	0	7	14	21	28	35	42	49	56	63
8	0	8	16	24	32	40	48	56	64	72
9	0	9	18	27	36	45	54	63	72	81

1. Let's find $56 \div 8$.

   (a) Find 8 on blue.
   (b) Find 56 under 8.
   (c) Move left to 7 on yellow.

   Complete: $56 \div 8 = $ ___.

2. Use the table to find the quotients.

   a. $6 \overline{)12}$ **b.** $7 \overline{)28}$ **c.** $4 \overline{)28}$ **d.** $8 \overline{)72}$

EXERCISES

Divide. Use the table if you need help.

1. $3 \overline{)24}$ **2.** $6 \overline{)24}$ **3.** $8 \overline{)24}$ **4.** $4 \overline{)24}$

5. $7 \overline{)42}$ **6.** $4 \overline{)20}$ **7.** $2 \overline{)16}$ **8.** $9 \overline{)45}$

ROUNDING MONEY

This dress costs $16.35. Rounded to the nearest dollar, the dress costs about $16.00.

1. A pen costs $1.59. Is this nearer to $1.00 or to $2.00?

   Rounded to the nearest dollar, the pen costs about $2.00.

2. Round these amounts to the nearest dollar.

   a. $3.43   **b.** $9.16   **c.** $2.55

EXERCISES

Round to the nearest dollar.

1. $4.99   **2.** $8.71   **3.** $12.49

4. $2.37   **5.** $6.83   **6.** $8.12

7. $9.19   **8.** $7.70   **9.** $5.91

ACTIVITY

Keep a record for one week of all the trips to the grocery store made by someone in your family. At the end of the week add the total cost. Round the total cost to the nearest dollar. About how many dollars will your family spend in a month for groceries?

Keeping Fit

Round to the nearest ten.

1. 72   **2.** 85   **3.** 47

Round to the nearest hundred.

4. 325   **5.** 450   **6.** 780

Add or subtract.

7. $2.10 + .89	**8.** $5.82 +4.27	**9.** $7.26 − .65	**10.** $7.53 −4.22
11. $6.57 + .35	**12.** $8.28 +2.47	**13.** $8.59 −3.64	**14.** $7.28 −5.86
15. $4.67 +4.91	**16.** $3.68 +7.68	**17.** $6.20 −4.16	**18.** $8.08 −6.27
19. $7.35 +2.84	**20.** $4.93 +4.56	**21.** $7.00 −5.96	**22.** $9.00 −3.82

What time will it be in 10 minutes?

23.    **24.**    **25.**

What time was it 20 minutes ago?

26.    **27.**    **28.**

WATCH REPAIRERS

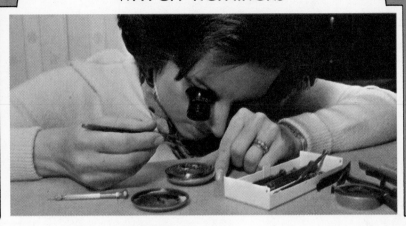

1. Mr. Jackson had 8 clocks in a row on a shelf. Each clock was 7 centimeters long. How long was the row of clocks?

2. Mrs. Robbins sold 2 watch bands. One band sold for $3.89. The other band sold for $2.35. What was the total sale?

3. Mr. Jackson bought a box of watch crystals. The box held 500 crystals. He used 176 of the crystals. How many did he have left?

4. Mrs. Robbins ordered 72 batteries for watches. The batteries are packed in boxes with 9 batteries in a box. How many boxes of batteries did she order?

★5. Mrs. Robbins repaired one watch for $24. She repaired another watch for twice as much. How much did she get paid for repairing both watches?

CHAPTER REVIEW

Write the next five even numbers. [188]

1. 42, 44, 46, ___ , ___ , ___ , ___ , ___

Write the next five odd numbers. [188]

2. 33, 35, 37, ___ , ___ , ___ , ___ , ___

Multiply.

3. $\begin{array}{r} 8 \\ \times 2 \\ \hline \end{array}$ [186] **4.** $\begin{array}{r} 7 \\ \times 3 \\ \hline \end{array}$ [190] **5.** $\begin{array}{r} 9 \\ \times 5 \\ \hline \end{array}$ [194] **6.** $\begin{array}{r} 6 \\ \times 4 \\ \hline \end{array}$ [192] **7.** $\begin{array}{r} 5 \\ \times 7 \\ \hline \end{array}$ [194]

8. $\begin{array}{r} 3 \\ \times 9 \\ \hline \end{array}$ [190] **9.** $\begin{array}{r} 1 \\ \times 8 \\ \hline \end{array}$ [202] **10.** $\begin{array}{r} 6 \\ \times 0 \\ \hline \end{array}$ [198] **11.** $\begin{array}{r} 5 \\ \times 8 \\ \hline \end{array}$ [194] **12.** $\begin{array}{r} 7 \\ \times 9 \\ \hline \end{array}$ [200]

13. $\begin{array}{r} 7 \\ \times 4 \\ \hline \end{array}$ [192] **14.** $\begin{array}{r} 3 \\ \times 8 \\ \hline \end{array}$ [190] **15.** $\begin{array}{r} 7 \\ \times 7 \\ \hline \end{array}$ [200] **16.** $\begin{array}{r} 8 \\ \times 9 \\ \hline \end{array}$ [202] **17.** $\begin{array}{r} 7 \\ \times 6 \\ \hline \end{array}$ [198]

Divide.

18. $2\overline{)18}$ [186] **19.** $7\overline{)56}$ [201] **20.** $4\overline{)36}$ [192] **21.** $8\overline{)64}$ [202]

22. $7\overline{)63}$ [201] **23.** $9\overline{)81}$ [202] **24.** $5\overline{)35}$ [194] **25.** $6\overline{)48}$ [198]

26. $6\overline{)42}$ [198] **27.** $9\overline{)9}$ [202] **28.** $5\overline{)40}$ [194] **29.** $9\overline{)72}$ [202]

30. $3\overline{)24}$ [190] **31.** $4\overline{)32}$ [192] **32.** $2\overline{)14}$ [186] **33.** $7\overline{)49}$ [200]

Solve these mini-problems. [199]

34. 7 candy bars.
5 cents each.
How much in all?

35. 36 birds.
6 in each cage.
How many cages?

CHAPTER TEST

Write the next five even numbers.

1. 16, 18, 20, ___, ___, ___, ___, ___

Write the next five odd numbers.

2. 19, 21, 23, ___, ___, ___, ___, ___

Multiply.

3.	5 ×7	**4.**	8 ×9	**5.**	6 ×7	**6.**	8 ×8	**7.**	9 ×9
8.	7 ×4	**9.**	7 ×7	**10.**	9 ×7	**11.**	6 ×2	**12.**	8 ×5
13.	8 ×6	**14.**	2 ×8	**15.**	9 ×3	**16.**	9 ×1	**17.**	6 ×6

Divide.

18. $2\overline{)14}$　　**19.** $3\overline{)18}$　　**20.** $9\overline{)36}$　　**21.** $8\overline{)72}$

22. $7\overline{)42}$　　**23.** $9\overline{)9}$　　**24.** $5\overline{)30}$　　**25.** $3\overline{)24}$

26. $4\overline{)28}$　　**27.** $6\overline{)36}$　　**28.** $3\overline{)27}$　　**29.** $7\overline{)49}$

30. $9\overline{)81}$　　**31.** $7\overline{)56}$　　**32.** $8\overline{)64}$　　**33.** $6\overline{)54}$

Solve these mini-problems.

34. 54 boys in all.
9 boys on a team.
How many teams?

35. 7 boxes.
8 apples in each box.
How many in all?

9 MULTIPLYING

We can change the grouping of factors.

(2 × 2) × 3   2 × (2 × 3)
  4 × 3   2 × 6
   12   12

Changing the grouping of the factors does not change the product.   (2 × 2) × 3 = 2 × (2 × 3)
This is the **grouping property of multiplication.**

1. Complete.

  a. (2 × 1) × 3   **b.** 2 × (1 × 3)
     ___ × 3   2 × ___

      ___   ___

  c. (2 × 1) × 3 = 2 × (1 × □)

2. Complete.

  a. (4 × 1) × 6 = ___   **b.** 3 × (2 × 1) = ___
     4 × (1 × 6) = ___   (3 × 2) × 1 = ___

3. Complete.

  a. (3 × 5) × 4 = 3 × (5 × □)

  b. 2 × (6 × 3) = (2 × 6) × □

  c. (3 × 2) × 7 = 3 × (□ × 7)

Complete.

1. $(4 \times 2) \times 3$
　　＿＿ $\times 3$
　　　＿＿

2. $4 \times (2 \times 3)$
　　$4 \times$ ＿＿
　　　＿＿

3. $(4 \times 2) \times 3 = 4 \times (2 \times \square)$ *3*

Complete.

4. $(2 \times 2) \times 4 = 2 \times (2 \times \square)$

5. $9 \times (1 \times 3) = (\square \times 1) \times 3$

6. $3 \times (3 \times 2) = (3 \times \square) \times 2$

7. $(4 \times 2) \times 4 = 4 \times (2 \times \square)$

8. $5 \times (2 \times 1) = (5 \times \square) \times 1$

9. $(2 \times 1) \times 4 = 2 \times (\square \times 4)$

10. $(4 \times 1) \times 3 = 4 \times (1 \times \square)$

11. $(6 \times 3) \times 5 = 6 \times (\square \times 5)$

12. $7 \times (4 \times 2) = (7 \times 4) \times \square$

13. $5 \times (2 \times 4) = (5 \times \square) \times 4$

14. $(9 \times 1) \times 5 = \square \times (1 \times 5)$

★ **15.** $25 \times (14 \times 4) = (\square \times 14) \times 4$

211

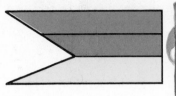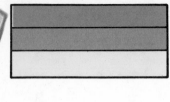

Race Time

Multiply.

1. 3 3	**2.** 9 1	**3.** 2 4	**4.** 5 8	**5.** 6 4	**6.** 7 7
7. 1 6	**8.** 5 0	**9.** 7 8	**10.** 2 9	**11.** 8 8	**12.** 5 6
13. 0 0	**14.** 7 9	**15.** 3 5	**16.** 6 7	**17.** 5 3	**18.** 1 1
19. 4 7	**20.** 3 9	**21.** 5 5	**22.** 6 9	**23.** 8 9	**24.** 9 4
25. 2 5	**26.** 4 3	**27.** 8 6	**28.** 3 2	**29.** 2 8	**30.** 2 1
31. 0 4	**32.** 3 8	**33.** 7 3	**34.** 5 4	**35.** 4 8	**36.** 3 6
37. 2 7	**38.** 1 3	**39.** 4 4	**40.** 6 3	**41.** 5 9	**42.** 7 0
43. 9 9	**44.** 7 1	**45.** 5 1	**46.** 6 6	**47.** 2 3	**48.** 6 2
49. 4 1	**50.** 2 2	**51.** 6 9	**52.** 5 7	**53.** 0 6	**54.** 4 9

Estimate the sums.

1. 56
  + 26

2. 42
  + 45

3. 59
  + 18

4. 341
  + 132

5. 378
  + 196

6. 441
  + 380

Estimate the differences.

7. 67
  − 35

8. 30
  − 17

9. 68
  − 22

10. 92
  − 53

11. 459
  − 164

12. 513
  − 292

13. 882
  − 371

14. 504
  − 286

15. 562
  − 158

16. 738
  − 392

17. 604
  − 286

18. 307
  − 178

Estimate each length in centimeters.

19.

20.

21.

213

MULTIPLES OF 10

We can find multiples of 10.

$10 + 10 = 20$ $10 + 10 + 10 + 10 + 10 = 50$
$2 \times 10 = 20$ $5 \times 10 = 50$
$10 \times 2 = 20$ $10 \times 5 = 50$

20 and 50 are multiples of 10.

1. Complete to find multiples of 10.

   a. $3 \times 10 = $ ___ and $10 \times 3 = $ ___

   b. $4 \times 10 = $ ___ and $10 \times 4 = $ ___

   c. $12 \times 10 = $ ___ and $10 \times 12 = $ ___

   d. $36 \times 10 = $ ___ and $10 \times 36 = $ ___

2. 60 is a multiple of 10 because $60 = 6 \times 10$. Complete.

   a. $20 = \square \times 10$ **b.** $70 = \square \times 10$

EXERCISES

Multiply.

   1. 2×10 **2.** 10×3 **3.** 8×10 **4.** 10×7

   5. 9×10 **6.** 10×6 **7.** 10×10 **8.** 16×10

   9. 4×10 **10.** 10×5 **11.** 12×10 **12.** 10×15

   13. 11×10 **14.** 10×13 **15.** 10×11 **16.** 10×9

214

USING THE GROUPING PROPERTY

We can use the grouping property to find 2×30.

$$2 \times 30 = 2 \times (3 \times 10)$$
$$= (2 \times 3) \times 10$$
$$= 6 \times 10$$
$$= 60$$

1. Copy and complete.

a. $4 \times 70 = 4 \times (7 \times 10)$
$\quad\quad = (4 \times 7) \times 10$
$\quad\quad = \underline{\quad} \times 10$
$\quad\quad = \underline{\quad}$

b. $4 \times 70 = \underline{\quad}$
$\quad$ so, $70 \times 4 = \underline{\quad}$

2. Multiply.

a. 3×20 **b.** 40×2 **c.** 7×20

EXERCISES

Multiply.

1. 2×30 **2.** 20×4

3. 50×4 **4.** 6×30

5. 4×80 **6.** 80×3

7. 4×60 **8.** 30×3 **9.** 5×40 **10.** 8×40

11. 7×70 **12.** 80×4 **13.** 70×7 **14.** 3×30

WAYS OF MULTIPLYING

We can use the multiplication-addition property to find products.

$$2 \times 12$$
$$2 \times (10 + 2)$$
$$(2 \times 10) + (2 \times 2)$$
$$20 \quad + \quad 4$$
$$24$$

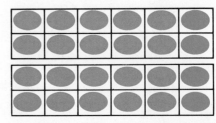

1. Copy and complete.

    a. 2×34
    $$2 \times (30 + 4)$$
    $$(2 \times 30) + (2 \times 4)$$
    $$60 \quad + \quad \rule{1cm}{0.15mm}$$
    $$\rule{1cm}{0.15mm}$$

    b. 4×23
    $$4 \times (20 + 3)$$
    $$(4 \times 20) + (4 \times 3)$$
    $$80 \quad + \quad \rule{1cm}{0.15mm}$$
    $$\rule{1cm}{0.15mm}$$

2. Here is another way to multiply.

MULTIPLY ONES	MULTIPLY TENS	ADD
52	52	52
×3	×3	×3
6 (3 × 2)	6 (3 × 2)	6 (3 × 2)
	150 (3 × 50)	150 (3 × 50)
		156

Copy and complete.

a. 21
  ×3
  ——
   3 (3 × ___)
  60 (3 × ___)
  ——
  63

b. 35
  ×4
  ——
   20 (4 × ___)
  120 (4 × ___)
  ——

216

3. Multiply.

a. 16	**b.** 75	**c.** 35	**d.** 67	**e.** 23
× 8	× 2	× 6	× 4	× 5

Multiply.

1. 43	**2.** 19	**3.** 32	**4.** 66	**5.** 82
× 2	× 8	× 2	× 6	× 4

6. 51	**7.** 76	**8.** 44	**9.** 93	**10.** 27
× 7	× 6	× 2	× 5	× 6

11. 14	**12.** 41	**13.** 45	**14.** 37	**15.** 23
× 2	× 6	× 3	× 5	× 4

16. 15	**17.** 26	**18.** 57	**19.** 65	**20.** 44
× 4	× 7	× 5	× 2	× 3

Solve these mini-problems.

21. 24 teams.
8 boys on a team.
How many boys in all?

22. 64 boxes.
4 bulbs in each box.
How many bulbs in all?

23. 35 chairs.
7 rows of chairs.
Same number of chairs
in each row.
How many chairs in each row?

217

SHORT FORM

We can use a short form to multiply 4 × 32.

Long Form

$$\begin{array}{r} 32 \\ \times\,4 \\ \hline 8\ \ (4 \times 2) \\ 120\ \ (4 \times 30) \\ \hline 128 \end{array}$$

Short Form

MULTIPLY ONES

$$\begin{array}{r} 3\,2 \\ \times\,4 \\ \hline 8 \end{array}$$

MULTIPLY TENS

$$\begin{array}{r} 3\,2 \\ \times\,4 \\ \hline 1\,2\,8 \end{array}$$

1. Complete.

   a. Multiply ones.
   $2 \times 3 = $ ____

   $$\begin{array}{r} 4\,3 \\ \times\,2 \\ \hline 6 \end{array}$$

   b. Multiply tens.
   2×4 tens $= $ ____ tens

   $$\begin{array}{r} 4\,3 \\ \times\,2 \\ \hline 8\,6 \end{array}$$

2. Multiply. Use the short form.

   a. $\begin{array}{r} 12 \\ \times\,3 \\ \hline \end{array}$
   b. $\begin{array}{r} 23 \\ \times\,2 \\ \hline \end{array}$
   c. $\begin{array}{r} 20 \\ \times\,3 \\ \hline \end{array}$
   d. $\begin{array}{r} 11 \\ \times\,4 \\ \hline \end{array}$

   e. $\begin{array}{r} 72 \\ \times\,4 \\ \hline \end{array}$
   f. $\begin{array}{r} 41 \\ \times\,2 \\ \hline \end{array}$
   g. $\begin{array}{r} 50 \\ \times\,3 \\ \hline \end{array}$
   h. $\begin{array}{r} 71 \\ \times\,8 \\ \hline \end{array}$

Multiply. Use the short form.

1. 14 ×2	**2.** 23 ×3	**3.** 21 ×6	**4.** 40 ×8	**5.** 52 ×2
6. 52 ×4	**7.** 31 ×5	**8.** 42 ×4	**9.** 61 ×6	**10.** 24 ×2
11. 20 ×6	**12.** 51 ×7	**13.** 72 ×4	**14.** 80 ×5	**15.** 13 ×3
16. 44 ×2	**17.** 63 ×2	**18.** 51 ×5	**19.** 93 ×2	**20.** 60 ×3

Solve these mini-problems.

21. 2 boxes of pears.
24 pears in each box.
How many pears in all?

22. 3 bunches of grapes.
42 grapes in each bunch.
How many grapes in all?

23. 4 rows of books.
31 books in each row.
How many books in all?

★ **24.** 40 pages.
3 rows of pictures on each page.
2 in each row.
How many pictures in all?

219

REGROUPING ONES

2 buses.
38 people on each bus.
How many in all?

Long Form

38
×2
―――
16 (2 × 8)
60 (2 × 30)
―――
76

Short Form

MULTIPLY ONES

¹
38
×2
――
6

MULTIPLY TENS

¹
38
×2
――
76

1. Complete to find 3 × 24.

    a. Multiply ones. 3 × 4 = ___

    b. Rename. 12 = ___ ten + ___

    c. Multiply tens.
       3 × 2 tens = ___ tens

    d. Add.
       6 tens + 1 ten = ___ tens

    ¹
    24
    ×3
    ――
    2

    ¹
    24
    ×3
    ――
    72

2. Complete to find 7 × 56.

    a. 7 × 6 = ___

    b. 42 = ___ tens + ___

    c. 7 × 5 tens = ___ tens

    d. 35 tens + 4 tens = ___ tens

    ⁴
    56
    ×7
    ――
    2

    ⁴
    56
    ×7
    ――
    392

220

3. Multiply. Use the short form.

a. 26
   × 3

b. 37
   × 4

c. 49
   × 5

d. 74
   × 6

Multiply. Use the short form.

1. 47
   × 2

2. 18
   × 3

3. 24
   × 4

4. 36
   × 2

5. 54
   × 3

6. 23
   × 6

7. 17
   × 8

8. 49
   × 3

9. 25
   × 4

10. 76
   × 5

11. 34
   × 7

12. 57
   × 6

13. 78
   × 6

14. 87
   × 7

15. 68
   × 9

16. 25
   × 3

17. 45
   × 4

18. 63
   × 4

19. 76
   × 7

20. 97
   × 8

Solve these problems.

21. 24 pirates on each ship.
7 ships.
How many pirates in all?

22. 5 sacks of gold pieces.
35 gold pieces in each sack.
How many gold pieces in all?

★ **23.** Pirates found 8 wooden chests.
Each chest had 9 gold rings
and 6 silver rings. How many
rings did the pirates find in all?

We can use the information from charts to solve problems.

OCEAN LINERS

Ship	Length	Dates
British Queen	275 ft	1839–1844
City of New York	528 ft	1888–1923
Lusitania	790 ft	1907–1915
Titanic	892 ft	1912
Bismarck	954 ft	1914–1940

1. Which ship was the longest?

2. Which ship was the shortest?

3. Find how much longer the Titanic was than the City of New York.

   a. How long was the Titanic?

   b. How long was the City of New York?

   c. Subtract: $892 - 528 =$ ___ .

4. How much longer was the Bismarck than the British Queen?

5. How long would the Bismarck and the Titanic be if placed end to end?

We can find multiples of 100.

$100 + 100 = 200$ $100 + 100 + 100 + 100 = 400$
$2 \times 100 = 200$ $4 \times 100 = 400$

200 and 400 are multiples of 100.

1. Complete.

   a. $1 \times 100 = 100$ and $100 \times 1 = $ ___

   b. $2 \times 100 = $ ___ and $100 \times 2 = $ ___

   c. $3 \times 100 = $ ___ and $100 \times 3 = $ ___

   d. $29 \times 100 = $ ___ and $100 \times 29 = $ ___

2. 800 is a multiple of 100 because $800 = 8 \times 100$. Complete.

   a. $500 = \square \times 100$ **b.** $700 = \square \times 100$

Multiply.

1. 6×100	**2.** 100×8	**3.** 100×9
4. 12×100	**5.** 37×100	**6.** 100×45
7. 9×100	**8.** 100×4	**9.** 25×100
10. 66×100	**11.** 100×14	**12.** 100×10
13. 7×100	**14.** 100×33	**15.** 31×100

3 mailbags.
200 letters in each.
How many letters in all?

We can use the grouping property to multiply hundreds.

$$3 \times 200$$
$$3 \times (2 \times 100)$$
$$(3 \times 2) \times 100$$
$$6 \quad \times 100$$
$$600$$

1. Complete.

a.
$$6 \times 400$$
$$6 \times (4 \times 100)$$
$$(6 \times 4) \times 100$$
$$24 \quad \times 100$$
_____

b.
$$5 \times 300$$
$$5 \times (3 \times 100)$$
$$(5 \times 3) \times 100$$
$$\underline{\quad} \times 100$$
_____

2. Look for patterns. Multiply.

a.
1	10	100
× 2	× 2	× 2

b.
2	20	200
× 4	× 4	× 4

c.
6	60	600
× 8	× 8	× 8

3. Multiply.

a. 300
      × 2

b. 400
      × 3

c. 600
      × 7

d. 800
      × 4

224

Multiply.

1. 200
$\times$ 3

2. 500
$\times$ 7

3. 600
$\times$ 6

4. 900
$\times$ 5

5. 300
$\times$ 6

6. 200
$\times$ 7

7. 700
$\times$ 6

8. 800
$\times$ 7

9. 400
$\times$ 8

10. 100
$\times$ 5

11. 500
$\times$ 4

12. 200
$\times$ 9

13. 600
$\times$ 8

14. 800
$\times$ 9

15. 500
$\times$ 8

16. 700
$\times$ 3

Solve these mini-problems.

17. 5 cartons.
300 books in each.
How many books in all?

18. 4 crates.
200 apples in each.
How many apples in all?

Brainteaser

1. Follow the steps to find my age.

(a) Find 3 times your own age.
(b) Add 27.
(c) Subtract 2 times your age.
(d) Add 23.
(e) Subtract your age. What is my age?

2. Use someone else's age instead of your own. Follow the same steps.

225

HUNDREDS, TENS, AND ONES

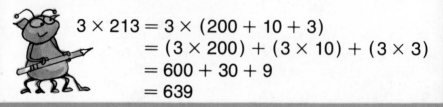

We can use the multiplication–addition property to multiply larger numbers.

$3 \times 213 = 3 \times (200 + 10 + 3)$
$= (3 \times 200) + (3 \times 10) + (3 \times 3)$
$= 600 + 30 + 9$
$= 639$

1. Copy and complete.

a. $4 \times 237 = 4 \times (200 + 30 + 7)$
$= (4 \times 200) + (4 \times 30) + (4 \times 7)$
$= \underline{} + 120 + \underline{}$
$= \underline{}$

b. $2 \times 348 = 2 \times (300 + \underline{} + 8)$
$= (2 \times 300) + (2 \times \underline{}) + (2 \times 8)$
$= \underline{} + \underline{} + \underline{}$
$= \underline{}$

2. We can use the long form. Copy and complete.

a. 237
$\times 4$
────
28 (4×7)
120 $(4 \times \underline{})$
800 $(4 \times \underline{})$
────
948

b. 348
$\times 2$
────
16 $(2 \times \underline{})$
80 $(2 \times \underline{})$
600 $(2 \times \underline{})$
────
────

3. Multiply.

a. 218
$\times 3$
────

b. 263
$\times 2$
────

c. 322
$\times 4$
────

d. 416
$\times 5$
────

226

Multiply.

1. 320 ×2	**2.** 192 ×3	**3.** 234 ×3	**4.** 431 ×6
5. 257 ×3	**6.** 108 ×4	**7.** 428 ×2	**8.** 637 ×4
9. 329 ×2	**10.** 471 ×2	**11.** 512 ×3	**12.** 315 ×5
13. 256 ×4	**14.** 521 ×7	★**15.** 1,420 ×3	★**16.** 2,608 ×7

Solve this mini-problem.

17. 6 rolls of tickets.
415 tickets in each roll.
How many tickets in all?

Brainteaser

Follow the steps to find the answer.

(a) Multiply the number of blind mice by the number of bears Goldilocks met.

(b) Then, subtract the number of pigs who met the Big Bad Wolf.

(c) Then, multiply by the number of dwarfs that Snow White met.

227

MULTIPLYING LARGER NUMBERS

We can use the short form to find 2 × 314.

Short Form

MULTIPLY ONES	MULTIPLY TENS	MULTIPLY HUNDREDS
314	314	314
× 2	× 2	× 2
8	2 8	6 2 8

1. Complete to find 3 × 231.

   a. Multiply ones. 3 × 1 = ___

   b. Multiply tens. 3 × 3 tens = ___ tens

   c. Multiply hundreds.
      3 × 2 hundreds = ___ hundreds

   $$\begin{array}{r} 231 \\ \times\,3 \\ \hline 693 \end{array}$$

2. Multiply.

   a. 421
      × 3

   b. 203
      × 6

   c. 343
      × 2

   d. 210
      × 4

EXERCISES

Multiply.

1. 214
   × 2

2. 120
   × 4

3. 332
   × 2

4. 233
   × 3

5. 301
   × 6

6. 321
   × 4

7. 310
   × 5

8. 723
   × 2

9. 201
   × 4

10. 323
    × 3

★ 11. 1,234
      × 2

★ 12. 2,312
      × 3

Multiply.

Keeping Fit

1. 6
    × 7

2. 9
    × 4

3. 5
    × 3

4. 4
    × 4

5. 8
    × 3

6. 6
    × 5

7. 3
    × 4

8. 5
    × 9

9. 1
    × 6

10. 7
     × 5

11. 3
     × 8

12. 1
     × 7

13. 8
     × 5

14. 2
     × 7

15. 4
     × 7

16. 8
     × 4

17. 2
     × 6

18. 1
     × 8

19. 3
     × 9

20. 1
     × 9

21. 2
     × 8

Divide.

22. 3)27

23. 5)15

24. 7)28

25. 9)45

26. 6)18

27. 2)12

28. 5)5

29. 4)32

30. 8)64

31. 6)54

32. 7)42

33. 7)35

34. 7)7

35. 9)36

36. 4)28

37. 2)18

38. 2)14

39. 6)42

40. 9)27

41. 8)40

42. 3)18

43. 5)30

44. 8)24

45. 9)54

46. 7)49

47. 6)48

REGROUPING ONCE

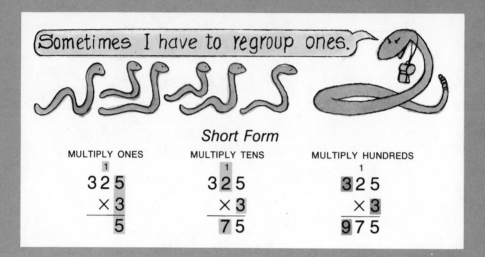

Sometimes I have to regroup ones.

Short Form

MULTIPLY ONES	MULTIPLY TENS	MULTIPLY HUNDREDS
1	1	1
325	325	325
× 3	× 3	× 3
5	7 5	9 7 5

1. Copy and complete.

a.
1
327
× 2
4

b.
1
226
× 3
8

c.
3
416
× 5
0

d.
2
204
× 6
4

2. Sometimes we regroup tens. Complete.

a. Multiply ones: $3 \times 3 =$ ___ .

243
× 3
9

b. Multiply tens.
3×4 tens = ___ tens

1
243
× 3
2 9

c. Rename.
12 tens = ___ hundred + ___ tens

d. Multiply hundreds.
3×2 hundreds = ___ hundreds

1
243
× 3
7 2 9

e. Add.
6 hundreds + 1 hundred = ___ hundreds

230

3. Copy and complete.

a. $\overset{3}{2}71$
   $\times 5$
   —––
   55

b. $\overset{1}{4}63$
   $\times 3$
   —––
   89

c. 583
   $\times 3$
   —––
   9

d. 362
   $\times 4$
   —––
   8

Multiply.

1. 426
   $\times 2$

2. 219
   $\times 4$

3. 173
   $\times 3$

4. 212
   $\times 7$

5. 206
   $\times 9$

6. 421
   $\times 6$

7. 361
   $\times 3$

8. 702
   $\times 5$

9. 431
   $\times 8$

10. 521
   $\times 4$

11. 307
   $\times 8$

12. 614
   $\times 3$

13. 114
   $\times 7$

14. 480
   $\times 3$

15. 524
   $\times 4$

16. 603
   $\times 9$

17. 241
   $\times 8$

18. 725
   $\times 2$

★**19.** 2,041
   $\times 7$

★**20.** 1,501
   $\times 6$

Solve these mini-problems.

21. 3 rows.
   162 plants in each row.
   How many plants in all?

22. Plant 650 seeds a day.
   Plant for 6 days.
   How many seeds planted?

231

We rename ones and tens to find 7×256.

Short Form

MULTIPLY ONES

$$\begin{array}{r} 2\,5\,^{4}6 \\ \times\,7 \\ \hline 2 \end{array}$$

MULTIPLY TENS

$$\begin{array}{r} 2\,^{3}5\,^{4}6 \\ \times\,7 \\ \hline 9\,2 \end{array}$$

MULTIPLY HUNDREDS

$$\begin{array}{r} 2\,^{3}5\,^{4}6 \\ \times\,7 \\ \hline 1{,}7\,9\,2 \end{array}$$

1. Complete to find 3×658.

  a. Multiply ones. $3 \times 8 =$ ___

$$\begin{array}{r} \,^{2}\, \\ 6\,5\,8 \\ \times\,3 \\ \hline 4 \end{array}$$

  b. Rename.
   $24 =$ ___ tens $+$ ___

  c. Multiply tens.
   3×5 tens $=$ ___ tens

$$\begin{array}{r} \,^{1}\,^{2}\, \\ 6\,5\,8 \\ \times\,3 \\ \hline 7\,4 \end{array}$$

  d. Add. 15 tens $+$ 2 tens $=$ ___ tens

  e. Rename. 17 tens $=$ ___ hundred $+$ ___ tens

  f. Complete the example.

2. Copy and complete.

  a. $\begin{array}{r} \,^{1}\,^{1}\, \\ 379 \\ \times\,2 \\ \hline 58 \end{array}$
  b. $\begin{array}{r} \,^{2}\,^{4}\, \\ 437 \\ \times\,6 \\ \hline 22 \end{array}$
  c. $\begin{array}{r} \,^{3}\, \\ 287 \\ \times\,5 \\ \hline 5 \end{array}$
  d. $\begin{array}{r} \,^{2}\, \\ 743 \\ \times\,8 \\ \hline 4 \end{array}$

3. Multiply.

  a. $\begin{array}{r} 265 \\ \times\,3 \\ \hline \end{array}$
  b. $\begin{array}{r} 639 \\ \times\,5 \\ \hline \end{array}$
  c. $\begin{array}{r} 436 \\ \times\,3 \\ \hline \end{array}$
  d. $\begin{array}{r} 654 \\ \times\,7 \\ \hline \end{array}$

Multiply.

1. 274 ×3	**2.** 336 ×4	**3.** 475 ×6	**4.** 367 ×5
5. 389 ×2	**6.** 274 ×3	**7.** 349 ×5	**8.** 186 ×7
9. 296 ×3	**10.** 519 ×6	**11.** 733 ×4	**12.** 365 ×8
13. 565 ×2	**14.** 486 ×5	**15.** 174 ×7	**16.** 936 ×9
17. 328 ×7	**18.** 416 ×8	**19.** 675 ×5	**20.** 807 ×9
21. 179 ×5	**22.** 254 ×7	★**23.** 1,325 ×6	★**24.** 2,453 ×9

Solve these mini-problems.

25. 6 girls.
Each has 372 marbles.
How many marbles in all?

26. 2 planes.
184 people in each.
How many people in all?

27. Plane flies 675 miles
in 1 hour.
How many miles in 4
hours?

233

Multiply.

1. 30
    × 2

2. 21
    × 3

3. 61
    × 5

4. 28
    × 4

5. 25
    × 3

6. 29
    × 7

7. 400
    × 3

8. 314
    × 2

9. 201
    × 4

10. 123
    × 4

11. 214
    × 3

12. 107
    × 8

13. 345
    × 4

14. 264
    × 5

15. 240
    × 6

16. 871
    × 3

17. 542
    × 4

18. 379
    × 3

19. 245
    × 9

20. 953
    × 6

21. 543
    × 7

22. 285
    × 4

23. 436
    × 5

24. 244
    × 3

25. 353
    × 9

ACTIVITY

Estimate the length of the following in centimeters:

an edge of a book

a cabinet

a table

a television

Now measure each of these articles. Compare these measurements with your estimates.

234

GARDENERS

1. Mrs. Washington planted 3 rows of tomato plants. Each row had 24 tomato plants. How many tomato plants did she plant in all?

2. Mr. García bought 6 cans of bug spray for the garden. Each can cost $2.40. How much did he spend for the bug spray?

3. Mrs. Washington planted 21 seeds. She planted 3 rows of seeds with the same number of seeds in each row. How many seeds in each row?

4. Mr. García and Mrs. Washington planted 30 tomato plants and 34 pepper plants. They planted 8 rows in all with the same number of plants in each row. How many plants in each row?

★ 5. Mr. García had $20.00 to buy some garden supplies. He spent $3.50 for seeds, and $12.75 for peat moss. How much change did he receive?

CHAPTER REVIEW

Multiply.

1. 60
[215]× 4

2. 24
[220]× 3

3. 36
[220]× 2

4. 74
[220]× 6

5. 300
[224] × 5

6. 50
[215]× 3

7. 344
[228] × 2

8. 900
[224] × 4

9. 21
[218]× 4

10. 40
[218]× 5

11. 32
[218]× 4

12. 47
[220]× 8

13. 210
[228] × 3

14. 401
[228] × 6

15. 348
[230] × 2

16. 605
[230] ×7

17. 231
[230] × 4

18. 371
[230] × 5

19. 523
[232] × 9

20. 836
[232] × 8

21. 687
[232] × 9

22. 444
[232] × 4

23. 239
[232] × 8

24. 281
[230] ×7

Solve these mini-problems. [235]

25. 4 boxes. 275 pens in each. How many pens in all?

26. 8 cases. 128 books in each. How many books in all?

27. 3 cans. 50 sardines in each. How many sardines in all?

28. 113 goldfish in each fishbowl. 4 fishbowls. How many goldfish in all?

29. 8 schoolbuses. 73 children in each. How many children in all?

236

CHAPTER TEST

Multiply.

1. 40
    × 5

2. 36
    × 5

3. 900
    × 3

4. 28
    × 7

5. 52
    × 2

6. 68
    × 5

7. 88
    × 9

8. 70
    × 6

9. 23
    × 3

10. 50
    × 7

11. 68
    × 4

12. 75
    × 6

13. 200
    × 6

14. 432
    × 2

15. 124
    × 3

16. 404
    × 6

17. 171
    × 5

18. 561
    × 7

19. 185
    × 4

20. 768
    × 9

Solve these mini-problems.

21. 4 jars.
    165 beads in each.
    How many beads in all?

22. 9 cages.
    50 monkeys in each cage.
    How many monkeys in all?

10 DIVISION

DIVIDING TENS AND HUNDREDS

Let's find patterns.

$2 \times 3 = 6$ $6 \div 3 = 2$ $3\overline{)6}$ with 2 above

$20 \times 3 = 60$ $60 \div 3 = 20$ $3\overline{)60}$ with 20 above

$200 \times 3 = 600$ $600 \div 3 = 200$ $3\overline{)600}$ with 200 above

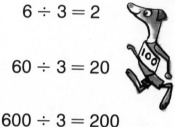

1. Look for a pattern. Make true.

a. $4 \times 2 = \underline{\hphantom{00}}$ $8 \div 2 = \underline{\hphantom{00}}$ $2\overline{)8}$
   $40 \times 2 = \underline{\hphantom{00}}$ $80 \div 2 = \underline{\hphantom{00}}$ $2\overline{)80}$
   $400 \times 2 = \underline{\hphantom{00}}$ $800 \div 2 = \underline{\hphantom{00}}$ $2\overline{)800}$

b. $3 \times 3 = \underline{\hphantom{00}}$ $9 \div 3 = \underline{\hphantom{00}}$ $3\overline{)9}$
   $30 \times 3 = \underline{\hphantom{00}}$ $90 \div 3 = \underline{\hphantom{00}}$ $3\overline{)90}$
   $300 \times 3 = \underline{\hphantom{00}}$ $900 \div 3 = \underline{\hphantom{00}}$ $3\overline{)900}$

2. Complete.

a. $30 \times 6 = \underline{\hphantom{00}}$ $180 \div 6 = \underline{\hphantom{00}}$ $6\overline{)180}$

b. $40 \times 6 = \underline{\hphantom{00}}$ $240 \div 6 = \underline{\hphantom{00}}$ $6\overline{)240}$

c. $\square \times 2 = 400$ $400 \div 2 = \underline{\hphantom{00}}$ $2\overline{)400}$

d. $\square \times 7 = 700$ $700 \div 7 = \underline{\hphantom{00}}$ $7\overline{)700}$

238

3. Divide.

    a. $2\overline{)40}$ **b.** $8\overline{)80}$ **c.** $4\overline{)120}$ **d.** $5\overline{)500}$

Make true.

1.
$2 \times 4 =$ ___ $8 \div 4 =$ ___ $4\overline{)8}$
$20 \times 4 =$ ___ $80 \div 4 =$ ___ $4\overline{)80}$
$200 \times 4 =$ ___ $800 \div 4 =$ ___ $4\overline{)800}$

Complete.

2. $10 \times 5 =$ ___ $50 \div 5 =$ ___ $5\overline{)50}$

3. $30 \times 7 =$ ___ $210 \div 7 =$ ___ $7\overline{)210}$

4. $100 \times 6 =$ ___ $600 \div 6 =$ ___ $6\overline{)600}$

5. $300 \times 2 =$ ___ $600 \div 2 =$ ___ $2\overline{)600}$

6. $\square \times 4 = 120$ $120 \div 4 =$ ___ $4\overline{)120}$

7. $\square \times 8 = 240$ $240 \div 8 =$ ___ $8\overline{)240}$

Divide.

8. $3\overline{)30}$ **9.** $2\overline{)140}$ **10.** $4\overline{)280}$ **11.** $2\overline{)80}$

12. $2\overline{)200}$ **13.** $4\overline{)360}$ **14.** $3\overline{)240}$ **15.** $2\overline{)400}$

16. $5\overline{)300}$ **17.** $6\overline{)360}$ **18.** $8\overline{)800}$ **19.** $6\overline{)480}$

20. $5\overline{)450}$ **21.** $7\overline{)700}$ ★**22.** $8\overline{)7,200}$ ★**23.** $3\overline{)2,700}$

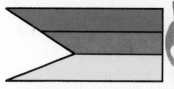 

Race Time

Divide.

1. $3\overline{)21}$ 2. $2\overline{)10}$ 3. $6\overline{)12}$ 4. $7\overline{)28}$

5. $6\overline{)48}$ 6. $7\overline{)42}$ 7. $4\overline{)32}$ 8. $9\overline{)72}$

9. $5\overline{)45}$ 10. $6\overline{)30}$ 11. $4\overline{)28}$ 12. $6\overline{)18}$

13. $6\overline{)24}$ 14. $5\overline{)35}$ 15. $8\overline{)40}$ 16. $7\overline{)14}$

17. $8\overline{)32}$ 18. $6\overline{)36}$ 19. $7\overline{)49}$ 20. $2\overline{)18}$

21. $7\overline{)56}$ 22. $8\overline{)64}$ 23. $6\overline{)42}$ 24. $8\overline{)72}$

25. $7\overline{)63}$ 26. $6\overline{)54}$ 27. $9\overline{)81}$ 28. $8\overline{)48}$

29. $8\overline{)16}$ 30. $9\overline{)45}$ 31. $3\overline{)18}$ 32. $7\overline{)35}$

33. $3\overline{)24}$ 34. $2\overline{)12}$ 35. $2\overline{)14}$ 36. $9\overline{)54}$

37. $4\overline{)12}$ 38. $7\overline{)7}$ 39. $4\overline{)16}$ 40. $8\overline{)56}$

41. $9\overline{)27}$ 42. $2\overline{)8}$ 43. $5\overline{)20}$ 44. $7\overline{)21}$

45. $5\overline{)10}$ 46. $9\overline{)18}$ 47. $2\overline{)16}$ 48. $4\overline{)36}$

49. $8\overline{)8}$ 50. $5\overline{)15}$ 51. $2\overline{)6}$ 52. $9\overline{)63}$

53. $5\overline{)40}$ 54. $3\overline{)27}$ 55. $5\overline{)25}$ 56. $9\overline{)36}$

REMAINDERS

We can subtract to find $27 \div 7$.

1 seven was subtracted each time.

3 sevens were subtracted in all.

The quotient is 3.

The remainder is 6.

```
           3 r 6
      7)27
           7   ( 1 seven)
          20
           7   ( 1 seven)
          13
           7   ( 1 seven)
           6    3 sevens
```

1. Copy and complete.

```
        r ___
a. 6)22
      6 (1 six)
     16
      6 (___ six)
     10
      6 (___ six)
      4  ___ sixes
```

```
        r ___
b. 4)23
      4 (___ four)
     19
      4 (___ four)
     15
```

2. Divide.

   a. $3)\overline{14}$ **b.** $2)\overline{9}$ **c.** $4)\overline{11}$ **d.** $3)\overline{16}$

EXERCISES

Divide.

1. $2)\overline{7}$ **2.** $4)\overline{19}$ **3.** $5)\overline{29}$ **4.** $7)\overline{38}$

5. $6)\overline{29}$ **6.** $5)\overline{32}$ **7.** $8)\overline{31}$ **8.** $4)\overline{27}$

USING MULTIPLICATION

Look at these two ways to find 8)37.
Multiplication can help us divide faster.

Jane's way

```
      4 r 5
  8)37
      8  ( 1 eight)
     29
      8  ( 1 eight)
     21
      8  ( 1 eight)
     13
      8  ( 1 eight)
      5    4 eights
```

Pat's way

```
      4 r 5
  8)37
     32  ( 4 eights or 4 × 8)
      5
```

1. Let's divide 7)39.

   Think: 4 × 7 = 28   7)39 $\overline{}$ r
              5 × 7 = 35   35 (5 × 7)
              6 × 7 = 42

   a. Is 35 less than 39?

   b. Is 42 greater than 39?

   c. Copy and complete the division.

2. Copy and complete.

```
        3 r ___
  a. 6)22
       18  (___ × 6)
        4
```

```
        7 r ___
  b. 4)30
       28  (___ × 4)
        2
```

Divide.

1. $8\overline{)36}$ 2. $3\overline{)19}$ 3. $5\overline{)49}$ 4. $7\overline{)51}$

5. $4\overline{)37}$ 6. $6\overline{)55}$ 7. $3\overline{)14}$ 8. $8\overline{)63}$

9. $9\overline{)83}$ 10. $2\overline{)17}$ 11. $4\overline{)22}$ 12. $9\overline{)74}$

13. $2\overline{)15}$ 14. $6\overline{)19}$ 15. $5\overline{)23}$ 16. $3\overline{)17}$

17. $4\overline{)27}$ 18. $3\overline{)25}$ 19. $7\overline{)26}$ 20. $9\overline{)33}$

21. $8\overline{)19}$ 22. $7\overline{)46}$ 23. $7\overline{)30}$ 24. $6\overline{)47}$

25. $9\overline{)41}$ 26. $7\overline{)59}$ 27. $8\overline{)54}$ 28. $6\overline{)53}$

29. $4\overline{)35}$ 30. $6\overline{)26}$ 31. $7\overline{)52}$ 32. $8\overline{)75}$

Solve these problems.

33. Have 37¢.
    Pencils cost 5¢ each.
    How many pencils bought?
    How many cents left?

34. 45 roses.
    6 to go in each vase.
    How many vases needed?
    How many roses left?

35. Mr. Lawrence has 26 pennies. He wants to give the same number of pennies to each of his 3 children. How many pennies will each child get? How many pennies will be left?

BARGAINS GALORE!

You can save money by buying at the sale price. How much money is saved if you buy at the sale price?

Example	REGULAR PRICE	SALE PRICE
	2 lollipops are 7¢ each	2 for 12¢

Think: 2 × 7 = 14

$$\begin{array}{r} 14¢ \\ -12¢ \\ \hline 2¢ \end{array}$$

2¢ are saved

REGULAR PRICE	SALE PRICE
1. Gum is 15¢ a pack.	5 packs for 70¢
2. Candy is 16¢ a bag.	4 bags for 60¢
3. Nuts are $1.38 a kilogram.	3 kilograms for $4.05
4. Figs are 27¢ a box.	4 boxes for 95¢
5. Potato chips are 39¢ a bag.	2 bags for 75¢
6. Candy apples are 17¢ each.	3 for 50¢
7. Candy bars are 15¢ each.	6 bars for 82¢
8. Popcorn is 27¢ a box.	4 boxes for $1.00

Add.

1. 376
  + 182

2. 46
  + 85

3. 408
  + 75

Keeping Fit

4. 269
  + 483

5. 560
  + 297

6. 684
  + 59

Subtract.

7. 763
  − 428

8. 92
  − 57

9. 627
  − 253

10. 170
  − 28

11. 570
  − 246

12. 900
  − 428

13. 736
  − 466

14. 802
  − 364

15. $6.42
  − 3.85

16. $5.00
  − 1.49

17. $1.00
  − .57

18. $7.00
  − .78

Multiply.

19. 4×10

20. 7×10

21. 5×10

22. 10×3

23. 10×9

24. 10×2

25. 2×30

26. 4×20

27. 5×30

28. 27
  × 3

29. 18
  × 5

30. 36
  × 4

31. 49
  × 7

32. 423
  × 3

33. 216
  × 4

34. 182
  × 4

35. 371
  × 6

36. 409
  × 7

37. 167
  × 5

38. 358
  × 6

39. 473
  × 9

36 balls in cans. 3 balls in each can. How many cans? Two ways to find $3\overline{)36}$.

Bob's way

$3\overline{)36}$
$\underline{15}$ (5 × 3)
21
$\underline{15}$ (5 × 3)
6
$\underline{6}$ (2 × 3)
0 12

Paul's way

THINK: 10 × 3 = 30
$3\overline{)36}$
$\underline{30}$ (10 × 3)
6
$\underline{6}$ (2 × 3)
0   12

The quotient is 12. There are 12 cans.

1. Let's find $2\overline{)28}$. Complete.

   $2\overline{)28}$
   $\underline{20}$ (10 × 2)
   8
   $\underline{8}$ (4 × 2)
   0

   a. Step 1: 10 × 2 = ___

   b. Step 2: 4 × 2 = ___

   c. What is the quotient?

2. Copy and complete.

   a. $5\overline{)70}$
      $\underline{50}$ (___ × 5)
      20
      $\underline{20}$ (___ × 5)
      0 ___

   b. $6\overline{)78}$
      $\underline{60}$ (___ × 6)
      18
      $\underline{18}$ (___ × 6)
      0 ___

3. Divide.

   a. $2\overline{)24}$ b. $5\overline{)55}$ c. $4\overline{)72}$ d. $8\overline{)96}$

   e. $4\overline{)56}$ f. $6\overline{)84}$ g. $5\overline{)95}$ h. $6\overline{)78}$

246

Divide.

1. $3\overline{)33}$ 2. $2\overline{)26}$ 3. $4\overline{)48}$ 4. $3\overline{)39}$

5. $2\overline{)38}$ 6. $4\overline{)60}$ 7. $3\overline{)45}$ 8. $5\overline{)65}$

9. $7\overline{)91}$ 10. $6\overline{)72}$ 11. $8\overline{)88}$ 12. $4\overline{)76}$

13. $9\overline{)9}$ 14. $3\overline{)54}$ 15. $5\overline{)75}$ 16. $2\overline{)34}$

17. $5\overline{)80}$ 18. $6\overline{)96}$ 19. $7\overline{)98}$ 20. $4\overline{)44}$

Solve these problems.

21. Pam put 52 arrowheads into 4 rows. Each row had the same number. How many were in each row?

22. Joe baked 84 cookies. He made 6 cookies for each friend. How many friends does he have?

23. Anita has 48 beads in all. She put them on 3 strings. Each string has the same number of beads. How many beads are on each string?

★ 24. There are 43 girls and 56 boys in the Third Grade. Mr. Allen put 9 children on a team for relay races. How many teams did he have?

Brainteaser

Trace the figure. Now, erase 5 line segments so that only 3 squares will be left.

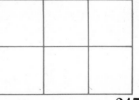

Here are two ways to find $3\overline{)78}$.
Pam subtracted the greatest multiple of ten.

Jim's way	Pam's way

```
    Jim's way                 Pam's way
   3)78                       3)78
     30  (10 × 3)               60  (20 × 3)
     48                         18
     30  (10 × 3)               18  ( 6 × 3)
     18                          0   26
     18  ( 6 × 3)
      0   26
```

The quotient is 26.

1. Let's look at $4\overline{)92}$. Complete.

    a. Step 1: $10 \times 4 =$ ___

    $20 \times 4 =$ ___

    $30 \times 4 =$ ___

```
   4)92
     80  (20 × 4)
     12
```

    b. Step 2: $3 \times 4 =$ ___

```
   4)92
     80  (20 × 4)
     12
```

    c. Complete the division.

```
   4)92
     80  (20 × 4)
     12
     12  ( 3 × 4)
      0     ___
```

2. Copy and complete.

    a.
```
   2)86
     80  (___ × 2)
      6
      6  (___ × 2)
      0      ___
```

    b.
```
   3)84
     60  (___ × 3)
     24
     24  (___ × 3)
      0      ___
```

248

3. Divide.

    a. $2\overline{)64}$ **b.** $4\overline{)84}$ **c.** $3\overline{)72}$ **d.** $2\overline{)90}$

Divide.

   1. $4\overline{)64}$ **2.** $2\overline{)82}$ **3.** $5\overline{)80}$ **4.** $2\overline{)98}$

   5. $6\overline{)66}$ **6.** $8\overline{)96}$ **7.** $3\overline{)99}$ **8.** $4\overline{)68}$

   9. $3\overline{)93}$ **10.** $4\overline{)88}$ **11.** $3\overline{)96}$ **12.** $7\overline{)70}$

13. $3\overline{)39}$ **14.** $2\overline{)62}$ **15.** $5\overline{)70}$ **16.** $4\overline{)84}$

17. $2\overline{)96}$ **18.** $6\overline{)72}$ **19.** $4\overline{)92}$ **20.** $3\overline{)75}$

21. $5\overline{)85}$ **22.** $4\overline{)72}$ **23.** $6\overline{)84}$ **24.** $2\overline{)94}$

Solve these problems.

25. 84¢ in all.
6¢ for each pencil.
How many pencils can you buy?

26. 96 buttons in all.
6 buttons on each card.
How many cards?

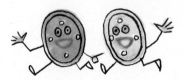

27. There were 78 children on 2 buses. Each bus had the same number of children. How many children were on each bus?

28. There are 36 cookies altogether. Each child gets 2 cookies. How many children are there?

249

93 pennies.
4 pennies for each ball. How many balls can you buy? How many pennies left?

quotient ⟶ 23 r 1 ⟵ remainder

```
      23 r 1
       3
      20
   4)93
      80  ( 20 × 4)
      13
      12  ( 3 × 4)
       1
```

You can buy 23 balls. 1 penny would be left.

1. Copy and complete.

a.
```
    ___ r ___
       1
      20
   3)65
      60  (20 × 3)
       5
       3  ( 1 × 3)
       2
```

b.
```
    ___ r ___
       3
      20
   4)95
      80  (___ × 4)
      15
      12  (___ × 4)
       3
```

c.
```
    ___ r ___
       3
      40
   2)87
      80  (___ × 2)
       7
       6  (___ × 2)
       1
```

d.
```
    ___ r ___
       0
      30
   2)61
      60  (___ × 2)
       1
       0  (___ × 2)
       1
```

2. Divide.

a. 2)63   b. 4)57   c. 2)73   d. 3)92

250

Divide.

1. $6\overline{)98}$ 2. $4\overline{)83}$ 3. $2\overline{)95}$ 4. $5\overline{)76}$

5. $3\overline{)83}$ 6. $4\overline{)89}$ 7. $7\overline{)93}$ 8. $3\overline{)91}$

9. $2\overline{)85}$ 10. $3\overline{)96}$ 11. $7\overline{)75}$ 12. $3\overline{)98}$

13. $2\overline{)53}$ 14. $3\overline{)47}$ 15. $6\overline{)95}$ 16. $8\overline{)97}$

17. $4\overline{)76}$ 18. $2\overline{)79}$ 19. $3\overline{)49}$ 20. $4\overline{)91}$

21. $6\overline{)89}$ 22. $3\overline{)77}$ 23. $2\overline{)93}$ 24. $5\overline{)99}$

Solve these mini-problems.

25. 86 birds in all.
4 birds on each branch.
How many branches?
How many birds not on
a branch?

26. 82 seeds. 3 rows of seeds.
Same number seeds in each
row.
How many in each row?
How many are left?

27. 98 donuts. 4 boxes.
Same number in
each box.
How many donuts in
each box?
How many are left?

28. 95 books. 3 shelves.
Same number on each
shelf.
How many books on
each shelf?
How many left?

We may check division with multiplication.

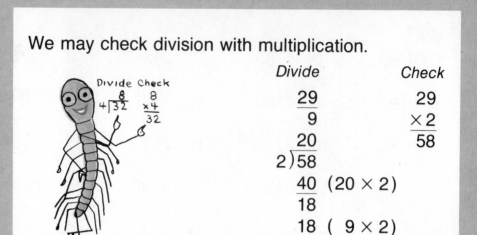

Divide	Check
29	29
9	× 2
20	58
2)58	
40 (20 × 2)	
18	
18 (9 × 2)	
0	

1. This flow chart shows how to check a quotient with a remainder.

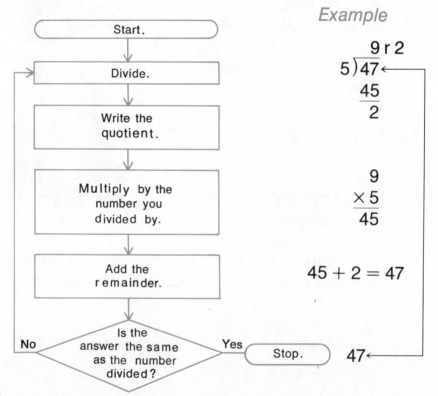

Example

$$9 \text{ r } 2$$
$$5)\overline{47}$$
$$45$$
$$2$$

$$9$$
$$\times 5$$
$$45$$

$$45 + 2 = 47$$

$$47$$

a. Jo checked a division example that had a remainder. Her answer was not the same as the number divided. What should she do next?

b. A flow chart for checking a division example with no remainder skips a step. What is the step?

2. Divide and check.

a. $6\overline{)68}$ **b.** $2\overline{)87}$ **c.** $3\overline{)85}$ **d.** $4\overline{)72}$

EXERCISES

Divide and check.

1. $2\overline{)69}$ **2.** $3\overline{)98}$ **3.** $4\overline{)85}$ **4.** $2\overline{)65}$

5. $3\overline{)38}$ **6.** $5\overline{)83}$ **7.** $4\overline{)79}$ **8.** $3\overline{)83}$

9. $6\overline{)82}$ **10.** $5\overline{)77}$ **11.** $5\overline{)95}$ **12.** $3\overline{)73}$

13. $2\overline{)54}$ **14.** $4\overline{)97}$ **15.** $2\overline{)75}$ **16.** $3\overline{)87}$

Solve these problems.

17. Mrs. Hontos sold 93 apples to 3 people. Each bought the same number of apples. How many apples did each one get?

18. Mrs. Chan has a pet shop. She has 72 goldfish. She wants to put 6 goldfish in each bowl. How many bowls does she need?

★**19.** Joe bought 5 boxes of candy and 9 kilograms of nuts. Candy costs 93¢ a box. Nuts cost $1.34 a kilogram. How much did he spend in all?

DIVIDING LARGER NUMBERS

We can divide larger numbers. Find $3\overline{)147}$.

Step 1: $20 \times 3 = 60$
           $30 \times 3 = 90$
           $40 \times 3 = 120$
           $50 \times 3 = 150$

Step 2: $9 \times 3 = 27$

$$
\begin{array}{r}
49 \\
\hline
9 \\
40 \\
3\overline{)147} \\
120 \quad (40 \times 3) \\
\hline
27 \\
27 \quad (9 \times 3) \\
\hline
0
\end{array}
$$

1. Let's find $7\overline{)479}$. Complete.

   a. Step 1: $50 \times 7 =$ ___
                     $60 \times 7 =$ ___
                     $70 \times 7 =$ ___

   b. Step 2: $7 \times 7 =$ ___
                     $8 \times 7 =$ ___
                     $9 \times 7 =$ ___

   c. Complete the division.

$$
\begin{array}{r}
\underline{\quad} \; r \underline{\quad} \\
8 \\
60 \\
7\overline{)479} \\
420 \quad (60 \times 7) \\
\hline
59 \\
56 \quad (8 \times 7) \\
\hline
3
\end{array}
$$

2. Copy and complete.

   a.
$$
\begin{array}{r}
70 \; r \underline{\quad} \\
4\overline{)282} \\
280 \quad (\underline{\quad} \times 4) \\
\hline
2
\end{array}
$$

   b.
$$
\begin{array}{r}
\underline{\quad} \; r \underline{\quad} \\
5 \\
30 \\
9\overline{)321} \\
270 \quad (\underline{\quad} \times 9) \\
\hline
51 \\
45 \quad (\underline{\quad} \times 9) \\
\hline
6
\end{array}
$$

254

3. Divide.

    a. $3\overline{)153}$ **b.** $6\overline{)128}$ **c.** $4\overline{)307}$ **d.** $8\overline{)524}$

Divide.

  1. $5\overline{)393}$ **2.** $3\overline{)261}$ **3.** $9\overline{)856}$ **4.** $4\overline{)326}$

  5. $2\overline{)184}$ **6.** $6\overline{)599}$ **7.** $7\overline{)421}$ **8.** $8\overline{)777}$

  9. $6\overline{)486}$ **10.** $5\overline{)354}$ **11.** $2\overline{)187}$ **12.** $6\overline{)350}$

13. $3\overline{)278}$ **14.** $9\overline{)729}$ **15.** $4\overline{)384}$ **16.** $3\overline{)267}$

17. $7\overline{)494}$ **18.** $6\overline{)387}$ **19.** $7\overline{)567}$ **20.** $9\overline{)507}$

21. $8\overline{)463}$ **22.** $4\overline{)300}$ **23.** $8\overline{)645}$ **24.** $7\overline{)532}$

25. $9\overline{)819}$ **26.** $5\overline{)468}$ **27.** $6\overline{)304}$ **28.** $9\overline{)758}$

Solve this problem.

29. 672 cookies.
8 classes.
Same number for
each.
How many cookies for
each class?

30. 534 apples.
6 apple trees.
Same number on
each.
How many apples on
each tree?

31. 420 legs.
5 insects.
Same number of legs.
How many legs on
each insect?

Keeping Fit

Multiply.

1. 6 ×5	**2.** 3 ×7	**3.** 6 ×9			

4. 9 ×9   **5.** 5 ×3   **6.** 5 ×8

7. 9 ×2   **8.** 7 ×7   **9.** 9 ×3   **10.** 5 ×5   **11.** 6 ×3

12. 3 ×8   **13.** 4 ×6   **14.** 8 ×6   **15.** 9 ×7   **16.** 8 ×7

17. 20 ×3   **18.** 30 ×2   **19.** 50 ×2   **20.** 200 ×3   **21.** 700 ×6

Divide.

22. 4)20   **23.** 8)32   **24.** 9)45   **25.** 3)24

26. 6)42   **27.** 8)64   **28.** 6)36   **29.** 9)72

30. 7)63   **31.** 4)24   **32.** 7)35   **33.** 6)48

34. 9)81   **35.** 8)56   **36.** 9)54   **37.** 5)45

38. 9)90   **39.** 2)40   **40.** 2)60   **41.** 7)700

42. 4)400   **43.** 3)900   **44.** 5)500   **45.** 4)800

Brainteaser

Complete.

$9 \times 8 \times 7 \times 0 \times 6 \times 5 \times 4 \times 3 \times 2 \times 1 =$ ___

BANK TELLERS

1. The Washingtons have $374 in one savings account and $268 in another savings account. How much do they have in both savings accounts?

2. Mrs. Jackson deposited $156 each month in her savings account for 5 months. How much did Mrs. Jackson put in her savings account in all?

3. Mr. Byrne gave the teller a $500 check. The teller returned $138 in cash. How much money did Mr. Byrne deposit in his account?

4. Mrs. Chin is one of the bank tellers. She had 550 rolls of dimes. She put them in boxes with 8 rolls in each box. How many boxes were used? How many rolls of dimes were left over?

5. Mr. Douglas is one of the bank tellers. One week he waited on 325 customers. 178 of them were women. How many were men?

★ 6. The Garcias pay service charges to keep their money in the bank. These charges are $3.00 each month for writing checks and $15.00 each year for a safety deposit box. How much do the Garcias pay for service charges in one year?

We can find $2\overline{)774}$.

Step 1: $200 \times 2 = 400$
$300 \times 2 = 600$
$400 \times 2 = 800$

Step 2: $70 \times 2 = 140$
$80 \times 2 = 160$
$90 \times 2 = 180$

Step 3: $7 \times 2 = 14$

```
        387
          7
         80
        300
      2)774
        600  (300 × 2)
        174
        160  ( 80 × 2)
         14
         14  (  7 × 2)
          0
```

1. Let's find $3\overline{)877}$. Complete.

   a. Step 1: $100 \times 3 = \underline{\hspace{1cm}}$
   $200 \times 3 = \underline{\hspace{1cm}}$
   $300 \times 3 = \underline{\hspace{1cm}}$

```
        200
      3)877
        600  (200 × 3)
         77
```

   b. Step 2: $70 \times 3 = \underline{\hspace{1cm}}$
   $80 \times 3 = \underline{\hspace{1cm}}$
   $90 \times 3 = \underline{\hspace{1cm}}$

```
          __ r __
          2
         90
        200
      3)877
        600  (200 × 3)
        277
```

   c. Step 3: $2 \times 3 = \underline{\hspace{1cm}}$

   d. Copy and complete the division.

```
        270  (__ × 3)
          7
          6  (__ × 3)
          1
```

258

2. Copy and complete.

```
        201 r 3
          1
        200
a. 4)807
        800  (___ × 4)
          7
          4  (___ × 4)
          3
```

```
        123 r 5
          3
         20
        100
b. 6)743
        600  (___ × 6)
        143
        120  (___ × 6)
         23
         18  (___ × 6)
          5
```

3. Divide.

   a. 2)608   **b.** 5)502   **c.** 4)952   **d.** 3)724

EXERCISES

Divide.

1. 4)428   **2.** 3)643   **3.** 2)447   **4.** 5)575

5. 2)406   **6.** 4)849   **7.** 3)737   **8.** 2)937

9. 3)468   **10.** 6)684   **11.** 7)368   **12.** 4)803

13. 3)791   **14.** 8)509   **15.** 6)611   **16.** 4)523

17. 5)300   **18.** 4)674   ★ **19.** 3)7,251   ★ **20.** 2)6,082

Solve this problem.

21. Jim sold 312 newspapers in 4 days. He sold the same number each day. How many newspapers did he sell each day?

259

Divide.

1. $2\overline{)80}$ 2. $4\overline{)280}$ 3. $3\overline{)600}$

4. $4\overline{)48}$ 5. $6\overline{)78}$ 6. $3\overline{)84}$

7. $3\overline{)96}$ 8. $4\overline{)65}$ 9. $2\overline{)79}$

10. $2\overline{)73}$ 11. $6\overline{)242}$ 12. $7\overline{)294}$

13. $5\overline{)219}$ 14. $3\overline{)926}$ 15. $5\overline{)840}$ 16. $3\overline{)764}$

17. $6\overline{)932}$ 18. $8\overline{)624}$ 19. $4\overline{)231}$ 20. $5\overline{)325}$

21. $9\overline{)423}$ 22. $3\overline{)333}$ 23. $7\overline{)300}$ 24. $8\overline{)800}$

ACTIVITY

1. Keep a chart of five visits to the grocery store like the one shown. For each visit, record the price of eggs per dozen and the date that you went. Did the price of eggs change at all? If so, how much?

Date of Visit	Price of Eggs

2. Find and tell the price of a food item (such as milk) in your newspaper. Do this for three different days. Keep a chart and for each day show: the name of the store, the name of the item, and the price. After three days, tell which store sold this item at the lowest price.

THE MARKET

1. Mr. Martin put 270 carrots in bunches. There were 7 carrots in a bunch. How many bunches of carrots did he have? How many carrots were left?

2. Mr. Leonard sold 288 loaves of bread in 6 days. He sold the same number of loaves each day. How many loaves of bread did he sell each day?

3. Mrs. Block packed 8 oranges to a box. She sold 448 oranges one week. How many boxes of oranges did she sell?

4. Mary Ann had 380 grapefruit in all. She put 9 grapefruit in each bag. How many bags of grapefruit were there? How many grapefruit were left?

5. Mrs. Sanders sold 120 onions. She sold them to 5 people. How many did each person buy?

6. Lyn works 8 hours each Saturday at the stand. How many hours does she work in 48 Saturdays?

ADDING HOURS AND MINUTES

Toni came home at 3:25. She must meet Maria in 1 hour and 30 minutes. What time will that be?

Think: 3:25 → 3 hours 25 minutes

ADD MINUTES

```
  3 hours   25 minutes
+ 1 hour    30 minutes
            55 minutes
```

ADD HOURS

```
  3 hours   25 minutes
+ 1 hour    30 minutes
  4 hours   55 minutes or
            4:55
```

Toni will meet Maria at 4:55.

1. The time is 5:38. What time will it be in 2 hours and 15 minutes? Complete.

ADD MINUTES

```
  5 hours  38 minutes
+ 2 hours  15 minutes
           53 minutes
```

ADD HOURS

```
  5 hours  38 minutes
+ 2 hours  15 minutes
  7 hours  53 minutes
```

The time will be 7:____ .

2. What time will it be in 3 hours and 20 minutes?

a. 　　b. 　　c.

262

What time will it be in 3 hours and 22 minutes?

1.    **2.**    **3.**

What time will it be in 1 hour and 32 minutes?

4.    **5.**    **6.**

What time will it be in 2 hours and 27 minutes?

7.    **8.**    **9.**

Solve these problems.

10. Donna ate breakfast at 7:30. She started for school 1 hour and 20 minutes later. At what time did she start for school?

11. Tom went fishing at 6:05. He came home 5 hours and 35 minutes later. What time did he come home?

★ **12.** Al started reading at 3:15. He stopped reading 1 hour and 48 minutes later. What time was it?

263

CHAPTER REVIEW

Multiply. [238]

1. 30	**2.** 10	**3.** 70	**4.** 80	**5.** 600
×6	×9	×7	×5	×5

Divide.

6. 7)70
[238]

7. 6)180
[238]

8. 8)640
[238]

9. 3)600
[238]

10. 6)44
[242]

11. 5)38
[242]

12. 3)54
[246]

13. 7)84
[246]

14. 3)57
[246]

15. 4)96
[248]

16. 3)93
[248]

17. 2)48
[248]

18. 2)73
[250]

19. 3)74
[250]

20. 4)89
[250]

21. 3)98
[250]

22. 4)95
[250]

23. 2)95
[250]

24. 5)386
[254]

25. 6)241
[254]

26. 7)249
[254]

27. 4)204
[254]

28. 2)164
[254]

29. 4)348
[254]

30. 8)750
[254]

31. 3)639
[258]

32. 8)877
[258]

33. 2)758
[258]

34. 4)934
[258]

35. 7)946
[258]

36. 6)726
[258]

37. 3)746
[258]

Solve these problems.

38. Sue left school at 3:15. She arrived home 1 hour
[262] and 23 minutes later. What time was that?

39. Jay watched TV at 7:26. He went to bed 1 hour
[262] and 15 minutes later. What time was that?

40. Lynn put 376 stamps in 6 rows. The same number
[243] of stamps were in each row. How many stamps
were in each row? How many were left?

CHAPTER TEST

Multiply.

1. 20 $\times 3$	**2.** 40 $\times 7$	**3.** 400 $\times 2$	**4.** 800 $\times 6$	**5.** 30 $\times 9$

Divide.

6. $3\overline{)60}$ **7.** $7\overline{)280}$ **8.** $6\overline{)360}$ **9.** $2\overline{)800}$

10. $3\overline{)28}$ **11.** $6\overline{)87}$ **12.** $5\overline{)72}$ **13.** $6\overline{)72}$

14. $4\overline{)83}$ **15.** $2\overline{)74}$ **16.** $2\overline{)95}$ **17.** $4\overline{)92}$

18. $7\overline{)287}$ **19.** $5\overline{)374}$ **20.** $4\overline{)302}$ **21.** $5\overline{)465}$

22. $3\overline{)942}$ **23.** $2\overline{)537}$ **24.** $3\overline{)854}$ **25.** $2\overline{)726}$

Solve these problems.

26. Ann began playing tag at 4:23. She stopped playing 1 hour and 22 minutes later. What time was that?

27. Kay began riding her bike at 2:37. She stopped 2 hours and 17 minutes later. What time was that?

28. Mr. Robbins packed 864 eggs into 3 boxes. Each box had the same number of eggs. How many eggs were in each box?

11 FRACTIONS

FRACTIONAL NUMERALS

Three children want to share a candy bar. The bar is cut into three parts. Each part is the same size.

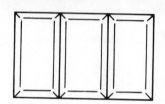

Each part is one third of the whole candy bar. $\frac{1}{3}$ is a **fractional numeral** for one third.

1. Look at this picture.

   a. How many parts are shown?

   b. How many parts are shaded?

   c. Write a fractional numeral for one fourth.

$$\frac{1}{4} \begin{array}{l} \longleftarrow \textbf{ number of parts shaded} \\ \longleftarrow \textbf{ parts of the same size in all} \end{array}$$

2. Which show halves?

   a.   b.   c.

3. Why doesn't the picture in Item 2b show halves?

4. Write fractional numerals for the shaded parts.

a. **b.** **c.**

Write fractional numerals.

1. one half   **2.** one sixth   **3.** one fourth

Which pictures show fourths?

4.   **5.**   **6.**

Which pictures show thirds?

7.   **8.**   **9.**

Write fractional numerals for the shaded parts.

10.   **11.**   **12.**

13.   **14.**   **15.**

16.   **17.**   ★ **18.**

267

COMPARING UNIT FRACTIONS

$\frac{1}{2}, \frac{1}{3}, \frac{1}{4}, \frac{1}{5}$, and so on, are **unit fractions.**

This picture shows that
$\frac{1}{3}$ is greater than $\frac{1}{5}$.

$$\frac{1}{3} > \frac{1}{5}$$

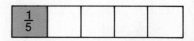

1. Which is greater?
   $\frac{1}{2}$ or $\frac{1}{4}$

2. Compare. Use > or <.

   a. $\frac{1}{4} \equiv \frac{1}{6}$

   b. $\frac{1}{6} \equiv \frac{1}{4}$

EXERCISES

Compare. Use > or <.

1. $\frac{1}{5} \equiv \frac{1}{10}$ 2. $\frac{1}{6} \equiv \frac{1}{8}$

3. $\frac{1}{8} \equiv \frac{1}{10}$ 4. $\frac{1}{5} \equiv \frac{1}{6}$

5. $\frac{1}{6} \equiv \frac{1}{10}$ 6. $\frac{1}{8} \equiv \frac{1}{5}$

★7. $\frac{1}{6} \equiv \frac{2}{8}$ ★8. $\frac{3}{5} \equiv \frac{2}{10}$

268

RECREATION WORKERS

1. Fourth Street School has 160 third graders. Only 40 of them do running exercises. How many do not do running exercises?

2. Last winter, there were 130 recreation workers in Logan City. In the summer, there were twice as many. How many recreation workers were there during the summer?

3. Ms. García is a recreation worker. The first week she worked, she earned $144.90. The next week she earned $149.40. How much did she earn for these two weeks?

4. During one week, Noriko swam these distances:

Monday	1,000 meters
Tuesday	2,000 meters
Wednesday	800 meters
Thursday	900 meters
Friday	1,000 meters
Saturday	3,000 meters

How many meters did she swim in all that week?

FRACTIONAL PARTS OF A WHOLE

We can think of more than one part of a whole.

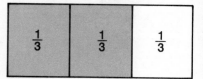

$\frac{2}{3}$ ← **number of parts shaded**

← **parts of the same size in all**

We read $\frac{2}{3}$ as two thirds.

1. Look at the circle.

   a. How many parts of the same size in all?

   b. How many parts shaded?

   c. Write a fractional numeral for the shaded parts.

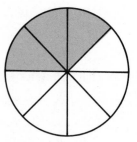

2. Look at the square.

   a. How many parts of the same size in all?

   b. How many parts shaded?

   c. Write a fractional numeral for the shaded parts.

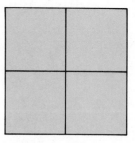

We read $\frac{4}{4}$ as four fourths.

$\frac{4}{4}$ is another name for 1.

270

3. Write fractional numerals for the shaded parts.

a.   **b.**   **c.**

Write fractional numerals for the shaded parts.

1.   **2.**   **3.**

4.   **5.**   **6.**

7.   **8.**   **9.**

★ **10.** Make a flow chart. Show how to write a fractional numeral for the shaded part of a whole.

ACTIVITY

Take a sheet of paper. Fold it in half. Write $\frac{1}{2}$ on each folded part.

Now fold it in half again. Write $\frac{1}{4}$ on each folded part. Do this one more time. Write a fraction on each fold.

$\frac{1}{2}$

$\frac{1}{2}$

COMPARING FRACTIONS

We can compare fractions.

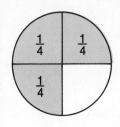  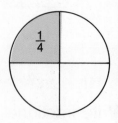

$\frac{3}{4} > \frac{1}{4}$ $\frac{3}{4}$ is greater than $\frac{1}{4}$.

$\frac{1}{4} < \frac{3}{4}$ $\frac{1}{4}$ is less than $\frac{3}{4}$.

1. Look at these pictures.

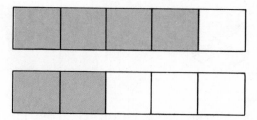 

   a. How many fifths are shaded in each?

   b. Which is greater, $\frac{4}{5}$ or $\frac{2}{5}$?

   c. Complete. Use > or <.
   $\frac{4}{5} \equiv \frac{2}{5}$ and $\frac{2}{5} \equiv \frac{4}{5}$

2. Compare. Use > or <. Draw pictures if you need help.

   a. $\frac{2}{3} \equiv \frac{1}{3}$ **b.** $\frac{3}{6} \equiv \frac{5}{6}$ **c.** $\frac{1}{8} \equiv \frac{3}{8}$

272

Compare. Use > or <.

1.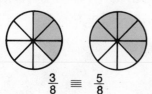

$$\frac{3}{8} \equiv \frac{5}{8}$$

2.

$$\frac{5}{6} \equiv \frac{1}{6}$$

Compare. Use > or <. Draw pictures if you need help.

3. $\frac{4}{5} \equiv \frac{1}{5}$ **4.** $\frac{3}{10} \equiv \frac{7}{10}$ **5.** $\frac{4}{9} \equiv \frac{2}{9}$

6. $\frac{3}{8} \equiv \frac{7}{8}$ **7.** $\frac{2}{7} \equiv \frac{5}{7}$ **8.** $\frac{3}{4} \equiv \frac{1}{4}$

9. $\frac{2}{5} \equiv \frac{3}{5}$ **10.** $\frac{5}{6} \equiv \frac{3}{6}$ ★**11.** $\frac{2}{3} \equiv \frac{1}{5}$

Keeping Fit

Multiply.

1. $\begin{array}{r} 45 \\ \times 7 \\ \hline \end{array}$ **2.** $\begin{array}{r} 23 \\ \times 3 \\ \hline \end{array}$ **3.** $\begin{array}{r} 46 \\ \times 5 \\ \hline \end{array}$ **4.** $\begin{array}{r} 54 \\ \times 9 \\ \hline \end{array}$

5. $\begin{array}{r} 407 \\ \times 8 \\ \hline \end{array}$ **6.** $\begin{array}{r} 506 \\ \times 6 \\ \hline \end{array}$ **7.** $\begin{array}{r} 905 \\ \times 7 \\ \hline \end{array}$ **8.** $\begin{array}{r} 704 \\ \times 9 \\ \hline \end{array}$

Divide.

9. $7\overline{)42}$ **10.** $8\overline{)64}$ **11.** $3\overline{)29}$ **12.** $5\overline{)80}$

13. $4\overline{)63}$ **14.** $7\overline{)46}$ **15.** $7\overline{)497}$ **16.** $9\overline{)243}$

17. $7\overline{)309}$ **18.** $4\overline{)107}$ **19.** $3\overline{)101}$ **20.** $5\overline{)201}$

USING FRACTIONS

Fractional numerals tell about parts of sets. What part of this set of animals has only 2 legs?

$\frac{2}{5}$ $\longleftarrow$ number of animals with only 2 legs
$\phantom{\frac{2}{5}}$ $\longleftarrow$ number of animals in all

$\frac{2}{5}$ of the animals have 2 legs.

1. Look at the geese.

   a. How many in all?

   b. How many are flying?

   c. Write a fractional numeral for the number of geese flying.

   d. How many are eating?

   e. Write a fractional numeral for the number of geese eating.

274

2. Look at the boxes of popcorn.

    a. How many boxes are full?

    b. Write a fractional numeral for the full boxes.

    c. How many boxes are empty?

    d. Write a fractional numeral for the empty boxes.

3. Write a fractional numeral for the shaded part of each set.

    a. △△△   **b.** ○○●○   **c.** ▪▪▫
       △△△   ●○○●   ▫▫

Write a fractional numeral for the shaded part of each set.

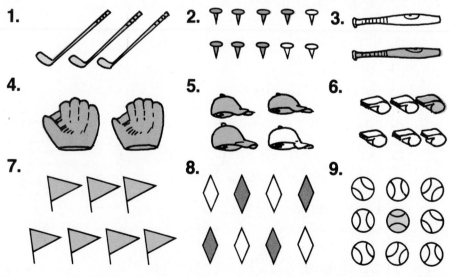

1.

2.

3.

4.

5.

6.

7.

8.

9.

FINDING FRACTIONAL PARTS

Joe colored 12 eggs. He colored $\frac{1}{2}$ of them pink. How many eggs were colored pink?

$$\frac{1}{2} \text{ of } 12 = 6$$

Think: $12 \div 2 = 6$

1. Gail also colored eggs. She placed them this way.

   a. How many in all?

   b. How many parts?

   c. What part of the whole is Part A? Part B? Part C?

   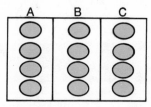

   d. How many in Part A? Part B? Part C?

   e. Complete: $\frac{1}{3}$ of 12 = ___ ; 12 ÷ 3 = ___ .

2. Eddy placed some cookies in 2 groups.

   a. How many cookies in all?

   b. What part of all the cookies is in Group D? Group K?

   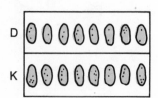

   c. How many in Group D? Group K?

   d. Complete: $\frac{1}{2}$ of 16 = ___ ; 16 ÷ 2 = ___ .

276

3. What part of each set is shaded? Complete.

a.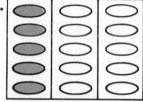

$\frac{1}{2}$ of 8 = ___

b.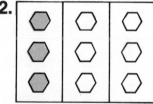

$\frac{1}{5}$ of 10 = ___

Complete.

1.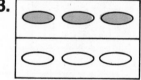

$\frac{1}{3}$ of 15 = ___

2.

$\frac{1}{3}$ of 9 = ___

3.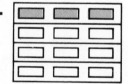

$\frac{1}{2}$ of 6 = ___

4.

$\frac{1}{4}$ of 12 = ___

5.

$\frac{1}{3}$ of 6 = ___

Solve these mini-problems.

6. 3 frogs.
1 jumped away.
What part jumped away?

7. 7 fish.
2 swim away.
What part stay?

277

Steve ate $\frac{2}{4}$ of a tart.   Lyn ate $\frac{1}{2}$ of a tart.

$\frac{2}{4}$ and $\frac{1}{2}$ are two names for the same number.

They are **equivalent.** $\frac{2}{4} = \frac{1}{2}$

1. Look at the pictures. Complete.

   a. What part of A is shaded?

   b. What part of B is shaded?

   c. Is the same amount shaded in each?

   Complete: $\frac{1}{3} = \frac{3}{\square}$

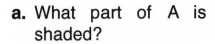
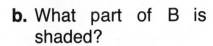
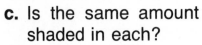

2. Complete.

   a.
   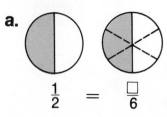

   $\frac{1}{2} = \frac{\square}{6}$

   b.
   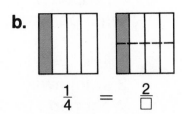

   $\frac{1}{4} = \frac{2}{\square}$

278

3. Draw pictures to show each.

a. $\frac{1}{4} = \frac{2}{8}$ **b.** $\frac{1}{3} = \frac{2}{6}$ **c.** $\frac{3}{12} = \frac{1}{4}$

Complete.

1.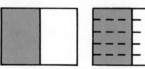

$\frac{1}{2} = \frac{\square}{10}$

2.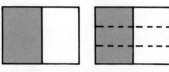

$\frac{1}{2} = \frac{3}{\square}$

3.

$\frac{1}{2} = \frac{4}{\square}$

4.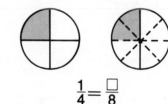

$\frac{1}{4} = \frac{\square}{8}$

Draw pictures to show each.

5. $\frac{1}{2} = \frac{3}{6}$ **6.** $\frac{1}{2} = \frac{5}{10}$ **7.** $\frac{1}{5} = \frac{2}{10}$

8. $\frac{1}{2} = \frac{2}{4}$ ★**9.** $\frac{2}{3} = \frac{4}{6}$ ★**10.** $\frac{2}{2} = \frac{4}{4}$

Brainteaser

Find the pattern. Complete.

1. $\frac{1}{2}, \frac{1}{3}, \frac{1}{4}, \frac{1}{5},$ ____ , ____ , ___

2. $\frac{1}{2}, \frac{2}{3}, \frac{3}{4}, \frac{4}{5},$ ____ , ____ , ___

3. $\frac{1}{2}, \frac{2}{4}, \frac{3}{6}, \frac{4}{8},$ ____ , ____ , ___

279

FRACTIONS ON A NUMBER LINE

We can show whole numbers on a number line.

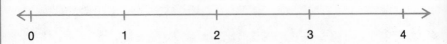

We can also show fractions on a number line.

1. Look at this number line.

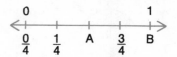

a. What fraction goes with A?

b. What fraction goes with B?

c. Complete:
$$1 = \frac{4}{\square}.$$

2. Is $\frac{1}{2}$ or $\frac{1}{4}$ farther to the right?

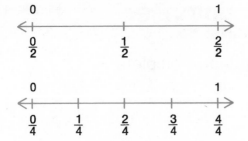

Complete. Use >, <, or =.

a. $\frac{1}{2} \equiv \frac{1}{4}$

b. $\frac{1}{4} \equiv \frac{1}{2}$

c. $\frac{1}{2} \equiv \frac{4}{4}$

Use the number lines to compare. Use >, <, or =.

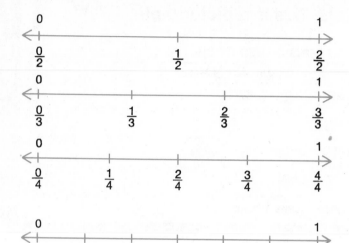

1. $\dfrac{1}{3}$ ▦ $\dfrac{1}{6}$

2. $\dfrac{1}{2}$ ▦ $\dfrac{5}{6}$

3. $\dfrac{2}{3}$ ▦ $\dfrac{1}{4}$

4. $\dfrac{2}{3}$ ▦ $\dfrac{4}{6}$

5. $\dfrac{2}{6}$ ▦ $\dfrac{2}{3}$

6. $\dfrac{5}{6}$ ▦ $\dfrac{3}{4}$

7. $\dfrac{1}{4}$ ▦ $\dfrac{1}{6}$

8. $\dfrac{2}{3}$ ▦ $\dfrac{6}{6}$

9. $\dfrac{1}{2}$ ▦ $\dfrac{5}{6}$

Keeping Fit

Add or subtract.

1. $\begin{array}{r} 83 \\ +45 \\ \hline \end{array}$

2. $\begin{array}{r} 24 \\ +17 \\ \hline \end{array}$

3. $\begin{array}{r} 427 \\ -132 \\ \hline \end{array}$

4. $\begin{array}{r} 814 \\ -215 \\ \hline \end{array}$

5. $\begin{array}{r} 795 \\ -262 \\ \hline \end{array}$

6. $\begin{array}{r} 502 \\ -226 \\ \hline \end{array}$

7. $\begin{array}{r} 82 \\ +79 \\ \hline \end{array}$

8. $\begin{array}{r} 192 \\ +232 \\ \hline \end{array}$

9. $\begin{array}{r} 373 \\ +465 \\ \hline \end{array}$

10. $\begin{array}{r} 189 \\ +327 \\ \hline \end{array}$

11. $\begin{array}{r} 200 \\ -176 \\ \hline \end{array}$

12. $\begin{array}{r} 457 \\ -298 \\ \hline \end{array}$

281

PICTOGRAPHS

Graphs tell facts. This is a **pictograph.**

BALLOONS OWNED BY CHILDREN

Name	Number of Balloons
Ted	🎈 🎈 🎈
Sue	🎈
Al	🎈 🎈 🎈 🎈
Greg	🎈 🎈

Each symbol 🎈 means 1 balloon.

1. In the above graph, each symbol means 1 balloon.

   a. How many balloons does Ted have?

   b. Who has the most balloons?

   c. How would the graph show 10 balloons?

2. One symbol may mean 2 things. Look at this graph.

FISH CAUGHT BY CHILDREN

Name	Number of Fish
Lora	🐟 🐟 🐟 🐟
Pat	🐟 🐟
Gene	🐟

Each symbol 🐟 means 2 fish.

   a. How many fish does each 🐟 mean?

   b. How many fish did Lora catch?

   c. How would the graph show 10 fish?

Use this pictograph to find the information.

DAYS ABSENT FROM SCHOOL

Name	Days Absent
Jack	😦 😦 😦 😦
Ellen	😦 😦 😦 😦 😦 😦
Rosa	😦 😦
Larry	😦

Each symbol 😦 means 1 day.

1. Who was absent the most days?

2. Who was absent the fewest days?

ACTIVITY

Make your own pictograph. Copy this chart.

TOY BOATS OWNED BY CHILDREN

Name	Number of Toy Boats

Now fill in your graph to show that:

Kathy has 2 boats

Dan has 1 boat

Jay has 3 boats

You can use a picture of a little boat to stand for 1 toy boat.

283

BAR GRAPHS

A **bar graph** tells information.
Sally saved pennies on four days this week.

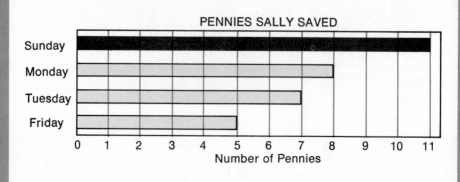

PENNIES SALLY SAVED

Sunday	
Monday	
Tuesday	
Friday	

0   1   2   3   4   5   6   7   8   9   10   11
Number of Pennies

1. Where are the days shown on the bar graph?

2. The bottom shows the scale. How is it marked?

3. Follow these steps to find how many pennies Sally saved on Sunday.

   (a) Put your finger on the black bar to the right of "Sunday."
   (b) Follow the black bar to the right until it ends.

   How many pennies did Sally save on Sunday?

4. How many pennies were saved on Monday?

5. How many pennies were saved on Tuesday?

6. How many pennies were saved on Friday?

7. On which day did Sally save the most pennies?

Some children in Al's class have marbles.

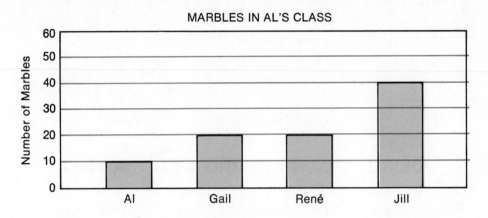

MARBLES IN AL'S CLASS

1. Where is the scale shown?

2. How is the scale marked?

3. Who has the same number of marbles as Gail?

4. Who has the most marbles? the fewest marbles?

ACTIVITY

Make your own bar graph. Copy this chart.

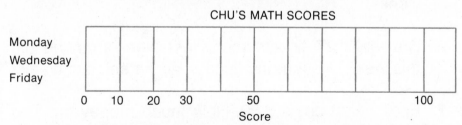

CHU'S MATH SCORES

Complete the scale along the bottom of the graph.
Now, draw in the bars to show Chu's scores:

Monday	80
Wednesday	90
Friday	100

285

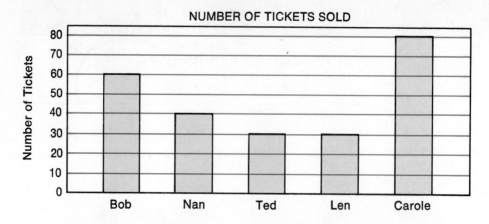

NUMBER OF TICKETS SOLD

Number of Tickets

80
70
60
50
40
30
20
10
0

Bob   Nan   Ted   Len   Carole

USING GRAPHS IN PROBLEM SOLVING

Five children sold tickets to the class play this week.

1. How many tickets did Bob and Len sell together?

2. How many tickets did Nan and Carole sell together?

3. How many more tickets did Nan sell than Ted?

4. Two children sold the same number of tickets. How many tickets did they sell together?

5. Last week, Nan sold twice as many tickets as she did this week. How many tickets did she sell last week?

6. Bob sold 27 tickets more last week than he did this week. How many tickets did he sell last week?

★ 7. Each ticket costs $.30. How much money did Ted earn for the class?

★ 8. How much money in all was earned this week by the five children?

Multiply.

1. 23
    × 3

2. 36
    × 7

3. 48
    × 5

Keeping Fit

4. 143
    × 2

5. 703
    × 8

6. 749
    × 6

Divide.

7. 2)26

8. 8)59

9. 4)80

10. 7)89

11. 6)140

12. 3)639

13. 8)568

14. 5)724

Complete.

15. 1 m = ___ cm

16. 100 cm = ___ m

17. 3 m = ___ cm

18. 6 m = ___ cm

19. 500 cm = ___ m

20. 800 cm = ___ m

What time will it be in 1 hour and 18 minutes?

21.

22.

23.

What time will it be in 2 hours and 12 minutes?

24.

25.

26.

CHAPTER REVIEW

Write fractional numerals for the shaded parts.

1. [266]

2. [270]

3. [274]

4. [274]

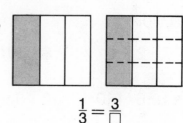

Make true sentences. [278]

5.

6.

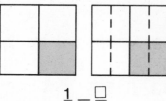

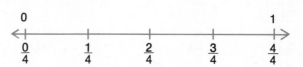

$\frac{1}{4} = \frac{\square}{8}$

$\frac{1}{3} = \frac{3}{\square}$

Compare. Use >, <, or =. [272, 280]

7. $\frac{5}{8} \equiv \frac{7}{8}$

8. $\frac{1}{4} \equiv \frac{2}{8}$

9. $\frac{3}{4} \equiv \frac{3}{8}$

10. $\frac{7}{8} \equiv \frac{4}{4}$

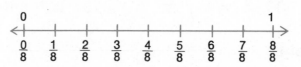

11. How many stamps [282] does Bob have?

12. How would 10 stamps [282] be shown?

STAMPS OWNED BY CHILDREN

Name	Number of Stamps
Bob	▪ ▪ ▪ ▪
Bill	▪ ▪
Ann	▪

Each symbol ▪ means 2 stamps.

13. How many buttons [284] did Sue save?

14. How many buttons [284] did Al save?

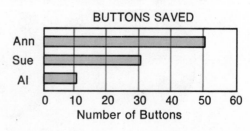

CHAPTER TEST

Write fractional numerals for the shaded parts.

1.   **2.**   **3.**  **4.**

Make true sentences.

5.

$$\frac{1}{2} = \frac{\square}{4}$$

6.

$$\frac{1}{3} = \frac{2}{\square}$$

Compare. Use >, <, or =.

7. $\frac{2}{6} \equiv \frac{5}{6}$

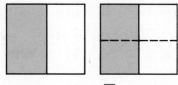

8. $\frac{2}{3} \equiv \frac{1}{6}$

9. $\frac{2}{6} \equiv \frac{1}{3}$

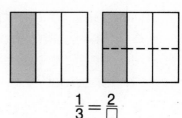

10. $\frac{5}{6} \equiv \frac{3}{3}$

11. How many pins does Elsa have?

12. How would 6 pins be shown?

Number of Safety Pins

Elsa	
Carl	
Rhoda	

Each symbol means 1 pin.

13. How many clips does Les have?

14. How many clips does Guy have?

Paper Clips

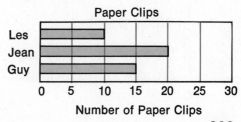

Number of Paper Clips

289

12 GEOMETRY

POINTS, PATHS, AND LINE SEGMENTS

Jane goes to camp. She swims in the lake. There are many paths from Jane's tent to the lake. Use your finger to trace each of the three paths. Which is the shortest?

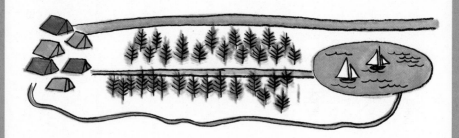

The shortest path between two points is called a **line segment**.

1. Follow these steps to make a line segment.

a. Mark 2 points on your paper.

b. Write A above one point.

c. Write B above the other point.

d. Use your ruler to connect the points.

290

2. Which are line segments?

a.   b.   c.   d.

3. Which have more than one line segment?

a.   b.   c.   d.

EXERCISES

1. Look at this map. What color is the line segment?

Which are line segments?

2.   **3.**   **4.**   **5.**

Which have more than one line segment?

6.   **7.**   **8.**   **9.**

10.   **11.**   **12.**   **13.**

291

LINES AND RAYS

1. Let's make a line.

    a. Mark two points on your paper.

    b. Write *K* above one point. Write *M* above the other point.

    c. Connect the points with a line segment.

    d. Make the line segment longer at each end.

    e. Make arrows at both ends.

A **line** goes on and on forever in two directions.

2. Let's make a ray.

    a. Mark 2 points on your paper.

    b. Write *A* above one point. Write *B* above the other point.

    c. Connect the points with a line segment.

    d. Make the line segment longer at the right end. Put an arrow on it.

    e. Make a ray that goes to the left.

A **ray** goes on and on forever in one direction.

3. Complete.

a. This line goes through point *P* and point ___ .

P   Q

b. This ray starts at point *S* and goes through point ___ .

T   S

c. This ray starts at point *N* and goes through point ___ .

N   M

4. Which are lines? Which are rays?

a.   **b.**   **c.**   **d.**

Which are line segments? Which are lines? Which are rays?

1.   **2.**   **3.**   **4.**

5. _____   **6.**   **7.**   **8.**

9. How many lines are shown?

★10. How many rays from point *X* are shown?

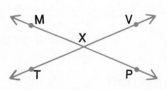

M   V
X
T   P

293

CIRCLES

These are **circles.**

center

C
D

radius

B
C
D

diameter

1. Look at this circle. Complete.

   a. Point ___ is the center.

   b. One radius goes through points *A* and *D*. Another radius goes through points *A* and ___.

   c. Measure each radius in centimeters. Are they the same length?

A **radius** is a line segment from the center to a point on the circle. We say **radii** for more than one radius.

2. Look at this circle. Complete.

   a. Point ___ is the center.

   b. A diameter goes through point *W* and between points *B* and ___ on the circle.

   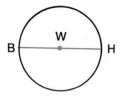

A **diameter** is a line segment that goes through the center of a circle. It goes between two points on the circle.

294

3. Look at this circle.

    a. How many diameters are shown?

    b. Measure the diameters. Are they the same length?

Which circles have radii shown?

1.   **2.**   **3.**   ★**4.**

How many radii are shown in each?

5.   **6.**   **7.**   ★**8.**

How many diameters are shown in each?

9.   **10.**    **11.**   **12.**

Look at this circle. Complete.

13. Point ___ is the center.

14. A radius goes between points *T* and ___ .

15. A diameter goes through point *S* and between points *R* and ___ .

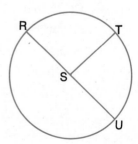

RECTANGLES AND SQUARES

This card has the shape of a **rectangle.**

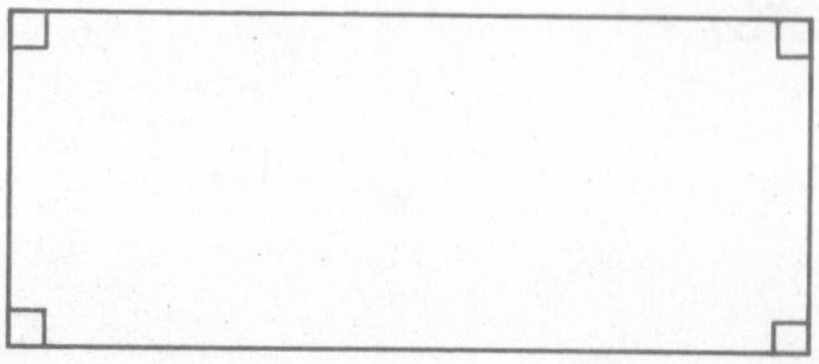

A rectangle has 4 sides and 4 square corners. Square corners are called **right angles.**

1. Let's make a rectangle.

   a. Copy the 4 points on your paper.

   b. Draw 4 line segments.

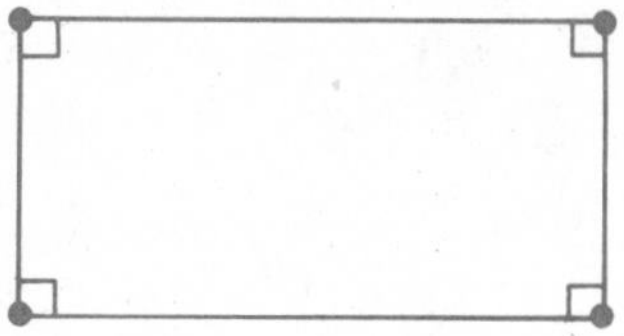

   c. Measure the segments with a centimeter ruler. Are any sides the same length?

   d. Are the corners right angles?

2. Look at this **square.**

   a. Are the 4 corners right angles?

   b. Is a square also a rectangle?

   c. Measure the segments with a centimeter ruler. How many sides are the same length?

3. Which are rectangles? Which are squares?

   a. **b.**  **c.**

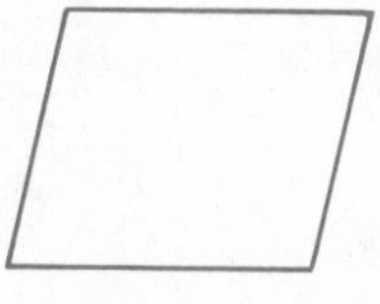

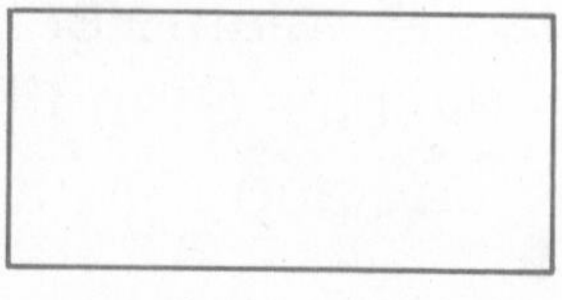

Look at this figure.

1. How many right angles are there?

2. Measure the sides in centimeters.
   How many sides are the same length?

3. Is the figure a rectangle? a
   square?

Which are rectangles? Which are squares?

4. 5. 6.

7. 8. 9.

★ **10.** How many squares are
   in this window?

★ **11.** How many rectangles
   are in the window?

ACTIVITY

Make a list of everything in your home that is shaped like a rectangle. Put a star next to things that are also shaped like squares.

TRIANGLES

These are **triangles.**
A triangle has 3 sides.

1. Let's make a triangle.

   a. Copy the points on your paper.

   b. Connect the points with segments.

   c. How many sides are there?

2. Which figures are triangles?

   a. **b.** **c.**  **d.**

Which figures are triangles?

1. **2.**  **3.** **4.**

5. **6.** **7.** **8.**

★**9.** How many triangles
   can you find?

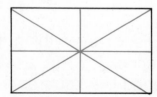

298

MOTION PICTURE PROJECTIONISTS

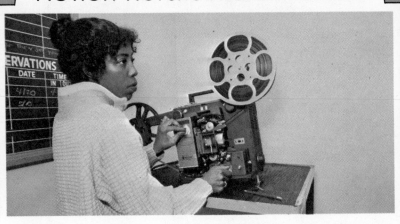

1. There are about 16,000 people who are motion-picture projectionists. About $\frac{1}{4}$ of them work for drive-in theaters. About how many work for drive-ins?

2. Mr. García earns $5.50 an hour at the Plaza Cinema. How much does he earn in a 40-hour week?

3. Miss Jones earns $232.00 a week at the Sunset Cinema. She gets 3 weeks of paid vacation a year. How much money does she get for vacation time?

4. A reel of film lasts 20 minutes. How many reels are needed for a 3-hour movie?

5. Mr. Ryan worked at the local television station for 10 years. Mrs. Weiss worked there for 8 years. How much longer has Mr. Ryan worked there than Mrs. Weiss?

6. A person must be 18 years old to work as a motion picture projectionist. Elida is $16\frac{1}{2}$ years old. How many months does she have to wait?

SYMMETRY

1. Trace the butterfly and the line. Fold along the line.

   Do both parts match?

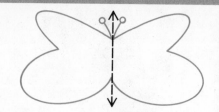

2. Trace the letter and the line. Fold along the line.

   Do both parts match?

We can fold a figure on a line. If the parts match, the figure is **symmetric.** The line is called a **line of symmetry.**

3. Some figures may have two lines of symmetry. Trace this figure.

   a. Fold on the black line.
      Do the parts match?

   b. Fold on the red line.
      Do the parts match?

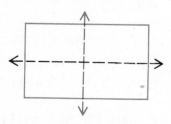

4. Which have one line of symmetry? two lines?

a.

b.

c.

d.

e.

f.

300

Which are symmetric?

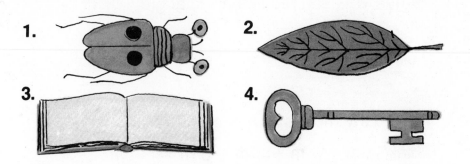

1.

2.

3.

4.

Which have one line of symmetry? two lines?

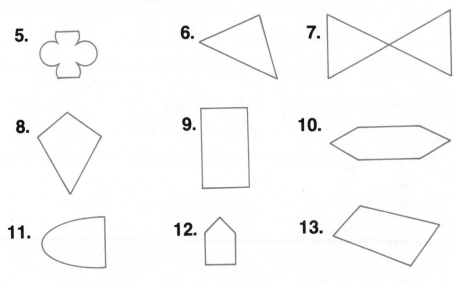

5.

6.

7.

8.

9.

10.

11.

12.

13.

14. Which figure above is not symmetric?

ACTIVITY

Find a picture of a symmetric figure in a magazine. Cut it out. Fold the picture to find all the lines of symmetry. Draw each in a different color.

PERIMETER

1. Mary wanted to put a fence around her garden. The garden was shaped like a rectangle.

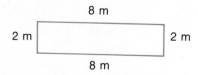

How many meters of fence does Mary need?

Think: 2 m + 8 m + 2 m + 8 m = ___ m

The **perimeter** of the rectangle is 20 m.

2. Let's find the perimeter of this triangle.

   a. How long is each side?

   b. Add the lengths of the sides.
      2 cm + 3 cm + 4 cm = ___ cm

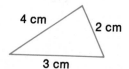

   c. What is the perimeter of the triangle?

   Perimeter is the distance around a figure.

3. Look at this square.
   Each side is 3 cm long.

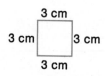

   Complete to find the perimeter.

   3 cm + 3 cm + 3 cm + 3 cm = ___ cm

4. Find the perimeters.

   a.
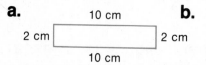

   b.
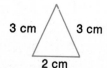

   c.
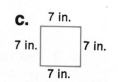

302

Find the perimeters.

1.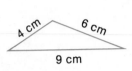

2.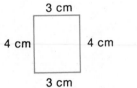

3.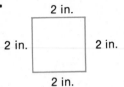

4.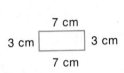

5.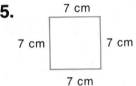

6.

7.

8.

★ **9.**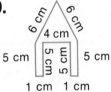

Add.

1.	24	**2.**	62	**3.**	703
	+ 35		+ 28		+ 278

Keeping Fit

4.	68	**5.**	42	**6.**	463
	11		38		122
	+ 80		+ 19		+ 354

Subtract.

7.	86	**8.**	75	**9.**	72	**10.**	485
	− 4		− 24		− 8		− 147

11.	564	**12.**	642	**13.**	835	**14.**	700
	− 254		− 306		− 597		− 447

AREA

We measure **area** in **square units**.

square unit

The **area** of this rectangle is 6 square units.

1. Look at this figure.

   a. How many square units are in the rectangle?

   b. What is the area of the rectangle?

2. Look at this figure.

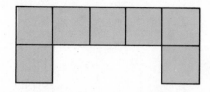

   a. How many square units are in the figure?

   b. What is the area?

Find the areas.

1.

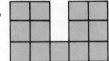

2.

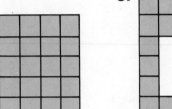

3.

4.

5.

6.

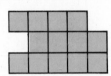

7.

8.

9.

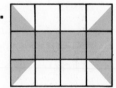

Find the areas of the shaded parts.

★**10.**

★**11.**

ACTIVITY

Draw a rectangle with a length of 10 cm and a width of 4 cm. Cut it out. Then cut out 4 more rectangles just like it. Cut each rectangle into at least two triangles. Mix up all the pieces. Now try to put the rectangles back together.

305

CHOOSING THE CORRECT OPERATION

Choose the correct operation: +, −, ×, or ÷.
Do not solve.

1. 2 hamburgers.
   Paid 70¢ in all.
   How much for one?

2. 24 cans in a carton.
   5 cartons.
   How many cans in all?

3. 3 buses.
   27 children in each.
   How many children
   in all?

4. 34 hot dogs.
   Each child eats
   2 hot dogs.
   How many children?

5. Hot dog costs 25¢.
   Drink costs 20¢.
   Find total cost.

6. Have 55¢.
   Sandwich costs 65¢.
   How much more need-
   ed?

7. 184 bottles.
   8 in each box.
   How many boxes?

8. Spent $1.45.
   Gave clerk $5.00.
   How much change?

9. Candy costs
   15¢ a bag.
   Buy 8 bags.
   Find total cost.

10. 223 seats filled.
    157 seats empty.
    How many seats
    in all?

SPACE

These objects take up space.

1. Look at the picture above. Which objects have these shapes?

a.   b.   c.   d.

2. Name other objects shaped like those above.

Look at these shapes. Which objects have these shapes?

 A   B   C   D

1.   2.   3.

4.   5.   6.

VOLUME

Objects in space can be measured.
A **cubic unit** is used to measure **volume.**

  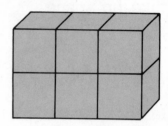

cubic unit   This volume is 6 cubic units.

1. Look at this picture.

   a. How many cubic units are shown?

   b. What is the volume?

2. Count the cubic units in this object.

   a. How many cubic units are there?

   b. What is the volume?

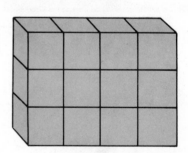

3. Find the volumes.

   a. 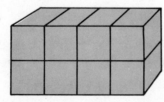   b.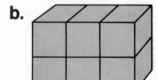

4. Find the volume.

    a. How many cubic units in the red layer?

    b. How many cubic units in the blue layer?

    c. How many cubic units in all?

    d. What is the volume?

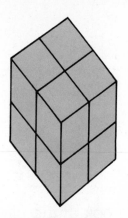

Find the volumes.

1.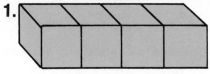

2.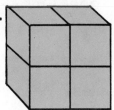

3.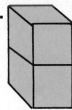

4.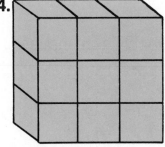

5.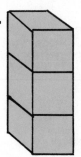

6.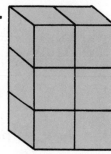

7.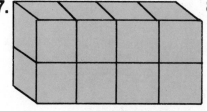

8.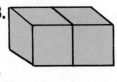

9.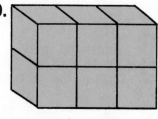

CHAPTER REVIEW

Which are line segments? Which are lines? Which are rays? [290, 292]

1.　　　　**2.**　　　　　　**3.**　　　　　　　**4.**

Look at the circle. Complete. [294]

5. Point ___ is the center.
6. A radius goes between points R and ___ .
7. A diameter goes through point M and between points B and ___ .

Which are rectangles? Which are squares? Which are triangles? [296, 298]

8.　　　**9.**　　　**10.**　　　**11.**

How many lines of symmetry does each figure have? [300]

12.　　**13.**　　**14.**　　**15.**

Find the perimeters. [302]

16.　　　　**17.**　　　　**18.**

　　　　　　　　　　　　　　　　5 cm
　　　　　　　　　　　　　2 cm ▭ 2 cm
　　　　　　　　　　　　　　　　5 cm

Find the area. [304]　　　Find the volume. [308]

19.　　　　　　**20.**

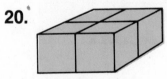

CHAPTER TEST

Which are line segments? Which are lines? Which are rays?

1.   2.   3.   4.

Look at the circle. Complete.

5. Point ___ is the center.
6. A radius goes between points S and ___ .
7. A diameter goes through point T and between points L and ___ .

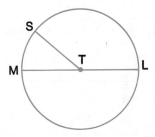

Which are rectangles? Which are squares? Which are triangles?

8.   9.    10.   11.

How many lines of symmetry does each figure have?

12.   13.   14. 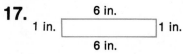   15.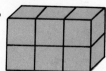

Find the perimeters.

16.
4 cm 4 cm
2 cm

17. 6 in.
1 in. [   ] 1 in.
6 in.

18. 6 m
6 m [ ] 6 m
6 m

Find the area.

19.

Find the volume.

20.

13 THOUSANDS; PROBABILITY

ADDING THOUSANDS

$$
\begin{array}{r}
345 \\
+453 \\
\hline
798
\end{array}
\qquad
\begin{array}{r}
5,345 \\
+1,453 \\
\hline
6,798
\end{array}
$$

IT'S EASY.

Adding thousands is just like adding hundreds.

1. Add.

a. $\begin{array}{r} 262 \\ +135 \end{array}$
b. $\begin{array}{r} 427 \\ +162 \end{array}$
c. $\begin{array}{r} 301 \\ +536 \end{array}$
d. $\begin{array}{r} 542 \\ 231 \\ +125 \end{array}$

2. Add.

a. $\begin{array}{r} 3,002 \\ +4,997 \end{array}$
b. $\begin{array}{r} 5,016 \\ +4,382 \end{array}$
c. $\begin{array}{r} 2,334 \\ 3,001 \\ +4,523 \end{array}$

EXERCISES

Add.

1. $\begin{array}{r} 4,623 \\ +3,240 \end{array}$
2. $\begin{array}{r} 5,027 \\ +2,931 \end{array}$
3. $\begin{array}{r} 6,230 \\ +3,726 \end{array}$
4. $\begin{array}{r} 2,138 \\ +4,201 \end{array}$

5. $\begin{array}{r} 8,012 \\ +1,375 \end{array}$
6. $\begin{array}{r} 3,253 \\ +6,142 \end{array}$
7. $\begin{array}{r} 1,425 \\ 3,273 \\ +5,101 \end{array}$
8. $\begin{array}{r} 4,124 \\ 2,315 \\ +2,260 \end{array}$

312

REGROUPING WITH THOUSANDS

We can rename to add hundreds or thousands.

¹ ¹	¹ ¹ ¹	¹ ¹	¹ ¹ ¹
598	3,598	469	2,469
+ 867	+ 2,867	+ 856	+ 6,856
1,465	6,465	1,325	9,325

1. Sometimes we rename once. Copy and complete.

a.　5,633　　　**b.**　2,580　　　**c.**　6,207
　　+ 1,229　　　　　+ 1,465　　　　　　1,431
　　　　　2　　　　　　　　45　　　　　+ 2,720
　　　　　　　　　　　　　　　　　　　　　358

2. Let's rename twice. Copy and complete.

a.　5,726　　　**b.**　4,238　　　**c.**　3,542
　　+ 2,195　　　　　+ 3,881　　　　　　1,825
　　　　21　　　　　　　119　　　　　+ 4,970
　　　　　　　　　　　　　　　　　　　　337

3. Copy and complete to rename three times.

a.　6,438　　　**b.**　7,302　　　**c.**　4,685
　　+ 1,684　　　　　+ 5,899　　　　　　2,158
　　　　122　　　　　　201　　　　　+ 3,586
　　　　　　　　　　　　　　　　　　　　429

4. Add.

a.　2,413　　　**b.**　5,825　　　**c.**　5,624
　　+ 1,622　　　　　+ 4,297　　　　　　1,468
　　　　　　　　　　　　　　　　　　　+ 1,975

Add.

1. 3,086 +4,805	**2.** 4,772 +3,218	**3.** 3,007 +5,928	**4.** 2,845 +5,129
5. 8,142 +1,285	**6.** 2,047 +5,661	**7.** 7,211 +1,498	**8.** 3,927 +3,081
9. 2,639 +3,182	**10.** 4,911 +2,089	**11.** 5,006 +2,999	**12.** 8,117 +1,294
13. 2,337 +4,773	**14.** 3,008 +4,994	**15.** 6,725 +2,385	**16.** 5,820 +1,299
17. 1,008 +4,994	**18.** 6,217 +1,298	**19.** 4,883 +2,337	**20.** 5,883 +2,775
21. 5,938 +2,183	**22.** 4,993 +3,008	**23.** 5,822 +2,377	**24.** 6,003 +2,997
25. 4,004 2,668 +1,274	**26.** 5,004 4,993 +1,115	**27.** 5,973 2,163 +1,008	**28.** 5,005 4,196 +1,227

Solve these mini-problems.

29. Drove 1,425 kilometers Monday.
Drove 2,698 kilometers Tuesday.
How many kilometers in all?

30. 5,267 blue trucks.
3,976 red trucks.
How many trucks in all?

314

SUBTRACTING THOUSANDS

We can subtract hundreds.		So, we can subtract thousands.
724 − 302 **422**		5,724 − 1,302 **4,422**

1. Subtract.

    a.   623   **b.**   576   **c.**   831
       − 102   − 345   − 730

2. Subtract.

    a.   9,285   **b.**   2,051   **c.**   4,307
       − 1,140   − 1,040   − 2,201

EXERCISES

Subtract.

1. 8,294 −2,162	**2.** 7,064 −5,031	**3.** 6,338 −2,126	**4.** 9,245 −6,124
5. 2,176 −1,025	**6.** 5,297 −3,152	**7.** 8,261 −4,150	**8.** 4,462 −3,141
9. 8,341 −2,101	**10.** 6,578 −3,215	**11.** 5,470 −2,310	**12.** 8,657 −3,214
13. 6,254 −1,123	**14.** 4,029 −3,014	**15.** 3,617 −2,205	**16.** 8,465 −7,241

315

We can rename to subtract hundreds.

SUBTRACT ONES	SUBTRACT TENS	SUBTRACT HUNDREDS
1 13	11 3 1 13	11 3 1 13
4 2 3	4 2 3	4 2 3
− 2 4 5	− 2 4 5	− 2 4 5
8	7 8	1 7 8

We can also rename to subtract thousands.

SUBTRACT ONES	SUBTRACT TENS	SUBTRACT HUNDREDS	SUBTRACT THOUSANDS
1 14	11 5 1 14	15 11 4 5 1 14	15 11 4 5 1 14
5,6 2 4	5,6 2 4	5,6 2 4	5,6 2 4
− 3,8 4 5	− 3,8 4 5	− 3,8 4 5	− 3,8 4 5
9	7 9	7 7 9	1,7 7 9

1. Copy and complete.

a.
```
     1  13
  7,5 2 3
 −2,4 1 9
        4
```

b.
```
  5 12  7 14
  6,2 8 4
 −3,5 3 7
    7 4 7
```

c.
```
        13 13
   2  3  3 16
  3,4 4 6
 −1,8 5 9
    5 8 7
```

2. We can subtract with zeros. Copy and complete.

a.
```
   14  9
 8  4 10 12
 9 5 0 2
−7,6 2 7
   8 7 5
```

b.
```
    9 12
 5 10 2 10
 6,0 3 0
−1,5 7 6
   4 5 4
```

c.
```
       9  9
 4 10 10 10
 5,0 0 0
−1,6 7 2
   3 2 8
```

3. Subtract.

a.
```
  9,502
 −7,627
```

b.
```
  6,435
 −3,297
```

c.
```
  8,001
 −1,256
```

Subtract.

1. 6,295 − 3,178	**2.** 7,163 − 2,085	**3.** 4,263 − 1,375	**4.** 7,603 − 2,184
5. 5,402 − 1,526	**6.** 8,926 − 2,938	**7.** 9,465 − 2,999	**8.** 3,004 − 1,216
9. 9,001 − 2,994	**10.** 7,495 − 3,286	**11.** 5,420 − 1,768	**12.** 3,040 − 1,278
13. 6,892 − 1,359	**14.** 8,114 − 1,368	**15.** 7,005 − 1,397	**16.** 9,030 − 7,466
17. 3,145 − 1,628	**18.** 5,490 − 2,768	**19.** 4,626 − 1,879	**20.** 7,051 − 5,620
21. 6,250 − 2,638	**22.** 8,200 − 4,726	**23.** 5,000 − 2,154	**24.** 9,258 − 3,476
25. 7,465 − 4,297	**26.** 4,010 − 2,321	**27.** 6,175 − 3,489	**28.** 8,605 − 5,327
29. 4,120 − 2,397	**30.** 5,103 − 3,168	**31.** 8,002 − 5,769	**32.** 9,000 − 6,784

Solve these mini-problems.

33. 3,450 people in all.
1,572 go home.
How many stay?

34. 5,070 kilometers in all.
Went 2,968 kilometers.
How many more to go?

1. Look at this spinner.

    a. How many equal parts are shown?

    b. What colors are the parts?

    c. To what color does the arrow point?

    d. To what color does the arrow point now?

    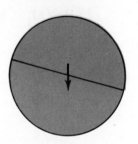

    e. The arrow will point to either ___ or ___ .

The chances of the arrow pointing to green are 1 out of 2.
The chances of the arrow pointing to red are 1 out of 2.

2. This chart shows a record of spins.

RED	GREEN
╫╫ ╫╫ ╫╫ ╫╫ I	╫╫ ╫╫ ╫╫ IIII

Did the arrow point to red about as often as it did to green?

3. Look at the box.

    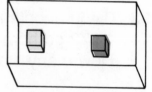

    a. How many blocks are there?

    b. How many are yellow?

    c. The chances of picking the yellow block are 1 out of 2. What are the chances of picking the blue block?

318

Let's play a game with a penny.

1. How many sides has a penny?

2. What do we call the sides?

3. Flip your penny. Which side came up?

4. Flip the penny again. Which side came up now?

5. Flip your penny 40 times. Record the results on a chart like this. Place a mark in the correct side each time.

HEADS	TAILS

6. Count your marks. Is the number of heads about the same as the number of tails?

Brainteaser

Find the pattern. Write the next 3 rows.

```
                1
              1   1
            1   2   1
          1   3   3   1
        1   4   6   4   1
      1   5  10  10   5   1
```

How far can the pattern be followed?

1. a. How many equal parts are on this spinner?

b. To what color does the arrow point?

> The chances of the arrow pointing to blue are 1 out of 3.

c. What are the chances of the arrow pointing to red? to green?

2. a. How many equal parts are on this spinner?

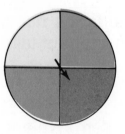

b. To what color does the arrow point?

> The chances of the arrow pointing to red are 1 out of 4.

c. What are the chances of the arrow pointing to blue? to green? to yellow?

Copy this chart. You will use it to play a game.

RED	YELLOW	BLUE

You will also need 3 blocks and a box. One block should be red; one yellow; and one blue.

1. Place the blocks in a box. Shake them.

2. Without looking, pick a block.

3. Record a mark in the correct place on the chart.

4. Put the block back into the box.

5. Shake the box again. Pick another block.

6. Record a mark in the correct place on the chart.

7. Pick a block 45 times.

8. How many times did you pick a red block? a yellow block? a blue block?

9. Are the numbers almost the same?

10. What are the chances of your picking a red block? a blue block? a yellow block?

11. Get a green block. Play the game with 4 blocks.

12. What are the chances of picking each color?

CHAPTER REVIEW

Add. [313]

1.	5,206 +3,450	**2.**	6,117 +1,238	**3.**	5,284 +2,193	**4.**	3,281 +5,985
5.	7,465 +1,719	**6.**	3,007 +4,993	**7.**	5,618 +2,395	**8.**	6,059 +2,983
9.	1,547 3,201 +4,150	**10.**	2,834 4,125 +2,041	**11.**	3,456 2,813 +1,520	**12.**	5,374 1,252 +2,791

Subtract. [316]

13.	5,947 −2,324	**14.**	7,283 −4,152	**15.**	2,784 −1,097	**16.**	5,469 −2,678
17.	6,947 −4,959	**18.**	8,634 −2,786	**19.**	7,050 −2,268	**20.**	9,006 −5,123

21. What are the chances [318] of the coin coming up heads?

22. What are the chances [320] of the arrow pointing to yellow?

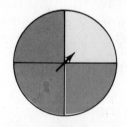

23. What are the chances [320] of the arrow pointing to blue?

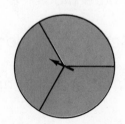

CHAPTER TEST

Add.

1. 2,371
  + 4,228

2. 3,416
  + 3,391

3. 2,536
  + 9,681

4. 3,907
  + 4,298

5. 5,364
  + 7,658

6. 4,153
    3,214
  + 1,321

7. 5,325
    2,141
  + 2,262

8. 3,916
    2,430
  + 1,862

Subtract.

9. 4,685
  − 1,273

10. 5,947
   − 2,324

11. 5,831
   − 3,627

12. 7,642
   − 2,351

13. 6,587
   − 3,998

14. 4,913
   − 1,938

15. 5,070
   − 2,641

16. 8,000
   − 6,834

17. What are the chances of the arrow pointing to green?

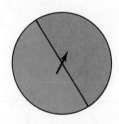

18. What are the chances of picking a blue block?

19. What are the chances of picking a red block?

PRACTICE EXERCISES

Add.

1.
$$\begin{array}{r} 1 \\ 8 \\ \hline \end{array}$$
2.
$$\begin{array}{r} 3 \\ 3 \\ \hline \end{array}$$
3.
$$\begin{array}{r} 5 \\ 2 \\ \hline \end{array}$$
4.
$$\begin{array}{r} 2 \\ 4 \\ \hline \end{array}$$
5.
$$\begin{array}{r} 4 \\ 3 \\ \hline \end{array}$$
6.
$$\begin{array}{r} 5 \\ 0 \\ \hline \end{array}$$

7.
$$\begin{array}{r} 3 \\ 1 \\ \hline \end{array}$$
8.
$$\begin{array}{r} 1 \\ 4 \\ \hline \end{array}$$
9.
$$\begin{array}{r} 4 \\ 5 \\ \hline \end{array}$$
10.
$$\begin{array}{r} 3 \\ 2 \\ \hline \end{array}$$
11.
$$\begin{array}{r} 2 \\ 7 \\ \hline \end{array}$$
12.
$$\begin{array}{r} 1 \\ 9 \\ \hline \end{array}$$

13.
$$\begin{array}{r} 5 \\ 3 \\ \hline \end{array}$$
14.
$$\begin{array}{r} 1 \\ 0 \\ \hline \end{array}$$
15.
$$\begin{array}{r} 2 \\ 8 \\ \hline \end{array}$$
16.
$$\begin{array}{r} 4 \\ 4 \\ \hline \end{array}$$
17.
$$\begin{array}{r} 5 \\ 1 \\ \hline \end{array}$$
18.
$$\begin{array}{r} 7 \\ 1 \\ \hline \end{array}$$

19.
$$\begin{array}{r} 6 \\ 3 \\ \hline \end{array}$$
20.
$$\begin{array}{r} 4 \\ 1 \\ \hline \end{array}$$
21.
$$\begin{array}{r} 4 \\ 6 \\ \hline \end{array}$$
22.
$$\begin{array}{r} 2 \\ 9 \\ \hline \end{array}$$
23.
$$\begin{array}{r} 4 \\ 8 \\ \hline \end{array}$$
24.
$$\begin{array}{r} 7 \\ 3 \\ \hline \end{array}$$

25.
$$\begin{array}{r} 6 \\ 1 \\ \hline \end{array}$$
26.
$$\begin{array}{r} 4 \\ 9 \\ \hline \end{array}$$
27.
$$\begin{array}{r} 5 \\ 5 \\ \hline \end{array}$$
28.
$$\begin{array}{r} 4 \\ 7 \\ \hline \end{array}$$
29.
$$\begin{array}{r} 3 \\ 8 \\ \hline \end{array}$$
30.
$$\begin{array}{r} 9 \\ 5 \\ \hline \end{array}$$

31.
$$\begin{array}{r} 8 \\ 4 \\ \hline \end{array}$$
32.
$$\begin{array}{r} 5 \\ 6 \\ \hline \end{array}$$
33.
$$\begin{array}{r} 8 \\ 8 \\ \hline \end{array}$$
34.
$$\begin{array}{r} 9 \\ 3 \\ \hline \end{array}$$
35.
$$\begin{array}{r} 7 \\ 7 \\ \hline \end{array}$$
36.
$$\begin{array}{r} 6 \\ 5 \\ \hline \end{array}$$

37.
$$\begin{array}{r} 8 \\ 7 \\ \hline \end{array}$$
38.
$$\begin{array}{r} 7 \\ 5 \\ \hline \end{array}$$
39.
$$\begin{array}{r} 6 \\ 8 \\ \hline \end{array}$$
40.
$$\begin{array}{r} 9 \\ 4 \\ \hline \end{array}$$
41.
$$\begin{array}{r} 9 \\ 6 \\ \hline \end{array}$$
42.
$$\begin{array}{r} 8 \\ 5 \\ \hline \end{array}$$

43.
$$\begin{array}{r} 6 \\ 6 \\ \hline \end{array}$$
44.
$$\begin{array}{r} 7 \\ 9 \\ \hline \end{array}$$
45.
$$\begin{array}{r} 8 \\ 9 \\ \hline \end{array}$$
46.
$$\begin{array}{r} 2 \\ 6 \\ \hline \end{array}$$
47.
$$\begin{array}{r} 0 \\ 5 \\ \hline \end{array}$$
48.
$$\begin{array}{r} 7 \\ 6 \\ \hline \end{array}$$

49.
$$\begin{array}{r} 7 \\ 8 \\ \hline \end{array}$$
50.
$$\begin{array}{r} 9 \\ 7 \\ \hline \end{array}$$
51.
$$\begin{array}{r} 3 \\ 9 \\ \hline \end{array}$$
52.
$$\begin{array}{r} 6 \\ 7 \\ \hline \end{array}$$
53.
$$\begin{array}{r} 8 \\ 3 \\ \hline \end{array}$$
54.
$$\begin{array}{r} 9 \\ 8 \\ \hline \end{array}$$

55.
$$\begin{array}{r} 6 \\ 4 \\ \hline \end{array}$$
56.
$$\begin{array}{r} 8 \\ 6 \\ \hline \end{array}$$
57.
$$\begin{array}{r} 1 \\ 5 \\ \hline \end{array}$$
58.
$$\begin{array}{r} 9 \\ 2 \\ \hline \end{array}$$
59.
$$\begin{array}{r} 0 \\ 4 \\ \hline \end{array}$$
60.
$$\begin{array}{r} 9 \\ 9 \\ \hline \end{array}$$

Subtract.

1. 9 3	2. 5 0	3. 10 1	4. 7 4	5. 9 4	6. 14 5
7. 13 9	8. 9 9	9. 10 3	10. 9 2	11. 8 7	12. 8 5
13. 10 5	14. 8 2	15. 10 7	16. 8 0	17. 16 9	18. 5 3
19. 8 4	20. 9 5	21. 12 9	22. 10 8	23. 13 7	24. 11 5
25. 14 6	26. 17 8	27. 14 7	28. 16 8	29. 11 2	30. 13 4
31. 12 3	32. 11 6	33. 12 8	34. 12 5	35. 18 9	36. 15 7
37. 13 5	38. 11 9	39. 14 9	40. 4 0	41. 13 6	42. 16 8
43. 12 4	44. 15 6	45. 9 8	46. 13 8	47. 9 6	48. 7 5
49. 10 4	50. 11 8	51. 6 6	52. 7 2	53. 15 8	54. 7 3
55. 11 7	56. 15 6	57. 9 1	58. 2 0	59. 17 9	60. 11 3
61. 12 7	62. 5 2	63. 3 3	64. 13 6	65. 12 6	66. 6 1

Multiply.

1.	0 2	**2.**	4 4	**3.**	1 3	**4.**	2 2	**5.**	8 8	**6.**	5 5
7.	2 3	**8.**	3 9	**9.**	0 3	**10.**	1 4	**11.**	7 7	**12.**	2 4
13.	1 2	**14.**	2 5	**15.**	3 3	**16.**	6 6	**17.**	9 7	**18.**	0 9
19.	4 5	**20.**	1 5	**21.**	5 6	**22.**	4 7	**23.**	1 6	**24.**	9 5
25.	0 4	**26.**	8 0	**27.**	2 6	**28.**	0 5	**29.**	9 8	**30.**	1 7
31.	6 7	**32.**	3 8	**33.**	5 9	**34.**	9 9	**35.**	6 9	**36.**	7 6
37.	3 4	**38.**	1 8	**39.**	0 6	**40.**	4 6	**41.**	5 4	**42.**	8 9
43.	2 7	**44.**	4 8	**45.**	7 9	**46.**	3 5	**47.**	5 7	**48.**	9 3
49.	8 7	**50.**	8 5	**51.**	9 2	**52.**	5 7	**53.**	0 7	**54.**	6 3
55.	0 1	**56.**	2 8	**57.**	1 9	**58.**	3 6	**59.**	8 9	**60.**	7 8
61.	3 7	**62.**	2 9	**63.**	4 9	**64.**	5 8	**65.**	0 8	**66.**	6 8

Divide.

1. $4\overline{)12}$ 2. $3\overline{)6}$ 3. $2\overline{)4}$ 4. $1\overline{)5}$

5. $5\overline{)5}$ 6. $2\overline{)8}$ 7. $1\overline{)3}$ 8. $3\overline{)12}$

9. $5\overline{)10}$ 10. $3\overline{)3}$ 11. $1\overline{)4}$ 12. $2\overline{)6}$

13. $3\overline{)9}$ 14. $1\overline{)1}$ 15. $4\overline{)8}$ 16. $4\overline{)20}$

17. $2\overline{)10}$ 18. $1\overline{)2}$ 19. $4\overline{)20}$ 20. $5\overline{)25}$

21. $1\overline{)6}$ 22. $3\overline{)21}$ 23. $5\overline{)30}$ 24. $9\overline{)9}$

25. $2\overline{)18}$ 26. $7\overline{)7}$ 27. $8\overline{)32}$ 28. $9\overline{)45}$

29. $9\overline{)54}$ 30. $8\overline{)8}$ 31. $6\overline{)36}$ 32. $1\overline{)8}$

33. $4\overline{)32}$ 34. $5\overline{)40}$ 35. $9\overline{)36}$ 36. $8\overline{)16}$

37. $1\overline{)9}$ 38. $4\overline{)36}$ 39. $8\overline{)64}$ 40. $7\overline{)49}$

41. $5\overline{)45}$ 42. $9\overline{)72}$ 43. $7\overline{)63}$ 44. $6\overline{)6}$

45. $4\overline{)28}$ 46. $9\overline{)63}$ 47. $2\overline{)12}$ 48. $1\overline{)7}$

49. $7\overline{)56}$ 50. $8\overline{)48}$ 51. $9\overline{)81}$ 52. $8\overline{)24}$

53. $3\overline{)27}$ 54. $9\overline{)18}$ 55. $7\overline{)35}$ 56. $6\overline{)54}$

57. $5\overline{)35}$ 58. $9\overline{)27}$ 59. $8\overline{)72}$ 60. $6\overline{)42}$

61. $7\overline{)42}$ 62. $8\overline{)40}$ 63. $8\overline{)56}$ 64. $7\overline{)21}$

65. $6\overline{)24}$ 66. $5\overline{)40}$ 67. $8\overline{)64}$ 68. $9\overline{)72}$

(6) Write two expanded numerals for each.

Example   26 = 2 tens + 6   20 + 6

1. 28 **2.** 73 **3.** 80 **4.** 12 **5.** 61

Write standard numerals.

6. 30 + 1 **7.** 50 + 8 **8.** 10 + 7 **9.** 70 + 2

10. 90 + 8 **11.** 40 + 4 **12.** 10 + 0 **13.** 60 + 3

(9) Compare. Use >, <, or =.

1. 35 ≡ 38 **2.** 46 ≡ 56 **3.** 81 ≡ 73 **4.** 26 ≡ 25

5. 15 ≡ 19 **6.** 79 ≡ 64 **7.** 55 ≡ 66 **8.** 93 ≡ 94

(12) Write a standard numeral for each.

1. 3 hundreds + 2 tens + 7 **2.** 400 + 60 + 5

3. 8 hundreds + 0 tens + 6 **4.** 700 + 0 + 8

5. 9 hundreds + 9 tens + 9 **6.** 200 + 90 + 0

Write expanded numerals.

Example   371 = 300 + 70 + 1

7. 685 **8.** 214 **9.** 850 **10.** 409

11. 550 **12.** 666 **13.** 137 **14.** 388

(14) What is the value of each underlined digit?

1. 3<u>4</u>7 **2.** <u>8</u>62 **3.** 95<u>3</u> **4.** <u>7</u>59

5. 7<u>6</u>0 **6.** 4<u>3</u>8 **7.** 2<u>3</u>4 **8.** 62<u>4</u>

(14) Write standard numerals.

9. Five hundred seventy-six

10. Seventy-six

11. Eight hundred ninety

12. Eight hundred

13. Eight hundred nine

14. Sixty-eight

(16) Compare. Use >, <, or =.

1. 546 ≡ 298   **2.** 776 ≡ 900   **3.** 824 ≡ 850

4. 489 ≡ 487   **5.** 590 ≡ 378   **6.** 400 ≡ 500

7. 719 ≡ 732   **8.** 653 ≡ 656   **9.** 820 ≡ 619

(24) Write standard numerals.

1. 7 thousands + 2 hundreds + 5 tens + 9

2. 3 thousands + 0 hundreds + 1 ten + 5

3. 6 thousands + 4 hundreds + 0 tens + 2

4. 9 thousands + 0 hundreds + 0 tens + 4

5. 4,000 + 100 + 80 + 6

6. 8,000 + 300 + 60 + 0

7. 5,000 + 0 + 30 + 7

(26) What is the value of each underlined digit?

1. 3,486   **2.** 1,089   **3.** 6,457   **4.** 9,372

5. 1,248   **6.** 3,456   **7.** 9,872   **8.** 7,461

(28) Compare. Use >, <, or =.

1. 2,407 ≡ 2,470   2. 6,748 ≡ 8,000

3. 1,000 ≡ 999   4. 3,624 ≡ 3,499

5. 5,628 ≡ 5,624   6. 2,000 ≡ 1,999

7. 4,798 ≡ 6,001   8. 8,396 ≡ 8,410

(30) Find the pattern. Copy and complete.

1. 9,994; 9,995; 9,996; ____ ____ ____ ____

2. 4,000; 5,000; 6,000; ____ ____ ____ ____

3. 10,001; 10,002; 10,003; ____ ; ____ ; ____ ; ____

4. 1,002; 1,004; 1,006; ____ ____ ____ ____

5. 7,010; 7,020; 7,030; ____ ____ ____ ____

6. 4,005; 4,010; 4,015; ____ ____ ____ ____

(32) What is the value of each underlined digit?

1. 48,617   2. 75,306   3. 475,306

4. 156,720   5. 490,328   6. 728,539

7. 318,056   8. 360,514   9. 576,280

In which period are the underlined digits?

10. 467,032   11. 930,728   12. 100,340

13. 503,186   14. 172,500   15. 340,670

16. 752,105   17. 250,300   18. 192,372

330

(78) Add.

1.	**2.**	**3.**	**4.**	**5.**
4	7	9	1	3
3	5	4	8	8
+8	+6	+5	+7	+8

6.	**7.**	**8.**	**9.**	**10.**
5	4	6	8	9
8	4	4	7	8
+6	+4	+7	+3	+1

(80) Add.

1.	**2.**	**3.**	**4.**	**5.**
12	35	60	14	71
+ 6	+ 4	+ 7	+ 3	+ 8

6.	**7.**	**8.**	**9.**	**10.**
83	50	95	86	70
+25	+70	+42	+41	+60

Add.

1.	**2.**	**3.**	**4.**
243	350	702	600
+ 5	+ 6	+ 7	+300

5.	**6.**	**7.**	**8.**
316	821	930	708
+ 52	+ 148	+ 47	+561

(86) Add.

1.	**2.**	**3.**	**4.**	**5.**
8	9	7	4	6
7	6	7	9	9
+5	+8	+7	+8	+9

6.	**7.**	**8.**	**9.**	**10.**
6	8	8	6	5
8	8	9	7	9
6	8	2	9	8
+3	+8	+6	+5	+7

331

(88) **Add.**

1.   35   **2.**   47   **3.**   53   **4.**   18   **5.**   46
     + 8   + 6   + 9   + 8   + 4

6.   68   **7.**   57   **8.**   86   **9.**   75   **10.**   94
    +48   +73   +46   +75   +38

11.   75   **12.**   75   **13.**   88   **14.**   29   **15.**   54
    +68   +15   +26   +83   +29

(90) **Add.**

1.   468   **2.**   524   **3.**   705   **4.**   809
    + 7   + 6   + 28   + 67

5.   327   **6.**   933   **7.**   408   **8.**   524
    + 46   + 57   +709   + 138

(92) **Add.**

1.   263   **2.**   842   **3.**   650   **4.**   785
    + 74   + 90   + 73   + 83

5.   474   **6.**   657   **7.**   783   **8.**   392
    + 175   + 280   + 572   + 874

(94) **Add.**

1.   298   **2.**   475   **3.**   649   **4.**   536
    + 7   + 75   + 73   +288

5.   497   **6.**   368   **7.**   276   **8.**   637
    + 306   +242   + 428   + 165

9.   637   **10.**   548   **11.**   216   **12.**   456
    + 385   +457   +795   +544

(96) Add.

1. $\begin{array}{r} 34 \\ 21 \\ +43 \\ \hline \end{array}$	**2.** $\begin{array}{r} 53 \\ 28 \\ +14 \\ \hline \end{array}$	**3.** $\begin{array}{r} 47 \\ 29 \\ +63 \\ \hline \end{array}$	**4.** $\begin{array}{r} 26 \\ 75 \\ +38 \\ \hline \end{array}$
5. $\begin{array}{r} 63 \\ 25 \\ +47 \\ \hline \end{array}$	**6.** $\begin{array}{r} 93 \\ 87 \\ +61 \\ \hline \end{array}$	**7.** $\begin{array}{r} 45 \\ 234 \\ +351 \\ \hline \end{array}$	**8.** $\begin{array}{r} 963 \\ 47 \\ +896 \\ \hline \end{array}$
9. $\begin{array}{r} 215 \\ 132 \\ +452 \\ \hline \end{array}$	**10.** $\begin{array}{r} 321 \\ 416 \\ +133 \\ \hline \end{array}$	**11.** $\begin{array}{r} 546 \\ 172 \\ +231 \\ \hline \end{array}$	**12.** $\begin{array}{r} 463 \\ 512 \\ +351 \\ \hline \end{array}$

(99) Add.

1. $\begin{array}{r} \$4.26 \\ +\ \ .43 \\ \hline \end{array}$	**2.** $\begin{array}{r} \$5.65 \\ +\ \ .70 \\ \hline \end{array}$	**3.** $\begin{array}{r} \$3.82 \\ +1.45 \\ \hline \end{array}$	**4.** $\begin{array}{r} \$6.78 \\ +2.05 \\ \hline \end{array}$
5. $\begin{array}{r} \$1.91 \\ +\ \ .87 \\ \hline \end{array}$	**6.** $\begin{array}{r} \$3.75 \\ +\ \ .79 \\ \hline \end{array}$	**7.** $\begin{array}{r} \$4.28 \\ +3.45 \\ \hline \end{array}$	**8.** $\begin{array}{r} \$2.84 \\ +3.16 \\ \hline \end{array}$

(106) Subtract and check.

1. $\begin{array}{r} 87 \\ -\ 5 \\ \hline \end{array}$	**2.** $\begin{array}{r} 49 \\ -28 \\ \hline \end{array}$	**3.** $\begin{array}{r} 76 \\ -36 \\ \hline \end{array}$	**4.** $\begin{array}{r} 97 \\ -40 \\ \hline \end{array}$	**5.** $\begin{array}{r} 88 \\ -58 \\ \hline \end{array}$
6. $\begin{array}{r} 29 \\ -\ 6 \\ \hline \end{array}$	**7.** $\begin{array}{r} 68 \\ -53 \\ \hline \end{array}$	**8.** $\begin{array}{r} 90 \\ -60 \\ \hline \end{array}$	**9.** $\begin{array}{r} 77 \\ -45 \\ \hline \end{array}$	**10.** $\begin{array}{r} 96 \\ -36 \\ \hline \end{array}$

(108) Subtract.

1. $\begin{array}{r} 300 \\ -100 \\ \hline \end{array}$	**2.** $\begin{array}{r} 463 \\ -\ 41 \\ \hline \end{array}$	**3.** $\begin{array}{r} 987 \\ -\ \ 5 \\ \hline \end{array}$	**4.** $\begin{array}{r} 714 \\ -303 \\ \hline \end{array}$
5. $\begin{array}{r} 679 \\ -438 \\ \hline \end{array}$	**6.** $\begin{array}{r} 854 \\ -323 \\ \hline \end{array}$	**7.** $\begin{array}{r} 596 \\ -485 \\ \hline \end{array}$	**8.** $\begin{array}{r} 956 \\ -841 \\ \hline \end{array}$

(112) Subtract.

1. 34 − 9	**2.** 23 − 7	**3.** 94 − 6	**4.** 87 − 8	**5.** 67 − 9
6. 53 − 6	**7.** 45 − 8	**8.** 73 − 9	**9.** 84 − 7	**10.** 62 − 8

(114) Subtract.

1. 42 −35	**2.** 70 −38	**3.** 63 −27	**4.** 57 −28	**5.** 71 −54
6. 60 −48	**7.** 85 −37	**8.** 90 −61	**9.** 72 −43	**10.** 95 −38

(115) Subtract.

1. 943 − 8	**2.** 687 − 39	**3.** 452 −328	**4.** 863 −729
5. 726 −318	**6.** 247 −129	**7.** 531 −329	**8.** 173 −167
9. 536 −229	**10.** 483 −278	**11.** 357 −139	**12.** 672 −143

(118) Subtract.

1. 849 − 73	**2.** 638 − 45	**3.** 789 −293	**4.** 644 −352
5. 327 −295	**6.** 989 −396	**7.** 453 −291	**8.** 226 −194
9. 647 −395	**10.** 833 −293	**11.** 346 −184	**12.** 524 −473

(120) Subtract.

1.	562 − 184	**2.**	923 − 738	**3.**	925 − 875	**4.**	715 − 378
5.	938 − 839	**6.**	745 − 397	**7.**	415 − 298	**8.**	652 − 179
9.	647 − 258	**10.**	347 − 287	**11.**	485 − 296	**12.**	752 − 383

(122) Subtract.

1.	500 − 6	**2.**	703 − 91	**3.**	809 − 279	**4.**	600 − 347
5.	900 − 245	**6.**	402 − 149	**7.**	307 − 298	**8.**	200 − 158

(127) Round to the nearest ten.

1. 34   **2.** 85   **3.** 59   **4.** 71   **5.** 47

(128) Round to the nearest hundred.

1. 324   **2.** 814   **3.** 793   **4.** 650

Round to the nearest dollar.

5. $6.98   **6.** $8.04   **7.** $9.15   **8.** $4.89

(130) Estimate the sums or differences.

1.	32 + 47	**2.**	89 + 29	**3.**	415 + 320	**4.**	784 + 199
5.	61 − 49	**6.**	78 − 27	**7.**	923 − 481	**8.**	654 − 347

1. 4 ×3	**2.** 2 ×1	**3.** 3 ×0	**4.** 5 ×4	**5.** 1 ×4

1. $\begin{array}{r}4\\ \times 3\\ \hline\end{array}$　　**2.** $\begin{array}{r}2\\ \times 1\\ \hline\end{array}$　　**3.** $\begin{array}{r}3\\ \times 0\\ \hline\end{array}$　　**4.** $\begin{array}{r}5\\ \times 4\\ \hline\end{array}$　　**5.** $\begin{array}{r}1\\ \times 4\\ \hline\end{array}$

6. $\begin{array}{r}3\\ \times 3\\ \hline\end{array}$　　**7.** $\begin{array}{r}0\\ \times 0\\ \hline\end{array}$　　**8.** $\begin{array}{r}5\\ \times 3\\ \hline\end{array}$　　**9.** $\begin{array}{r}2\\ \times 2\\ \hline\end{array}$　　**10.** $\begin{array}{r}5\\ \times 1\\ \hline\end{array}$

11. $\begin{array}{r}4\\ \times 5\\ \hline\end{array}$　　**12.** $\begin{array}{r}0\\ \times 4\\ \hline\end{array}$　　**13.** $\begin{array}{r}5\\ \times 5\\ \hline\end{array}$　　**14.** $\begin{array}{r}1\\ \times 1\\ \hline\end{array}$　　**15.** $\begin{array}{r}0\\ \times 5\\ \hline\end{array}$

16. $\begin{array}{r}2\\ \times 3\\ \hline\end{array}$　　**17.** $\begin{array}{r}5\\ \times 0\\ \hline\end{array}$　　**18.** $\begin{array}{r}2\\ \times 4\\ \hline\end{array}$　　**19.** $\begin{array}{r}3\\ \times 5\\ \hline\end{array}$　　**20.** $\begin{array}{r}1\\ \times 2\\ \hline\end{array}$

21. $\begin{array}{r}3\\ \times 1\\ \hline\end{array}$　　**22.** $\begin{array}{r}4\\ \times 0\\ \hline\end{array}$　　**23.** $\begin{array}{r}2\\ \times 0\\ \hline\end{array}$　　**24.** $\begin{array}{r}1\\ \times 5\\ \hline\end{array}$　　**25.** $\begin{array}{r}4\\ \times 4\\ \hline\end{array}$

26. $\begin{array}{r}5\\ \times 2\\ \hline\end{array}$　　**27.** $\begin{array}{r}4\\ \times 1\\ \hline\end{array}$　　**28.** $\begin{array}{r}1\\ \times 3\\ \hline\end{array}$　　**29.** $\begin{array}{r}2\\ \times 5\\ \hline\end{array}$　　**30.** $\begin{array}{r}1\\ \times 0\\ \hline\end{array}$

31. $\begin{array}{r}0\\ \times 1\\ \hline\end{array}$　　**32.** $\begin{array}{r}4\\ \times 2\\ \hline\end{array}$　　**33.** $\begin{array}{r}3\\ \times 4\\ \hline\end{array}$　　**34.** $\begin{array}{r}0\\ \times 2\\ \hline\end{array}$　　**35.** $\begin{array}{r}3\\ \times 2\\ \hline\end{array}$

1. $2\overline{)8}$　　　**2.** $5\overline{)5}$　　　**3.** $1\overline{)3}$　　　**4.** $5\overline{)20}$

5. $3\overline{)9}$　　　**6.** $4\overline{)16}$　　　**7.** $1\overline{)5}$　　　**8.** $3\overline{)6}$

9. $4\overline{)8}$　　　**10.** $1\overline{)1}$　　　**11.** $5\overline{)10}$　　　**12.** $2\overline{)4}$

13. $1\overline{)2}$　　　**14.** $4\overline{)12}$　　　**15.** $2\overline{)10}$　　　**16.** $5\overline{)15}$

17. $2\overline{)6}$　　　**18.** $1\overline{)4}$　　　**19.** $3\overline{)3}$　　　**20.** $3\overline{)12}$

21. $2\overline{)2}$　　　**22.** $3\overline{)15}$　　　**23.** $5\overline{)25}$　　　**24.** $4\overline{)20}$

(203) Multiply.

1. 6
    ×7

2. 8
    ×8

3. 9
    ×5

4. 7
    ×9

5. 7
    ×8

6. 8
    ×7

7. 9
    ×8

8. 5
    ×6

9. 7
    ×5

10. 9
    ×9

11. 8
    ×5

12. 8
    ×9

13. 6
    ×5

14. 9
    ×6

15. 5
    ×9

16. 5
    ×7

17. 6
    ×6

18. 9
    ×7

19. 7
    ×8

20. 6
    ×8

21. 6
    ×9

22. 8
    ×7

23. 7
    ×6

24. 7
    ×7

25. 5
    ×8

(204) Divide.

1. $6\overline{)30}$ 2. $8\overline{)48}$ 3. $9\overline{)81}$ 4. $5\overline{)45}$

5. $7\overline{)56}$ 6. $8\overline{)40}$ 7. $9\overline{)72}$ 8. $5\overline{)30}$

9. $7\overline{)35}$ 10. $6\overline{)54}$ 11. $8\overline{)64}$ 12. $9\overline{)54}$

13. $7\overline{)42}$ 14. $6\overline{)36}$ 15. $5\overline{)40}$ 16. $9\overline{)63}$

17. $7\overline{)49}$ 18. $5\overline{)35}$ 19. $8\overline{)72}$ 20. $9\overline{)45}$

21. $8\overline{)56}$ 22. $7\overline{)63}$ 23. $6\overline{)48}$ 24. $9\overline{)72}$

(215) Multiply.

1. 3×10 2. 10×6 3. 10×8 4. 2×10

5. 20×9 6. 40×5 7. 3×70 8. 90×6

(218) Multiply.

1. 34 $\times 2$	**2.** 13 $\times 2$	**3.** 42 $\times 4$	**4.** 51 $\times 6$	**5.** 82 $\times 3$
6. 71 $\times 9$	**7.** 92 $\times 4$	**8.** 63 $\times 3$	**9.** 52 $\times 3$	**10.** 44 $\times 2$

(220) Multiply.

1. 47 $\times 2$	**2.** 18 $\times 6$	**3.** 24 $\times 4$	**4.** 43 $\times 5$	**5.** 45 $\times 6$
6. 78 $\times 5$	**7.** 67 $\times 4$	**8.** 46 $\times 8$	**9.** 79 $\times 6$	**10.** 86 $\times 9$
11. 93 $\times 8$	**12.** 79 $\times 7$	**13.** 53 $\times 8$	**14.** 47 $\times 9$	**15.** 36 $\times 6$

(224) Multiply.

1. 200 $\times 3$	**2.** 400 $\times 6$	**3.** 800 $\times 7$	**4.** 600 $\times 9$
5. 600 $\times 4$	**6.** 700 $\times 9$	**7.** 500 $\times 8$	**8.** 900 $\times 9$

(228) Multiply.

1. 234 $\times 2$	**2.** 143 $\times 2$	**3.** 413 $\times 3$	**4.** 632 $\times 3$
5. 412 $\times 4$	**6.** 823 $\times 3$	**7.** 614 $\times 2$	**8.** 322 $\times 4$
9. 411 $\times 8$	**10.** 533 $\times 3$	**11.** 714 $\times 2$	**12.** 811 $\times 9$

(230) Multiply.

1. 128 　　× 2	**2.** 314 　　× 3	**3.** 208 　　× 4	**4.** 307 　　× 6
5. 224 　　× 3	**6.** 241 　　× 3	**7.** 151 　　× 9	**8.** 218 　　× 4
9. 316 　　× 5	**10.** 518 　　× 5	**11.** 832 　　× 4	**12.** 751 　　× 8

(232) Multiply.

1. 436 　　× 4	**2.** 857 　　× 3	**3.** 644 　　× 5	**4.** 783 　　× 9
5. 385 　　× 7	**6.** 764 　　× 8	**7.** 958 　　× 7	**8.** 869 　　× 8
9. 647 　　× 5	**10.** 876 　　× 8	**11.** 493 　　× 6	**12.** 987 　　× 6

(238) Divide.

1. 4$\overline{)80}$	**2.** 6$\overline{)120}$	**3.** 7$\overline{)420}$	**4.** 8$\overline{)640}$
5. 7$\overline{)560}$	**6.** 5$\overline{)400}$	**7.** 8$\overline{)320}$	**8.** 9$\overline{)630}$
9. 5$\overline{)350}$	**10.** 4$\overline{)360}$	**11.** 9$\overline{)540}$	**12.** 6$\overline{)420}$

(242) Divide.

1. 9$\overline{)75}$	**2.** 8$\overline{)63}$	**3.** 7$\overline{)52}$	**4.** 9$\overline{)86}$
5. 7$\overline{)43}$	**6.** 3$\overline{)19}$	**7.** 6$\overline{)53}$	**8.** 5$\overline{)47}$
9. 4$\overline{)39}$	**10.** 6$\overline{)49}$	**11.** 5$\overline{)48}$	**12.** 8$\overline{)62}$

(246) Divide.

1. 4)52   **2.** 5)75   **3.** 6)72   **4.** 3)45

5. 8)96   **6.** 7)84   **7.** 5)95   **8.** 3)57

(248) Divide.

1. 3)84   **2.** 3)87   **3.** 4)76   **4.** 3)99

5. 4)80   **6.** 3)96   **7.** 5)95   **8.** 4)92

9. 2)78   **10.** 4)88   **11.** 3)87   **12.** 2)98

(252) Divide and check.

1. 4)87   **2.** 3)76   **3.** 5)99   **4.** 6)93

5. 2)75   **6.** 5)83   **7.** 3)95   **8.** 2)87

9. 4)67   **10.** 3)88   **11.** 6)91   **12.** 3)92

(254) Divide.

1. 3)196   **2.** 5)383   **3.** 7)647   **4.** 9)462

5. 7)583   **6.** 9)806   **7.** 6)542   **8.** 5)426

9. 8)473   **10.** 4)313   **11.** 7)431   **12.** 9)634

(258) Divide.

1. 3)623   **2.** 4)843   **3.** 2)625   **4.** 3)647

5. 5)814   **6.** 7)962   **7.** 4)926   **8.** 5)947

9. 3)947   **10.** 8)999   **11.** 2)846   **12.** 7)847

(87) Write number sentences. Do not solve.

1. 8 red balloons.
   5 green ballons.
   How many in all?

2. 14 birds.
   6 flew away.
   How many are left?

3. 27 boys.
   31 girls.
   How many in all?

4. 25 red pencils.
   4 green pencils.
   How many in all?

5. 23 apples.
   45 oranges
   How many in all?

6. 17 monkeys.
   9 hats.
   How many more monkeys?

7. 178 trucks.
   21 cars.
   How many in all?

8. 11 scouts.
   2 leaders.
   How many more scouts?

(100) Solve these problems.

1. There are 328 girls in school. There are 297 boys in school. How many children are in school?

2. Maria and her mother went shopping. They paid $5.75 for a shirt and $3.98 for shoes. How much did they spend?

3. Bob and John went to the sea shore to look for sea shells. Bob found 136 shells. John found 264 shells. How many shells did they find in all?

4. Andy caught 9 fish on Monday and 12 fish on Tuesday. How many more fish did he catch on Tuesday?

5. Jodi bought 34 stamps for her brother and 25 stamps for her sister. How many stamps did she buy in all?

341

(126) Solve these mini-problems.

1. Had $6.75.
   Spent $2.25.
   How much left?

2. Doll: $2.95.
   Have $1.29.
   How much needed?

3. Earned $2.25.
   Given $3.50.
   How much in all?

4. Bat and ball: $8.97.
   Ball: $2.49.
   How much for the bat?

5. Red dress: $8.98.
   Blue dress: $7.59.
   How much more
   for the red dress?

6. Scarf: $1.98.
   Gloves: $2.98.
   Hat: $2.29.
   How much in all?

7. Cookies: $1.98.
   Candy: $1.29.
   How much in all?

8. Had $7.58.
   Lost $1.25.
   How much left?

(131) Estimate the answers.

1. Wendy bought a book for $4.98. She gave the clerk $10.00. About how much change did she get?

2. Jeff wants a radio for $8.98. He has saved $5.05. About how much more does he need?

3. Mrs. Glick bought a chicken for $3.89 and a turkey for $5.16. About how much did she spend in all?

4. Mike's haircut cost $2.25. He gave the barber $5.00. About how much change did he get?

5. Mr. Black paid $6.94 for gas and $1.21 for oil. How much did he pay in all?

(137) Copy the extra information. Solve these mini-problems.

1. 35 boys.
   27 girls.
   9 teachers.
   How many children?

2. 135 cars.
   24 buses.
   8 jeeps.
   How many cars and jeeps?

3. Milk: 30¢.
   Coffee: 20¢.
   Tea: 20¢.
   How much for
   coffee and tea?

4. 19 hens.
   75 eggs.
   38 broken.
   How many eggs
   not broken?

5. May: 31 days.
   June: 30 days.
   July: 31 days.
   How many days in
   May and June in all?

6. Book: 279 pages.
   Read: 185 pages.
   Chapters: 7
   How many pages left
   to read?

(167) Solve these problems. If information is missing, make it up.

1. Alan bought a fishing rod for $4.98. How much money did he have left?

2. Sally baked 36 cookies. Her brother ate 9 of them. How many cookies were left?

3. Mrs. Jones paid $2.25 for a belt and $1.75 for a zipper. How much did she spend in all?

4. Jennifer has 3 bags of marbles. How many marbles are in each bag?

(235) Solve these problems.

1. A race car went 168 miles an hour for 4 hours. How many miles did it go?

2. Tim collects coins. He has a coin book with 56 coins in it. Each page in the book has 8 coins. How many pages of coins does he have?

3. Bill delivers papers 7 days a week. He delivers 158 papers each day. How many papers does he deliver in a week?

4. Ann baked 6 pans of cookies. Each pan had 28 cookies. How many cookies did she bake?

5. Gerry practiced 45 minutes on Thursday and 58 minutes on Friday. How long did she practice in all?

6. Mr. Foster packed 8 boxes of apples. Each box had 288 apples. How many apples did he pack in all?

7. Rau earned $3.50 for mowing lawns and $2.75 for pulling weeds. How much more did he earn for mowing lawns?

8. Mrs. Lander has 24 hats. She keeps 4 hats in a box. How many boxes does she have?

9. Sam bought 19 balloons for a party. Each balloon cost 3¢. How much did he spend in all?

10. A factory made 467 boxes of pens on Monday, 539 boxes on Tuesday and 398 boxes on Wednesday. How many boxes of pens were made in all?

Solve these problems.

1. Ms. Allen baked 80 cookies. She has 6 children. She gave the same number of cookies to each child. How many cookies did each child get? How many cookies left?

2. Maria had 27 cents in her piggy bank. Her dad gave her 8 cents. How many cents does she have in all?

3. Fred is making bean bags. It takes 3 pounds of beans for each bag. He has 149 pounds of beans. How many bean bags can he make. How many pounds of beans left?

4. Mr. Angelo grew 962 apples in his orchard. He put them in boxes with 8 apples in each box. How many boxes did he have? How many apples left?

5. A truck has 146 bricks. Each brick weighs 4 kilograms. How much do the bricks weigh in all?

6. Mr. Sax has 162 red yo-yos and 137 blue yo-yos in his store. How many more red yo-yos does he have?

7. A store has 96 liters of milk. There are 6 liters in each carton. How many cartons are there?

8. One roll of yarn has 45 meters of yarn. Another roll has 55 meters. How many meters are there in all?

9. There are 672 dolls in a store. They are kept 4 in a box. How many boxes are there?

10. Nuts cost 39¢ a kg. How much do 8 kg cost?

TABLE OF MEASURES

Length
1 meter (m) = 100 centimeters (cm)

Liquid
1 liter (L) = 2 half liters
1 half liter = 2 quarter liters

Weight
1 kilogram (kg) = 1,000 grams (g)

Time
1 minute = 60 seconds
1 hour = 60 minutes
1 day = 24 hours
1 week = 7 days

GLOSSARY

This glossary contains an example, an illustration, or brief description of important terms used in this book.

Addends The numbers that are added.
Example $3 + 5 = 8$ 3 and 5 are addends.

Area The number of square units it takes to cover the inside of a flat figure. The area of this figure is 8 square units.

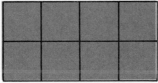

Bar graph A graph that shows number information with bars of different lengths.

Circle A path that begins and ends at the same point. All the points of the circle are the same distance from a point inside, called the center.

Degree The unit used when measuring temperature with a thermometer.

Diameter A line segment that goes through the center of a circle with its two endpoints on the circle. The diameter goes through points *A* and *B*.

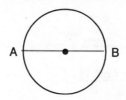

Difference The answer in subtraction.
  Example $9 - 5 = 4$ 4 is the difference.
Digit   Any one of the basic numerals.
  0, 1, 2, 3, 4, 5, 6, 7, 8, 9.

Equation A number sentence in which the equals sign, =, is used.
  Examples $6 + 4 = 10$ $8 - 3 = 5$
Equivalent fractional numbers Fractional numerals that name the same number.
  Example $\frac{1}{2} = \frac{2}{4}$

Estimate An answer that is found by using rounded numbers.
  Example $22 + 39 = \square$ $20 + 40 = 60$
                          60 is the estimate.
Even number   A number that has 2 as a factor.
  Examples   2, 4, 6
Expanded numeral A name for a number that shows the value of the digits.
  Example $35 = 30 + 5$

Factors   Numbers to be multiplied.
  Example $2 \times 4 = 8$ 2 and 4 are factors.
Fraction A number named by a numeral such as $\frac{1}{2}, \frac{5}{6}, \frac{4}{4}$.
Fractional numeral Numerals such as $\frac{1}{2}, \frac{5}{6}$ or $\frac{4}{4}$. They are names for fractions.

Function machine A machine that follows a rule. The rule for this machine is add 4.

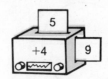

348

Graph A graph shows two sets of related information by the use of pictures or bars.

Grouping property of addition Changing the grouping of the addends does not change the sum.
Example $(3 + 4) + 2 = 3 + (4 + 2)$

Grouping property of multiplication Changing the grouping of factors does not change the product.
Example $(5 \times 2) \times 3 = 5 \times (2 \times 3)$.

Line A straight path that goes on in two directions without end.

Line of symmetry A line that separates a figure so that the two halves match when folded.

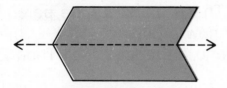

Line segment A straight path that has two endpoints.

Measure To compare a unit of measure with the thing to be measured.

Multiple The product of a number and a given number.
Example 40 is a multiple of 10 because $4 \times 10 = 40$.

Multiplication-addition property A property that relates addition and multiplication.
Example $2 \times (4 + 3) = (2 \times 4) + (2 \times 3)$

Number line A line on which numbers are matched with equally spaced marks.

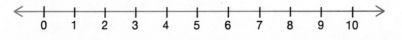

349

Number sentence A number sentence tells about numbers.
  Examples $2 + 6 = 8$, $8 - 6 = 2$, $8 > 6$, $6 < 8$

Numeral A symbol used to name a number. A name for the number, three, is 3.

Odd number A number that is not even.
  Examples 3, 5, 7
Order property of addition Changing the order of the addends does not change the sum.
  Example $7 + 5 = 5 + 7$
Order property of multiplication Changing the order of the factors does not change the product.
  Example $4 \times 9 = 9 \times 4$

Parentheses These marks ( ) are parentheses. They are used to show grouping. In $(4 + 3) + 2$, 4 and 3 are grouped and are added first. Then 2 is added to their sum.
Path A set of points such as in a curve, a line segment, or a circle.

Perimeter The distance around a figure. The perimeter of this figure is 10 inches.

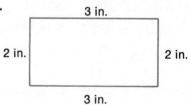

350

Periods in numerals   The groups of three digits set off by commas in a numeral.
    Example   In 143,257, the digits 1, 4, and 3 are in the thousands period, and the digits 2, 5 and 7 are in the ones period.

Pictograph   A graph that uses picture symbols to show number information.

Point   An exact location in space.

Probability   The chance of something happening.

Product   The answers in multiplication.
    Example   2 × 3 = 6   6 is the product.

Quotient   The answer in division.
    Example   8 ÷ 2 = 4   4 is the quotient.

Radius   A line segment from the center of a circle to a point on the circle. Radii are more than one radius. The radius goes from point *A* to point *B*.

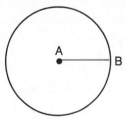

Ray   A straight path that begins with a point and goes in one direction, without end.

Rectangle   A figure formed by four line segments. It has four right angles.

Related sentences Related sentences use the same numbers and the same or opposite operation.
   Examples $4 + 3 = 7$, $3 + 4 = 7$, $7 - 4 = 3$ and
   $7 - 3 = 4$ are related sentences.
   $2 \times 5 = 10$ $5 \times 2 = 10$ $10 \div 5 = 2$,
   $10 \div 2 = 5$ are related sentences.

Remainder In the division $17 \div 5$, the quotient is 3 and the remainder is 2.

$$\begin{array}{r} 3\,r\,2 \\ 5\overline{)17} \\ \underline{15} \\ 2 \end{array}$$

Right angle An angle that looks like a square corner, such as a page of a book.

Square A figure that has all four sides the same length and four right angles.

Standard numeral The usual name for a number. The standard numeral for eight is 8.

Standard unit of measure A unit of measure that is agreed upon by a group of people.
   Examples   centimeter, liter, ounce

Sum The answer in addition.
   Example $3 + 2 = 5$ 5 is the sum.

Symmetric If the parts match when a figure is folded on a line, the figure is symmetric.

Temperature Tells how hot or cold something is.
Thermometer Measures the temperature.

Triangle A figure formed by three line segments.

Volume The number of cubic units that it takes to fill a space. The volume of this box is 24 cubic units.

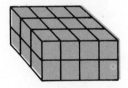

SYMBOL LIST

INDEX

A

Activity(ies), 1, 15, 19, 27, 37, 59, 89, 95, 103, 117, 119, 139, 165, 179, 180, 201, 205, 234, 260, 271, 283, 285, 297, 301, 305

Addends

four, 86 • grouping of, 61 • in addition, 46, 47 • meaning of, 46 • missing, 53, 54 • order of, 48 • three, 78, 86

Addition

basic facts, 79 • column, 78, 86, 96 • expanded form, 76 • four addends, 86 • grouping property of, 61 • hundreds, tens, ones, 82–83, 90, 92–95 • hundreds and thousands, 312, 313 • multiplication—addition property, 186 • multiplication and, 156–157 • number line and, 49 • order property of, 48 • relation to multiplication, 156, 157 • relation to subtraction, 54, 55 • renaming in, 84–85, 88–89, 92–93, 313–314 • sentences, 48, 49 • short form, 76, 84–85 • sum eighteen, 68 • sum eleven, 62 • sum fifteen, 64 • sum fourteen, 64 • sum seventeen, 68 • sum sixteen, 68 • sum thirteen, 64 • sum twelve, 62 • tens and ones, 76–77, 80–81, 84–85 • thousands, 312–314 • three addends, 78 • vertical, 47 • with dollars and cents, 99

Addition table, 70

Area, 304, 305

B

Bar graphs, 284–285

Basic facts

in addition, 79 • in division, 240 • in multiplication, 212 • in subtraction, 107

Brainteaser(s), 13, 29, 39, 66, 81, 85, 93, 98, 105, 124, 175, 187, 225, 227, 247, 256, 279, 319

C

Calendar, 180

Career(s)

bank tellers, 257 • bus drivers, 131 • cooks and chefs, 87 • dentists, 5 • gardeners, 235 • motion picture projectionists, 299 • newspaper reporters, 181 • real estate agents, 67 • recreation workers, 269 • roofers, 35 • surveyors, 151 • watch repairers, 207

Cent, 36

Centimeter, 136

Chapter review(s), 20, 44, 74, 102, 132, 152, 182, 208, 236, 264, 288, 310, 322

Chapter test(s), 21, 45, 75, 103, 133, 153, 183, 209, 237, 265, 287, 311, 323

Check up(s), 66, 98, 124, 234, 260

Checking

division, 252 • subtraction, 106

Circle

diameter of, 294–295 • meaning of, 294–295 • radius of, 294–295

Geometry

center of circle, 294–295 • circle, 294–295 • diameter, 294–295 • line, 292, 293 • line segment, 290–291 • part, 290 • point, 290, 292 • radius, 294, 295 • ray, 292, 293 • rectangle, 296–297 • right angle, 296–297 • square, 296–297 • symmetry, 300, 301 • triangle, 298

Gram, 141

Graph(s)

bar graphs, 284, 285 • in problem solving, 286 • pictographs, 282, 283

Greater than, 2, 9, 10

Grouping property of addition, 61

Grouping property of multiplication, 210–211, 215

H

Half dollar, 36–37
Half-gallon, 148
Half hour, 18–19
Half liter, 140
Half-pint, 148
Hour, 18–19
Hundreds, 12–13
Hundred thousands, 32–33

I

Inch, 144–145

K

Keeping Fit, 4, 10, 23, 29, 60, 97, 101, 110, 129, 135, 166, 176, 197, 206, 213, 229, 245, 256, 273, 281, 287, 303

L

Length

centimeter, 136 • feet, 146–147 • inches, 146–147 • meaning of, 134 • meter, 138

Less than, 2, 9, 10
Line, 292
Line of symmetry, 300–301
Line segment, 290
Liter, 140

M

Measurement(s)

of area, 304 • of length, 134 • of liquid, 140, 148–149 • of perimeter, 302–303 • of temperature, 142–143 • of time, 18–19, 40–43, 178–179, 262–263 • of weight, 141, 150 • to the nearest half inch, 144 • to the nearest inch, 144 • to the nearest quarter inch, 145 • volume, 308–309

Meter, 138

Metric system

centimeter, 136 • gram, 141 • half liter, 140 • liter, 140

Missing addend, 53–55
Missing factor, 168–169

Money

addition with, 99 • dollars and cents, 38–39 • in problem solving, 126 • making change, 125 • rounding to nearest dollar, 205 • value of coins, 36

Multiple(s)

of one hundred, 223 • of ten, 214

Multiplication

addition and, 156–157 • basic facts, 212 • division and, 170, 171–172 • eight as a factor, 202–203 • five as a factor,

357

164–165, 194–195 • four as a
factor, 164–165, 192–193 •
grouping property of, 210–211,
215 • in division, 242–243 •
nine as a factor, 202–203 •
of hundreds, 224–225 • one as a
factor, 162 • regrouping once,
230–231 • regrouping ones,
220–221 • regrouping twice,
232–233 • renaming in, 184–185
• seven as a factor, 200–201 •
short form, 218–219 • six as a
factor, 198–199 • three as a
factor, 160–161, 186 • three-digit
by a one-digit, 226–233 • two as
a factor, 160–161, 186 • two-digit
by a one-digit, 215–221 • zero
as a factor, 163
Multiplication-addition property,
186–187, 190–194, 198–202,
216–217
Multiplication sentence, 156–157
Multiplication table, 196, 204

N

Nickel, 36–37
Number(s)
comparing less than one hundred,
9–10 • comparing less than one
thousand, 16–17 • comparing
less than ten, 2 • comparing less
than ten thousand, 28 • even,
188 • odd, 188
Number line(s)
addition on, 48–49 • fractions on,
280–281 • rounding numbers on,
127, 128 • subtraction on, 52
Number sentence(s)
addition, 156–157 • choosing
correct, 56–57 • division, 170 •
inequalities, 71 • multiplication,
156 • related addition and
subtraction, 54 • related

multiplication and division, 170 •
writing, 55
Numeral(s)
expanded, 6, 12–13 • fractional,
266–267 • periods in, 32–33 •
standard, vi–1, 6–7, 12–13, 22–23

O

Odd number, 188
Ones, 12–13
Order property of addition, 48
Order property of multiplication,
158–159
Order word(s), 8
Ounce, 150

P

Path, 290–291
Penny, 36–37
Perimeter, 302
Periods in numerals, 32–33
Pictographs, 282–283
Pint, 148, 149
Place value, 16–17, 26–27, 30–33
Point, 290–291
Pound, 150
Probability, 318–321
Problem solving
basic operations, 177, 207, 235,
257, 269 • charts, 222 •
choosing correct number
sentence, 56–57 • choosing
correct operation, 306 • division,
261 • estimating, 131 • extra
information, 145, 189 • graphs,
286 • making change, 126 •
missing information, 167, 189 •
multiplication, 181 • reading
problems, 35 • with money, 100,
244 • with time, 178–179 •
writing number sentences, 58–59,
87

Problem solving skills
choosing number sentences, 56 • choosing the correct operation, 306 • estimating answers, 131 • extra and missing information, 189 • extra information, 137 • missing information, 167 • money problems, 126 • using graphs in problem solving, 286 • writing number sentences, 58
Product, 158

Q
Quart, 148–149
Quarter, 36–37
Quotient(s)
finding with multiplication table, 204 • greater than one hundred, 258–259 • less than fifty, 248–249 • less than one hundred, 254–255 • less than twenty, 246–247 • meaning of, 170 • with remainders, 241, 250–251

R
Race time, 79, 107, 212, 240
Radius of a circle, 294–295
Ray, 292–293
Rectangle, 296–297
Regrouping in multiplication
once, 230–231 • ones, 220–221 • twice, 232–233
Related number sentences
addition and subtraction, 54–55 • multiplication and division, 170–172
Remainders in division, 241, 250–251
Renaming in addition
hundreds and tens, 91–93 • tens

and ones, 84–85, 88–89 • thousands, 313 • three times, 313–314
Renaming in subtraction
hundreds, 116–119 • tens, 111–113 • tens and ones, 114 • thousands, 316–317 • twice, 120–121
Rounding money, 205
Rounding numbers
to nearest hundred, 128–129 • to nearest ten, 127

S
Short form
in addition, 76, 85 • in multiplication, 218–219 • in subtraction, 104
Space figures, 307
Square, 296–297
Square units, 304–305
Standard numeral
hundreds, 12–13 • tens and ones, 6–7 • thousands, 22–23
Subtraction
addition and, 54–55 • basic facts, 107 • checking, 106 • division and, 173 • from eighteen, 69 • from eleven, 63 • from fifteen, 65 • from fourteen, 65 • from seventeen, 69 • from sixteen, 69 • from thirteen, 65 • from twelve, 63 • function machine for, 72 • hundreds, tens, and ones, 108–109, 115 • meaning of, 50 • missing addend in, 54 • number line and, 52 • related sentences, 54–55 • renaming hundreds in, 118–119 • renaming tens and ones in, 114 • renaming tens in, 112 • renaming thousands in, 316–317 • renaming twice, 120–121 • sentence, 50, 54–55,

56–59, 71, 87 • short form, 104 •
tens and ones, 104–105 •
thousands, 315–317 • zero in,
122–123

Sum(s)
eighteen, 68 • eleven, 62 •
estimating, 130 • fifteen, 64 •
fourteen, 64 • meaning of, 46 •
seventeen, 68 • sixteen, 68 •
thirteen, 64 • twelve, 62

Symmetry, 300–301

T

Table(s)
addition, 70 • input-output, 73 •
multiplication, 196, 204

Temperature, 142–143

Tens, 12–13

Ten thousands, 30–31

Thousands
place value, 26 • standard
numerals for, 22–23

Time
adding hours and minutes,
262–263 • half hour, 18–19 •
hour, 18–19 • minutes later and

earlier, 178–179 • to five minutes,
40–41 • to the minute, 42–43 •
writing time, 18–19

Triangle, 298

U

Unit fractions, 268

V

Volume, 308–309

W

Week, 180

Y

Yard, 146–147

Z

Zero
as a factor, 163 • in subtraction,
122–123

ANSWERS

CHAPTER 1 ● **PAGE vi**
  1.a. 2   **b.** 1   **c.** 0
  2.a. a and c
PAGE 2
  1.a. >   **b.** <
  2.a. <   **b.** >   **c.** =   **d.** >
PAGE 3
  1.a. 2   **b.** 3   **c.** 23
  2.a. 3   **b.** 3; 3
PAGE 6
  1.a. 3   **b.** 30
  2.a. 30   **b.** 52   **c.** 73
PAGE 7
  1.a. 12   **b.** 42   **c.** 90
  2.a. 50   **b.** 16   **c.** 81
PAGE 8
  1.a. Third; Fourth
   b. Seventh; Ninth; Tenth
  2.a. Sixth; Eighth
   b. Eighth; Tenth
PAGE 9
  1.a. <; >   **b.** >; <   **c.** <; >
  2.a. >; <   **b.** <; >   **c.** >; <
  3.a. <   **b.** >   **c.** =
   d. >   **e.** =   **f.** >
PAGE 12
  1.a. 120   **b.** 120
  2.a. 2   **b.** 200
PAGE 14
  1.a. hundreds   **b.** tens; 20   **c.** ones; 4
  2.a. 400   **b.** 70   **c.** 7   **d.** 700
  3.a. 128   **b.** 210
PAGES 16–17
  1.a. >; >   **b.** <; <   **2.** <
  3.a. =   **b.** =   **c.** >   **d.** >
  4.a. <   **b.** <   **c.** =   **d.** >   **e.** <   **f.** >
PAGE 18
  1.a. 12; 12:00   **b.** 30; 12; 12; 12:30
  2.a. 1:00   **b.** 3:30   **c.** 4:00

362

CHAPTER 2 ● PAGE 22

    1.a. 995, 998, 999
      b. 950, 960, 970, 990
      c. 500, 600, 900
    2.a. 3,000   **b.** 5,000

PAGE 24

    1.a. One thousand, five hundred sixty-seven
      b. Three thousand, two hundred fifty-nine
      c. Four thousand nineteen
      d. Eight thousand two
    2.a. 1,008; 1,010   **b.** 1,018; 1,020
    3.a. 4   **b.** 1,000; 40
    4.a. 2,746   **b.** 3,825

PAGE 26

    1.a. hundreds, 200   **b.** thousands, 1,000
    2.a. 200   **b.** 90   **c.** 6,000
    3.a. 2,907   **b.** 3,068   **c.** 4,001

PAGE 28

    1.a. =   **b.** =   **c.** >   **d.** >
    2.a. >   **b.** =

PAGE 30

    1. 9,996; 9,998; 9,999
    2.a. 3,000   **b.** 70,000
      c. 2   **d.** 0

PAGES 32–33

    1.a. 99,993, 99,994
      b. 99,998, 99,999
    2.a. 200,000   **b.** 8,000
      c. 90,000   **d.** 70,000
      e. 600,000   **f.** 5,000
    3. Thousands; ones; 3
    4. 4, 2, and 0
    5.a. Thousands   **b.** ones   **c.** thousands
    6.a. One hundred fifty-seven thousand, six hundred twenty-two
      b. Five hundred ninety-four thousand, one hundred three
      c. Six hundred twenty thousand, four
      d. Four hundred thousand, one hundred twenty-five
      e. Seven hundred fifteen thousand, eight hundred fifty
      f. Nine hundred eighty-four thousand, seventeen

PAGE 36

    1.a. 24   **b.** 35
    2.a. 60   **b.** 80
    3.a. 3 dimes   **b.** 1 half dollar

PAGE 55
    1.a. $3 + 4 = 7$
      b. $4 + 3 = 7$
      c. $7 - 3 = 4$
      d. $7 - 4 = 3$
    2.a. 5, 5; 4, 4
      b. 6, 6

PAGES 56–57
    1.a. add   **b.** $4 + 3 = \triangledown$
    2.a. How many more puppies than bones?
      b. $6 - 2 = \triangledown$
    3. $4 + \square = 6$, $6 - 4 = \square$

PAGE 58
    1.a. 8   **b.** 1
      c. 4, 4
    2. $5 - 3 = \square$; 2

PAGE 61
    1.a. 4, 6   **b.** 5, 6
    2. 3

PAGE 62
    1.a. 1   **b.** 1
      c. 10   **d.** 12
    2.a. 12   **b.** 11
      c. 12   **d.** 12   **e.** 11

PAGE 63
    1.a. 9, 2   **b.** 8, 4
    2.a. 6, 6   **b.** 2, 2   **c.** 6, 6

PAGE 64
    1.a. 2   **b.** 2
      c. 10   **d.** 14
    2.a. 13   **b.** 15
      c. 14   **d.** 15   **e.** 14

PAGE 65
    1.a. 9, 4   **b.** 9, 5
    2.a. 7, 7   **b.** 8, 8   **c.** 6, 6

PAGE 68
    1.a. 1, 10, 16   **b.** 1, 10, 17
    2.a. 16   **b.** 16
      c. 17   **d.** 17

PAGE 69
    1.a. 8, 9   **b.** 7, 9
    2.a. 9, 9   **b.** 9, 9   **c.** 8, 8

PAGE 70
    1.c. 12   **2.c.** 5
PAGE 71
    1.a. >, >   **b.** <, <   **c.** =, =
    2.a. =   **b.** <   **c.** >
PAGE 72
    1.a. subtract 4   **b.** 3   **c.** 7
    2.a. 13   **b.** 6   **c.** 12
PAGE 73
    1. 3, 4, 11
    2.a. −6   **b.** −6   **c.** −6
    3.a. 10, 16   **b.** 14, 9

CHAPTER 4 • **PAGE 76**
    1. 7; 8; 78
    2. 9; 19; 29; 39; 49; 59
    3.a. 27   **b.** 37   **c.** 48   **d.** 65
PAGE 78
    1.a. 9; 9   **b.** 7; 7
    2.a. 16; 16   **b.** 18; 18
PAGE 80
    1.a. 90   **b.** 7; 8; 78
    2.a. 138   **b.** 128; 128
    3.a. 129   **b.** 99
      c. 139   **d.** 119
PAGE 82
    1.a. 700   **b.** 7; 5; 8; 758
    2.a. 1,290; 1,290   **b.** 786; 786
    3.a. 137   **b.** 216
      c. 459   **d.** 1,119
PAGES 84–85
    1. 2; 22
    2.a. 3; 6; 4; 0; 40
      b. 2; 8; 3; 7; 37
      c. 4; 7; 5; 2; 52
    3.a. 23   **b.** 30   **c.** 43   **d.** 92
      e. 71   **f.** 54   **g.** 30   **h.** 44
PAGE 86
    1. 20; 20
    2. 23; 23

PAGE 111
   1. 1; 6; 16
   2.a. 8   **b.** 2
PAGE 112
   1.a. 12   **b.** 5   **c.** 2
   2.a. 5; 9; 59; 59
   3.a. 19   **b.** 66   **c.** 88   **d.** 75
PAGE 114
   1. 3; 8; 38; 38
   2.a. 7   **b.** 46
   c. 45   **d.** 57
PAGE 115
   1.a. 266   **b.** 333
   c. 734   **d.** 525
   2.a. 27   **b.** 4
   c. 404   **d.** 538
PAGE 116
   1.a. 1; 10; 17   **b.** 5; 5; 18
   2.a. 1   **b.** 15   **c.** 6
PAGE 118
   1.a. 1   **b.** 6   **c.** 5   **d.** 3
   2.a. 256   **b.** 480   **c.** 86   **d.** 453
PAGES 120- 121
   1. 1; 7; 5; 175
   2.a. 5   **b.** 5   **c.** 3
   d. 7   **e.** 1
   3.a. 144   **b.** 265
   c. 77   **d.** 564
PAGE 122
   1.a. 10   **b.** 9
   2.a. 10; 10   **b.** 9   **c.** 56
   3.a. 596   **b.** 877
   c. 122   **d.** 72
PAGE 125
   1.a. 3 pennies and 1 nickel; answers may vary
   b. 1 nickel and 2 quarters; answers may vary
PAGE 127
   1.a. 70   **b.** 70
   2. 65
PAGE 128
   1. 400; 400
   2. 450
   3.a. $1.00   **b.** $6.00   **c.** $7.00
368

PAGE 130
    1.a. 100   **b.** 122
    2.a. 90   **b.** 170
      c. 100   **d.** 200

CHAPTER 6 ● **PAGE 134**
    1.a. a pen   **b.** no
    2.b. no   **3.a.** no   **b.** no
PAGE 136
    1. 3 cm   **2.** 9 cm
PAGE 138
    1. 100
    2.a. 200   **b.** 400
    3. 3   **4.** 4; 35
    5.a. meter   **b.** centimeter
      c. centimeter   **d.** meter
PAGE 140
    1. 4   **2.** 4
    3.a. 3 half liters   **b.** 8 half liters
PAGE 141
    1.a. 3,000   **b.** 5,000
    2.a. 6   **b.** 10
PAGES 142–143
    1. 26° below zero; 42°; 12° below zero
    2. the liquid in the thermometer goes down
    3. 40°   **4.** 18°
PAGES 144–145
    1. 2 inches
    2. 4 in., 2 in.
    3. $2\frac{1}{2}$ in.
    4.a. $\frac{3}{4}$ in.   **b.** $1\frac{1}{4}$ in.
PAGES 146–147
    2. 24   **3.** 6   **4.** 36
    5.a. 15   **b.** 108
PAGES 148–149
    1. 4; 8   **2.** 2; 6
    3. 2   **4.** 1
    5. gal 2, 4; qt 4; pt 16, 32; cups 16, 32, 64
    6.a. 1 gal   **b.** 3 cups

PAGE 150
    1.a. 16   **b.** 16   **c.** 8
    2.a. 16; 32   **b.** 64

CHAPTER 7 • **PAGE 154**
    1.a. 2   **b.** 4   **c.** 8; 8; 8
    2.a. 8   **b.** 6
      c. 12; 12   **d.** 4; 4
PAGES 156–157
    1. 6   **2.a.** $2 \times 5 = 10$ **b.** $5 \times 1 = 5$
    3.a. $4 + 4 = 8$ **b.** $5 + 5 + 5 = 15$
      c. $3 + 3 + 3 + 3 = 12$
    4.a. 3   **b.** 2   **c.** 6
    5.a. $3 \times 3 = 9$
      b. $2 \times 4 = 8$
      c. $2 \times 5 = 10$
PAGE 158
    1.a. factors 2, 4; product 8
      b. factors 4, 1; product 4
      c. factors 3, 2; product 6
    2.a. 12   **b.** 12   **c.** 3
    3.a. 6; 2   **b.** 8; 4
      c. 1   **d.** 3
PAGES 160–161
    1.a. 8   **b.** 10
    2.a. 6   **b.** 9
      c. 12   **d.** 15
    3.a. 8; 8   **b.** 15; 15   **c.** 10; 10
    4.a. 6   **b.** 15
      c. 4   **d.** 9   **e.** 6
PAGE 162
    1.a. 4; 5   **b.** 2; 3; 4; 5
    2.a. 3   **b.** 4
      c. 1   **d.** 5
PAGE 163
    1.a. 0; 0; 0
      b. 0; 0; 0   **c.** 0
    2.a. 0   **b.** 0
      c. 0   **d.** 0

PAGE 164

1. 16; 25

2.a. 4; 8; 12; 16; 20

   b. 5; 10; 15; 20; 25

3.a. 15   **b.** 10   **c.** 20

PAGE 167

1.a. the price of one candy bar

   b. Answers may vary.

2. Answers may vary.

PAGE 168

1.a. 5   **b.** 3

2.a. 3   **b.** 3   **c.** 0

3.a. 4   **b.** 3   **c.** 0

   d. 3   **e.** 2   **f.** 2

PAGE 170

1.a. 5   **b.** 3   **c.** 3

2.a. 3; 3   **b.** 4; 4   **c.** 2; 2

PAGE 171

1.a. $15 \div 5 = 3$; $15 \div 3 = 5$

   b. $12 \div 4 = 3$; $12 \div 3 = 4$

   c. $8 \div 2 = 4$; $8 \div 4 = 2$

2. $9 \div 3 = 3$

3.a. $3 \times 4 = 12$; $4 \times 3 = 12$

   b. $2 \times 5 = 10$; $5 \times 2 = 10$

   c. $3 \times 1 = 3$; $1 \times 3 = 3$

4. $2 \times 2 = 4$

5.a. 5; 5   **b.** 3; 3   **c.** 3; 3

PAGE 173

1.a. 2   **b.** 2

2.a. 5   **b.** 4   **c.** 5

PAGE 174

1.a. 15, 20, 25   **b.** 5   **c.** 5

2.a. 12, 16   **b.** 4   **c.** 4

3.a. 2; 2   **b.** 3; 3   **c.** 1; 1

4.a. 2   **b.** 3   **c.** 5

PAGE 178

1.a. 4:32   **b.** 10:05   **c.** 1:54   **2.** 8:43

3.a. 4:10   **b.** 9:55   **c.** 8:05

CHAPTER 8 • **PAGE 184**

1. 3   **2.a.** 1   **b.** 2

371

1.a. 6; 16   **b.** 4; 12
2.a. 18   **b.** 14   **c.** 16
3.a. 6; 6   **b.** 8; 8   **c.** 2; 2

1.a. 16; 18; 20; 22; 24
  b. 15; 17; 19; 21; 23
2.a. 0   **b.** 6
  c. 12   **d.** 10

1.a. 6; 21   **b.** 5; 12; 15; 27
2.a. 18; 18   **b.** 15; 15
3.a. 24   **b.** 27   **c.** 21
4.a. 7; 7   **b.** 6; 6   **c.** 8; 8

1.a. 3; 12; 32   **b.** 8; 20; 28
2.a. 32; 28; 36
3.a. 7; 7   **b.** 4; 4   **c.** 5; 5
  d. 9; 9   **e.** 4; 4   **f.** 4; 4

1.a. 2; 10; 30
  b. 3; 25; 15; 40
2.a. 15; 25; 30; 40; 45   **b.** 45
3.a. 35; 35   **b.** 40; 40   **c.** 45; 45
4.a. 6; 6   **b.** 5; 5   **c.** 7; 7
5.a. 2   **b.** 8   **c.** 5   **d.** 7

1.a. 3   **b.** 8   **c.** 24

2.

X	0	1	2	3	4	5	6	7	8	9
0	0	0	0	0	0	0	0	0	0	0
1	0	1	2	3	4	5	6	7	8	9
2	0	2	4	6	8	10	12	14	16	18
3	0	3	6	9	12	15	18	21	24	27
4	0	4	8	12	16	20	24	28	32	36
5	0	5	10	15	20	25	30	35	40	45
6	0	6	12	18	24	30	36	42	48	54
7	0	7	14	21	28	35	42	49	56	63
8	0	8	16	24	32	40	48	56	64	72
9	0	9	18	27	36	45	54	63	72	81

1.a. 3; 18; 48   **b.** 1; 1; 30; 6; 36
2.a. 54; 54   **b.** 48; 48   **c.** 42; 42
3.a. 6; 6   **b.** 7; 7
  c. 5; 5   **d.** 8; 8   **e.** 6; 6   **f.** 9; 9
4.a. 48   **b.** 42   **c.** 36   **d.** 54
5.a. 6   **b.** 8   **c.** 6   **d.** 6

1.a. 3; 21; 49   **b.** 4; 4; 35; 28; 63
2.a. 56; 56   **b.** 63; 63   **c.** 49
3.a. 7; 7   **b.** 8; 8   **c.** 7; 7
4.a. 7   **b.** 6   **c.** 7   **d.** 7

1.a. 3; 3; 24; 64   **b.** 4; 4; 45; 36; 81
2.a. 72   **b.** 64
  c. 81   **d.** 54   **e.** 56   **f.** 63
3.a. 9; 9   **b.** 8; 8   **c.** 9; 9
4.a. 9   **b.** 6   **c.** 8   **d.** 9
  e. 7   **f.** 7   **g.** 8   **h.** 6

1. 7   **2.a.** 2   **b.** 4   **c.** 7   **d.** 9

1. $2.00   **2.a.** $3.00   **b.** $9.00   **c.** $3.00

1.a. 2; 6   **b.** 3; 6   **c.** 3
2.a. 24; 24   **b.** 6; 6
3.a. 4   **b.** 3   **c.** 2

1.a. 30; 30   **b.** 40; 40
  c. 120; 120   **d.** 360; 360
2.a. 2   **b.** 7

1.a. 28; 280   **b.** 280; 280
2.a. 60   **b.** 80   **c.** 140

1.a. 8; 68   **b.** 12; 92
2.a. 1; 20   **b.** 5; 30; 140
3.a. 128   **b.** 150   **c.** 210   **d.** 268   **e.** 115

1.a. 6   **b.** 8   **2.a.** 36   **b.** 46   **c.** 60
d. 44   **e.** 288   **f.** 82   **g.** 150   **h.** 568

PAGES 220–221

1.a. 12   **b.** 1; 2   **c.** 6   **d.** 7
2.a. 42   **b.** 4; 2   **c.** 35   **d.** 39
3.a. 78   **b.** 148   **c.** 245   **d.** 444

PAGE 223

1.a. 100   **b.** 200; 200   **c.** 300; 300   **d.** 2,900; 2,900
2.a. 5   **b.** 7

PAGE 224

1.a. 2,400   **b.** 15; 1,500
2.a. 2; 20; 200   **b.** 8; 80; 800   **c.** 48; 480; 4,800
3.a. 600   **b.** 1,200   **c.** 4,200   **d.** 3,200

PAGE 226

1.a. 800; 28; 948
b. 40; 40; 600; 80; 16; 676
2.a. 30; 200   **b.** 8; 40; 300; 696
3.a. 654   **b.** 526   **c.** 1,288   **d.** 2,080

PAGE 228

1.a. 3   **b.** 9   **c.** 6
2.a. 1,263   **b.** 1,218   **c.** 686   **d.** 840

PAGES 230–231

1.a. 65   **b.** 67   **c.** 208   **d.** 122
2.a. 9   **b.** 12   **c.** 1; 2   **d.** 6   **e.** 7
3.a. 13   **b.** 13   **c.** 174   **d.** 144

PAGE 232

1.a. 24   **b.** 2; 4   **c.** 15
d. 17   **e.** 1; 7   **f.** 19
2.a. 7   **b.** 26   **c.** 143   **d.** 594
3.a. 795   **b.** 3,195   **c.** 1,308   **d.** 4,578

CHAPTER 10 • PAGES 238–239

1.a. 8, 80, 800; 4, 40, 400; 4, 40, 400
b. 9, 90, 900; 3, 30, 300; 3; 30, 300
2.a. 180, 30, 30   **b.** 240, 40, 40
c. 200, 200, 200; 100, 100, 100
3.a. 20   **b.** 10   **c.** 30   **d.** 100

PAGE 241

1.a. 3; 4; 1, 1, 3   **b.** 5; 3, 1, 1
2.a. 4 r 2   **b.** 4 r 1
   c. 2 r 3   **d.** 5 r 1

PAGE 242

1.a. yes   **b.** yes   **c.** 5 r 4
2.a. 4; 3   **b.** 2; 7

PAGE 246

1.a. 20   **b.** 8   **c.** 14
2.a. 10; 4; 14   **b.** 10; 3; 13
3.a. 12   **b.** 11   **c.** 13   **d.** 12
   e. 14   **f.** 14   **g.** 19   **h.** 13

PAGE 248

1.a. 40; 80; 120   **b.** 12   **c.** 23
2.a. 40; 3; 43
   b. 20; 8; 28
3.a. 32   **b.** 21
   c. 24   **d.** 45

PAGE 250

1.a. 21 r 2   **b.** 23 r 3
   c. 43 r 1; 40; 3   **d.** 30 r 1; 30; 0
2.a. 31 r 1   **b.** 14 r 1
   c. 36 r 1   **d.** 30 r 2

PAGES 252–253

1.a. Divide again.   **b.** Add the remainder.
2.a. 11 r 2; $6 \times 11 = 66 + 2 = 68$
   b. 43 r 1; $2 \times 43 = 86 + 1 = 87$
   c. 28 r 1; $3 \times 28 = 84 + 1 = 85$
   d. 18; $4 \times 18 = 72$

PAGES 254–255

1.a. 350; 420; 490   **b.** 49; 56; 63   **c.** 68 r 3
2.a. 2; 70   **b.** 35 r 6; 30; 5
3.a. 51   **b.** 21 r 2
   c. 76 r 3   **d.** 65 r 4

PAGES 258–259

1.a. 300; 600; 900   **b.** 210; 240; 270
   c. 6   **d.** 292 r 1; 90; 2
2.a. 200; 1   **b.** 100; 20; 3
3.a. 304   **b.** 100 r 2
   c. 238   **d.** 241 r 1

PAGE 262

1. 7:53   **2.a.** 7:25   **b.** 6:40   **c.** 4:43

CHAPTER 11 • PAGES 266–267

1.a. 4   **b.** 1   **c.** $\frac{1}{4}$

2.a. yes   **b.** no   **c.** yes

3. Picture is not divided equally.

4.a. $\frac{1}{3}$ **b.** $\frac{1}{2}$ **c.** $\frac{1}{6}$

PAGE 268

1. $\frac{1}{2}$

2.a. $>$ **b.** $<$

PAGES 270–271

1.a. 8   **b.** 3   **c.** $\frac{3}{8}$

2.a. 4   **b.** 4   **c.** $\frac{4}{4}$

3.a. $\frac{2}{4}$ **b.** $\frac{3}{8}$ **c.** $\frac{2}{2}$

PAGES 274–275

1.a. 8   **b.** 3

  c. $\frac{3}{8}$ **d.** 5   **e.** $\frac{5}{8}$

2.a. 3   **b.** $\frac{3}{4}$

  c. 1   **d.** $\frac{1}{4}$

3.a. $\frac{5}{6}$ **b.** $\frac{3}{8}$ **c.** $\frac{5}{5}$

PAGES 276–277

1.a. 12   **b.** 3

  c. $\frac{1}{3}$; $\frac{1}{3}$; $\frac{1}{3}$ **d.** 4; 4; 4   **e.** 4; 4

2.a. 16   **b.** $\frac{1}{2}$; $\frac{1}{2}$

  c. 8; 8   **d.** 8; 8

3.a. 4   **b.** 2

PAGES 278–279

1.a. $\frac{1}{3}$ **b.** $\frac{3}{9}$

  c. yes; 9

2.a. 3   **b.** 8

3.a–c. Answers may vary.

PAGE 280

1.a. $\frac{2}{4}$ **b.** $\frac{4}{4}$ **c.** 4

2.a. $>$ **b.** $<$ **c.** $<$

PAGE 282

1.a. 3   **b.** Al

  c. It would show a picture of 10 balloons.

2.a. 2   **b.** 8

  c. It would show a picture of 5 fish.

PAGE 284

1. to the left
2. from 0 to 11
3. 11   **4.** 8
5. 7   **6.** 5   **7.** Sunday

CHAPTER 12 • PAGE 291

2. b and c
3. a, b, and d
PAGE 293

3.a. Q   **b.** T   **c.** M
4.a. ray   **b.** line
    c. ray   **d.** line
PAGES 294–295

1.a. A   **b.** E   **c.** yes
2.a. W   **b.** H
3.a. 2   **b.** yes
PAGE 296

1.c. yes; opposite sides
2.a. yes   **b.** yes   **c.** 4
3.a. neither   **b.** rectangle, square   **c.** rectangle
PAGE 298

1.c. 3
2.a. yes   **b.** no   **c.** yes   **d.** yes
PAGE 300

1. yes   **2.** no
3.a. yes   **b.** yes
4.a. 2   **b.** 2
    c. 1   **d.** 1   **e.** 2   **f.** 1
PAGE 302

1. 20
2.a. 4 cm, 2 cm, 3 cm   **b.** 9   **c.** 9 cm
3. 12
4.a. 24 in.   **b.** 8 cm   **c.** 28 in.
PAGE 304

1.a. 12   **b.** 12 sq. units
2.a. 7   **b.** 7 sq. units
PAGE 307

1.a. can   **b.** ice cream cone
    c. scoop of ice cream   **d.** box
2. Answers may vary.

    1.a. 3   **b.** 3 cubic units
    2.a. 12   **b.** 12 cubic units
    3.a. 8 cubic units   **b.** 6 cubic units
    4.a. 4   **b.** 4
      c. 8   **d.** 8 cubic units

CHAPTER 13 ● PAGE 312
    1.a. 397   **b.** 589   **c.** 837   **d.** 898
    2.a. 7,999   **b.** 9,398   **c.** 9,858

PAGE 313
    1.a. 686   **b.** 40   **c.** 10
    2.a. 79   **b.** 8   **c.** 10
    3.a. 8   **b.** 13   **c.** 10
    4.a. 4,035   **b.** 10,122   **c.** 9,067

PAGE 315
    1.a. 521   **b.** 231   **c.** 101
    2.a. 8,145   **b.** 1,011   **c.** 2,106

PAGE 316
    1.a. 510   **b.** 2   **c.** 1
    2.a. 1   **b.** 4   **c.** 3
    3.a. 1,875   **b.** 3,138   **c.** 6,745

PAGE 318
    1.a. 2   **b.** green and red
      c. green   **d.** red   **e.** green; red
    2. yes   **3.a.** 2   **b.** 1   **c.** 1 out of 2

PAGE 320
    1.a. 3   **b.** blue
      c. 1 out of 3; 1 out of 3
    2.a. 4   **b.** red
      c. 1 out of 4; 1 out of 4; 1 out of 4